Microsoft Certified Azure Data Fundamentals (Exam DP-900) Certification Guide

The comprehensive guide to passing the DP-900 exam on your first attempt

Marcelo Leite

BIRMINGHAM—MUMBAI

Microsoft Certified Azure Data Fundamentals (Exam DP-900) Certification Guide

Group Product Manager: Reshma Raman

Publishing Product Manager: Birjees Patel

Content Development Editor: Shreya Moharir

Technical Editor: Sweety Pagaria

Copy Editor: Safis Editing

Project Coordinator: Farheen Fathima

Proofreader: Safis Editing

Indexer: Hemangini Bari

Production Designer: Joshua Misquitta

Marketing Coordinators: Shifa Ansari

First published: November 2022

Production reference: 1281022

Published by Packt Publishing Ltd.

Livery Place

35 Livery Street

Birmingham

B3 2PB, UK.

ISBN 978-1-80324-063-3

www.packt.com

For my wife, Rayane, and my parents, Diva and Marco, who have always supported me in every decision in my career.

Contributors

About the author

Marcelo Leite is a data and artificial intelligence specialist at Microsoft. He got the DP-900 in October 2020 and holds the advanced titles of Azure Data Engineer and Azure AI Engineer. He graduated in technology with a database specialization and has MBA in project and IT management. Marcelo has been working at Microsoft for over 5 years. He's also a professor of MBA courses for databases, data architecture, and cloud computing. With 17+ years of experience in roles such as software engineer, consulting manager, and solutions sales specialist, he shares his knowledge of data technologies on his YouTube channel "Dicas de Dados" and is very active on LinkedIn.

I dedicate this book to everyone who is in search of a successful career in data but is still walking this journey. It's possible, and this book was written to support you on it.

About the reviewers

James Reeves is a self-described technology nerd who has spent far too much time around data and yet keeps going back for more. As an experienced data engineer and architect, James loves to "think outside of the box" to create innovative solutions and believes that doing data discovery is like being a detective!

Abhishek Mittal is a cloud solution architect who has more than 9 years of experience in business intelligence and data warehousing space. He delivers exceptional value to customers by designing high-quality solutions and leading their successful implementations. His work entails architecting solutions for complex data problems for various clients across various business domains, managing technical scope and client expectations, and managing the implementation of a solution. He is a Microsoft Azure-certified professional and works as a senior architect with Nagarro. He is very passionate about learning and exploring new skills. He is gregarious in nature and always believes in sharing knowledge and helping others. You can reach out to him on LinkedIn.

Kasam Shaikh, a hybrid and cross-cloud practitioner, is a seasoned professional with 14 years of demonstrated industry experience, working as a Microsoft Azure cloud specialist with one of the leading IT companies in Mumbai, India. He is a Microsoft MVP in AI and among the only three AI MVPs from India. He is a global Azure AI speaker and author of four best-selling books on Microsoft Azure and AI. He is also the founder of Dear Azure – Azure INDIA (az-india), an online community for learning Azure AI. He owns a YouTube channel, where he shares his expertise on Microsoft Azure AI.

First, I would like to thank the Almighty, ALLAH, my mother, wife, and especially my little daughter, Maryam, for motivating me throughout the process, and Packt for believing in and considering me for this awesome contribution.

Anindita Basak is a cloud architect with almost 15+ years of experience, the last 12 years of which she has been extensively working on Azure. She has delivered various real-time implementations on Azure data analytics, and cloud-native and real-time event-driven architecture for Fortune 500 enterprises, ranging from banking, financial services, and insurance (BFSI)to retail sectors. She is also a cloud and DataOps trainer and consultant, and author of cloud AI and DevOps books.

Table of Contents

Preface   xv

Part 1: Core Data Concepts

1

Understanding the Core Data Terminologies   3

Understanding the core data
concepts   3
What is data?   4
How is data stored in a modern cloud
environment?   7

Describing a data solution   8
Transactional databases   8
Analytical databases   9

Defining the data type and
proper storage   11
Characteristics of relational and non-
relational databases   12

A transactional workload   15
An analytical workload   17

Understanding data
ingestion   18
Understanding batch load   19
Understanding data streaming   20

Case study   21
Summary   22
Sample questions and
answers   23
Answer key   23

2

Exploring the Roles and Responsibilities in Data Domain   25

Different workforces in a data
domain   25
Most common roles in a data domain   25
Database Administrator   26
Data engineer   26

Data analyst   26

Tasks and tools for database
administration profiles   27
Tasks of the DBA   27

Tools for the DBA   28
Tasks of the data analyst   33
Tools for the data analyst   33

**Tasks and tools for data
engineer profiles**   30
Tasks of the data engineer   31
Tools for the data engineer   31

Case study   34
Summary   36
**Sample questions and
answers**   36
Answer key   37

**Tasks and tools for the data
analyst**   33

3

Working with Relational Data   39

**Exploring the characteristics of
relational data**   39
Tables and entities   40
Relationship between entities   40

DDL   45
DML and DQL   46

**Describing the database
components**   48
Views   48
Stored procedures   49
Triggers   49
Indexes   50

**Exploring relational data
structures**   40
Data normalization   40

Introducing SQL   42
Key advantages of SQL   43
Key disadvantages of SQL   43
Understanding the categories of SQL
commands   44

Case study   50
Summary   52
Sample questions and answers   53
Answer key   53

4

Working with Non-Relational Data   55

**Exploring the characteristics
of non-relational data**   55
**Understanding the types of
non-relational data**   56
Non-structured data   56
Semi-structured data   57
Non-relational data basic storage   57

Exploring NoSQL databases   58

What is a NoSQL database?   58
Key-value store   58
Document database   59
Column family database   60
Graph database   62

**Identifying non-relational database
use cases**   64
Case study   64

A 360-degree customer view   65
Fraud detection – financial
institutions   67

Summary   67
Sample questions and answers   67
Answer key   69

5

Exploring Data Analytics Concepts   71

Exploring data ingestion
and processing   71
Data pipelines   72
Data ingestion types   74
Data source connectors   74

Exploring the analytical data
store   76
Data warehouse   76
Data lake   76
Hybrid approaches   76

Exploring an analytical data
model   77
Facts and dimensions   78

Exploring data visualization   79
Case study   81
Data-driven culture   81

Summary   82
Sample questions and answers   82
Answer key   84

Part 2: Relational Data in Azure

6

Integrating Relational Data on Azure   87

Exploring relational Azure
data services   87
Elastic pool   89

Use cases   98

Summary   99
Sample questions and
answers   100
Answer key   100

7

Provisioning and Configuring Relational Database Services
in Azure   101

Technical requirements   101
Provisioning relational Azure
data services   102

Provisioning Azure SQL Database   102
Provisioning Azure Database for
PostgreSQL and MySQL   110

Configuring relational databases
on Azure   114
Configuring Azure SQL
Database   115

Configuring and managing Azure
Database for PostgreSQL and
MySQL   119
Summary   120
Sample questions and answers   121
Answer key   122

8

Querying Relational Data in Azure   123

Technical requirements   123
Introducing SQL on Azure   124
Querying relational data in
Azure SQL Database   124
Common connection issues   129

Querying relational data in Azure
Database for PostgreSQL   137

Connecting to Azure Database for
PostgreSQL   138
Querying Azure Database for
PostgreSQL   140
Summary   143
Sample questions and answers   143
Answer key   144

Part 3: Non-Relational Data in Azure

9

Exploring Non-Relational Data Offerings in Azure   147

Exploring Azure non-relational
data stores   148
Exploring Azure Blob storage   148
Azure Data Lake Storage Gen2   149
Exploring Azure Files   150
Exploring Azure Table storage   151

Exploring Azure NoSQL
databases   152
Exploring Azure Cosmos DB   153

Azure Cosmos DB APIs   153
Core (SQL) API   154
MongoDB API   154
Table API   155
Cassandra API   155
Gremlin API   156

Summary   157
Sample questions and
answers   157
Answer key   158

10

Provisioning and Configuring Non-Relational Data Services in Azure   159

Technical requirements   159

Provisioning non-relational
data services   160

Provisioning Azure Cosmos DB   160

Configuring Azure Cosmos DB   167

Creating a sample Azure Cosmos DB
database   168

Provisioning an Azure
storage account and Data
LakeStorage   171

Summary   173

Sample questions and
answers   173

Answer key   174

Part 4: Analytics Workload on Azure

11

Components of a Modern Data Warehouse   177

Describing modern data
warehousing   177

Challenges of traditional data
warehouses   178

The birth of big data   179

Azure HDInsight   180

Modern data warehouse   181

Azure for the modern data warehouse   181

Exploring Azure data services
for modern data warehouses   182

Data ingestion and preparation
(ELT/ETL)   182

Data storage – Azure Data Lake
Storage Gen2   183

Data ingestion – Azure Data Factory and
Azure Synapse Analytics   183

Data preparation – Azure
Databricks   184

Modern data warehouse – Azure
Synapse Analytics   185

Real-time data analytics –
Azure Stream Analytics, Azure
Synapse Data Explorer, and
Spark streaming   192

Azure Stream Analytics   192

Azure Data Explorer and Azure
Synapse Data Explorer pools   193

Apache Spark Streaming   193

Delta Lake   194

Summary   194

Sample questions and answers   194

Answer key   195

12

Provisioning and Configuring Large-Scale Data Analytics in Azure   197

Technical requirements	198	Azure dedicated SQL pool	211
Understanding common practices for data loading	198	Azure Spark pools	216
		Azure Synapse Link	220
Provisioning an Azure Synapse		Azure Synapse Data Explorer	220
workspace	198	Azure Machine Learning	222
Practicing data load	202	Summary	223
Data storage and processing	208	Sample questions and answers	224
Azure serverless SQL pool	209	Answer key	225

13

Working with Power BI   227

Technical requirements	228	Publishing a report	236
Introducing Power BI	228	Exploring Power BI Service	238
The building blocks of Power BI	228	Creating a dashboard	238
Exploring Power BI Desktop	230	Power BI mobile app	240
		Summary	242
Creating a Power BI file	232	Sample questions and answers	242
Creating a connection	234	Answer key	243

14

DP-900 Mock Exam   245

Practice test – questions	245	Modern data warehouse analytics on Azure	249
Core data concepts	246		
Relational data on Azure	247	Practice test – answers and explanations	250
Non-relational data on Azure	248		

Core data concepts   251
Relational data on Azure   254
Non-relational data on Azure   257

Modern data warehouse analytics
on Azure   260

Summary   **262**

Index   265

Other Books You May Enjoy   276

Preface

Today, the world's leading companies are data-driven, and a good strategy for using data is one of the key success factors for organizations worldwide. Following this trend, there is a growing demand for professionals trained to work with this data, orchestrating, processing, and generating intelligence from it.

Microsoft Certified Azure Data Fundamentals (Exam DP-900) Certification Guide will introduce you to the fundamental knowledge required to ensure successful data projects in Azure, preparing you for the DP-900 certification test.

Going through basic concepts of data as well as hands-on exercises with Azure data services, this book will teach you about the different technologies offered in Azure and when to use each one.

The book is structured in four parts. The first covers core data concepts, the second relational data in Azure, the third covers non-relational data in Azure and the fourth part covers analytics workloads on Azure, ending with a mockup of the DP-900 test evaluating the knowledge acquired.

Who this book is for

This book is for data engineers, database administrators, or aspiring data professionals getting ready to take the DP-900 exam. It will also be helpful for those looking for a bit of guidance on how to be better equipped for Azure-related job roles such as Azure database administrator or Azure data engineer. A basic understanding of core data concepts and relational and non-relational data will help you make the most out of this book, but they're not a pre-requisite.

What this book covers

Chapter 1, Understanding the Core Data Terminologies, is all about creating a knowledge foundation around data types, transactional databases, analytical databases, data ingestion, and data stores.

Chapter 2, Exploring the Roles and Responsibilities in Data Domain, continues your introduction to the different job roles associated with creating, managing, and using databases. You will learn about the key responsibilities of these roles and the tools that these roles use on the Azure and Microsoft cloud portfolios.

Chapter 3, Working with Relational Data, explores the relational model for databases, how tables are structured, how you can use indexes to improve query performance, and how you can use views to simplify complex queries.

Chapter 4, Working with Non-Relational Data, explores non-relational databases and how they compare to relational databases. You will learn about the different types of non-relational databases commonly used by applications.

Chapter 5, Exploring Data Analytics Concepts, covers how to generate insights by processing data into a data analytics system, enabling the business to carry out data-driven operations.

Chapter 6, Integrating Relational Data on Azure, covers the Azure data services for relational databases, including Azure SQL Database, Azure Database for PostgreSQL, Azure Database for MySQL, and Azure Database for MariaDB. You will explore scenarios for using these database management systems.

Chapter 7, Provisioning and Configuring Relational Database Services in Azure, teaches you how to provision and configure Azure SQL Database, Azure Database for PostgreSQL, and Azure Database for MySQL.

Chapter 8, Querying Relational Data in Azure, explores **Structured Query Language** (**SQL**) and how you can use it to query, insert, update, and delete data in Azure SQL Database.

Chapter 9, Exploring Non-Relational Data Offerings in Azure, explores Azure data services for non-relational data, including Azure Table storage, Azure Blob Storage, Azure Files, and Azure Cosmos DB, as well as situations for using them.

Chapter 10, Provisioning and Configuring Non-Relational Data Services in Azure, looks at how to provision and configure Azure Cosmos DB and Azure Data Lake Storage.

Chapter 11, Components of a Modern Data Warehouse, examines the components of a modern data warehouse. You will understand the role of services such as Azure Databricks, Azure Synapse Analytics, and Azure HDInsight. You will also see how to use Azure Synapse Analytics to load and process data.

Chapter 12, Provisioning and Configuring Large-Scale Data Analytics in Azure, explores data ingestion options to build a data warehouse with Azure, services to perform data analytics, and features of Azure Synapse Analytics. You will create a Synapse Analytics workspace and use it to ingest and analyze data.

Chapter 13, Working with Power BI, is where you will learn what Power BI is, including its building blocks and how they work together.

Chapter 14, DP-900 Mock Exam, provides practice tests to prepare you for the DP-900 exam.

To get the most out of this book

You will need a computer with Windows or macOS with internet access to download the Azure Data Studio and Power Bi Desktop software, as well as access to the Azure portal and the Azure service websites. All code examples have been tested using Azure Data Studio on the Windows 11 operating system. However, they should work with macOS, Linux, and future version releases too.

Software covered in the book	Operating system requirements
Azure Data Studio	Windows, macOS, or Linux
Power BI Desktop	Windows or macOS
Power BI mobile app	Windows or macOS

Power BI Desktop and the mobile app can be downloaded from here:

`https://powerbi.microsoft.com/en-us/downloads/`

Azure Data Studio can be downloaded from here:

`https://learn.microsoft.com/en-us/sql/azure-data-studio/download-azure-data-studio`

If you are using the digital version of this book, we advise you to type the code yourself or access the code from the book's GitHub repository (a link is available in the next section). Doing so will help you avoid any potential errors related to the copying and pasting of code.

Download the example code files

You can download the example code files for this book from GitHub at `https://github.com/PacktPublishing/Microsoft-Certified-Azure-Data-Fundamentals-Exam-DP-900-Certification-Guide`. If there's an update to the code, it will be updated in the GitHub repository.

We also have other code bundles from our rich catalog of books and videos available at `https://github.com/PacktPublishing/`. Check them out!

Download the color images

We also provide a PDF file that has color images of the screenshots/diagrams used in this book. You can download it here: `https://packt.link/LTQeN`.

Conventions used

There are a number of text conventions used throughout this book.

`Code in text`: Indicates code words in text, database table names, folder names, filenames, file extensions, pathnames, dummy URLs, user input, and Twitter handles. Here is an example: "Mount the downloaded `WebStorm-10*.dmg` disk image file as another disk in your system."

A block of code is set as follows:

```
html, body, #map {
  height: 100%;
  margin: 0;
  padding: 0
}
```

Bold: Indicates a new term, an important word, or words that you see onscreen. For instance, words in menus or dialog boxes appear in **bold**. Here is an example: "Select **System info** from the **Administration** panel."

> **Tips or important notes**
> Appear like this.

Get in touch

Feedback from our readers is always welcome.

General feedback: If you have questions about any aspect of this book, email us at customercare@ packtpub.com and mention the book title in the subject of your message.

Errata: Although we have taken every care to ensure the accuracy of our content, mistakes do happen. If you have found a mistake in this book, we would be grateful if you would report this to us. Please visit www.packtpub.com/support/errata and fill in the form.

Piracy: If you come across any illegal copies of our works in any form on the internet, we would be grateful if you would provide us with the location address or website name. Please contact us at copyright@packt.com with a link to the material.

If you are interested in becoming an author: If there is a topic that you have expertise in and you are interested in either writing or contributing to a book, please visit authors.packtpub.com.

Share your thoughts

Once you've read *Microsoft Certified Azure Data Fundamentals (Exam DP-900) Certification Guide*, we'd love to hear your thoughts! Scan the QR code below to go straight to the Amazon review page for this book and share your feedback.

https://packt.link/r/1-803-24063-6

Your review is important to us and the tech community and will help us make sure we're delivering excellent quality content. Download a free PDF copy of this book

Download a free PDF copy of this book

Thanks for purchasing this book!

Do you like to read on the go but are unable to carry your print books everywhere?

Is your eBook purchase not compatible with the device of your choice?

Don't worry, now with every Packt book you get a DRM-free PDF version of that book at no cost.

Read anywhere, any place, on any device. Search, copy, and paste code from your favorite technical books directly into your application.

The perks don't stop there, you can get exclusive access to discounts, newsletters, and great free content in your inbox daily!

Follow these simple steps to get the benefits:

1. Scan the QR code or visit the link below:

https://packt.link/free-ebook/9781803240633

2. Submit your proof of purchase

3. That's it! We'll send your free PDF and other benefits to your email directly

Part 1:
Core Data Concepts

This part will provide complete coverage of the knowledge and skills required for the *Skills measured* under the *Describe Core Data Concepts* section of the exam syllabus. We will also cover knowledge and skills that go beyond exam content so that you are prepared for a real-world, day-to-day Azure data-focused role.

In this part, you will learn about the concepts surrounding data projects, from the terminology and the roles of a data team to the different types of data workloads, such as relational, non-relational, and analytical.

This part comprises the following chapters:

- *Chapter 1, Understanding the Core Data Terminologies*
- *Chapter 2, Exploring the Roles and Responsibilities in Data Domain*
- *Chapter 3, Working with Relational Data*
- *Chapter 4, Working with Non-Relational Data*
- *Chapter 5, Exploring Data Analytics Concepts*

1

Understanding the Core Data Terminologies

Welcome, dear reader!

This book has been prepared based on the knowledge that you need to pass the Azure DP-900 Data Platform Fundamentals exam. So, you will find detailed use cases, hand's-on exercises, as well as sample questions and answers to help you during the exam.

This book will not only prepare you for certification but also complement the knowledge needed for planning and working in a data organization. You can look forward to learning about transactional and analytical database concepts, SQL and NoSQL, when to use each option, and the most modern tools and techniques for implementation on Azure.

Data generation and data processing have been growing exponentially in recent years. Data is being generated and processed everywhere: in information systems, cell phones, smart watches, smart TVs, city buses, subways, and cars, among others. Knowing how to capture and process this data to generate intelligence provides today's main competitive advantage in the market.

To start understanding how these technologies and solutions work, it is necessary to know the concepts of data storage and processing, which we will cover in this introductory chapter.

By the end of this chapter, you will be able to understand the following:

- The types of data and how to store it
- Relational and non-relational data
- Data Analytics
- How to differentiate the data workloads

Understanding the core data concepts

To start, let's understand the terminologies used in the data world so that all the following concepts are easily interpreted to be applied to technologies.

What is data?

Data is a *record*, also called a *fact*, which can be a number, text, or description used to make decisions. Data only generates intelligence when processed and then this data is called *information* or *insights*.

Data is classified into three basic formats: *structured*, *semi-structured*, and *unstructured* data. We will learn about them all in the following sections.

Structured data

Structured data is formatted and typically stored in a table represented by columns and rows. This data is found in relational databases, which organize their table structures in a way that creates relationships between these tables.

The following figure shows an example of a simple table with structured data:

TABLE CUSTOMER

CUSTOMER_ID	LAST_NAME	FIRST_NAME	STREET	CITY	ZIP_CODE	COUNTRY
10505	Cortez	Leo	609 St Patrick Rd	Sydney	3004	Australia
10506	Carter	Tomas	Berliner Weg 15	Tamm	71799	Germany
11040	Brown	Noah	Av Grande, 105	Madrid	28034	Spain
15020	Wilson	John	4212 S 7th St	Chester	33098	USA
10220	Jones	Frank	71 San Antonio Av	Arlington	69003	USA
11892	Ness	Sarah	456 Vivid Island Dr	Plano	75024	USA

Figure 1.1 – Example of structured data in a database

In this example, the table called CUSTOMER has seven columns and six records (rows) with different values.

The CUSTOMER table could be part of a **customer relationship management** (**CRM**) database, for example, financial and **enterprise resource planning** (**ERP**), among other types of business applications.

Semi-structured data

Semi-structured data is a structure in which records have attributes such as columns but are not organized in a tabular way like structured data. One of the most used formats for semi-structured data is **JavaScript Object Notation** (**JSON**) files. The following example demonstrates the structure of a JSON file containing the registration of one customer:

```
## JSON FILE - Document 1 ##
{
   "CUSTOMER_ID": "10302",
   "NAME":
```

```
{
  "FIRST_NAME": "Leo",
  "LAST_NAME": "Boucher"
},
"ADDRESS":
{
  "STREET": "54, rue Royale",
  "CITY": "Nantes",
  "ZIP_CODE": "44000",
  "COUNTRY": "France"
  }
}
```

In this example, we can see that each JSON file contains a record, like the rows of the structured data table, but there are other formats of JSON and similar files that contain multiple records in the same file.

In addition to the JSON format, there is data in key-value and graph databases, which are considered semi-structured data, too.

The key-value database stores data in a related array format. These arrays have a unique identification key per record. Values written to a record can have a variety of formats, including numbers, text, and even full JSON files.

The following is an example of a key-value database:

Students		Professors	
Key	Value	Key	Value
1	Name: Jean Grey DateOfBirth: 19-05-1963 IDCard: 1234567 PlaceOfOrigin: Austin Country: USA AcademicProgram_ID:1	1	Name: Charles Xavier DateOfBirth: 13-07-1940 IDCard: 111111 PlaceOfOrigin: Mirfield Country: UK

2	Name: Scott Summers
	 DateOfBirth: 12-10-1968
	 IDCard: 765414A
	 Supervisor: {
	   Name: Emma Frost
	   DateOfBirth: 1-1-1936
	   IDCard: 222222
	   }
		2	Name: Emma Frost
			 DateOfBirth: 1-1-1936
			 IDCard: 222222

Figure 1.2 – Example of a key-value database

As you can see in the preceding figure, each record can contain different attributes. They are stored in a single collection, with no predefined schema, tables, or columns, and no relationships between the entities; this differentiates the key-value database from the relational database.

The graph database is used to store data that requires complex relationships. A graph database contains nodes (object information) and edges (object relationship information). It means that the graph database predetermines what objects are and the relationships they will have with each other, but the records can contain different formats. The following is a representation of nodes and edges in a graph database of sales and deliveries:

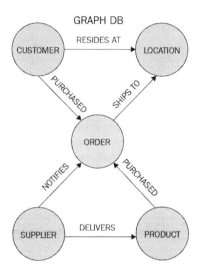

Figure 1.3 – Example of a graph database

The diagram demonstrates how the relations around the **ORDER** entity are created in a graph database, considering the **CUSTOMER**, **LOCATION**, **SUPPLIER**, and **PRODUCT** nodes in the process. It represents an interesting acceleration in terms of query processing in the database because the graph is already structured to deliver the relations faster.

Unstructured data

In addition to structured and semi-structured data, there is also unstructured data, such as audio, videos, images, or binary records without a defined organization.

This data can also be processed to generate information, but the type of storage and processing for this is different from that of structured and semi-structured data. It is common, for example, for unstructured data such as audio to be transcribed using artificial intelligence, generating a mass of semi-structured data for processing.

Now that you understand the basics of data types, let's look at how that data is stored in a cloud environment.

How is data stored in a modern cloud environment?

Depending on the data format, structured, semi-structured, and unstructured cloud platforms have different solutions. In Azure, we can count on Azure SQL Database, Azure SQL Database for PostgreSQL, Azure Database for MySQL, and database servers installed on virtual machines, such as SQL Server on a virtual machine in Azure, to store *structured data*. These are called relational databases.

Semi-structured data can be stored in Azure Cosmos DB and *unstructured data* (such as videos and images) can be stored in Azure Blob storage in a platform called Azure Data Lake Storage, optimized for queries and processing.

These services are delivered by Azure in the following formats:

- **Infrastructure as a service (IaaS)** – Databases deployed on virtual machines
- **Platform as a service (PaaS)** – Managed database services, where the responsibility for managing the virtual machine and the operating system lies with Azure

For these database services to be used, they must be provisioned and configured to receive the data properly.

One of the most important aspects after provisioning a service is the access control configuration. Azure allows you to create custom access role control, but in general, we maintain at least three profiles:

- **Read-only** – Users can read existing data on that service, but they cannot add new records or edit or delete them
- **Read/Write** – Users can read, create, delete, and edit records
- **Owner** – Higher access privilege, including the ability to manage permission for other users to use this data

With these configured profiles, you will be able to add users to the profiles to access the data storage/databases.

Let's look at an example. You are an administrator of a CUSTOMER database, and you have the Owner profile. So, you configure access to this database for the leader of the commercial area to Read/Write, and for salespeople to Read-only.

In addition to the permissions configuration, it is important to review all network configurations, data retention, and backup patterns, among other administrative activities. These management tasks will be covered in *Chapter 7, Provisioning and Configuring Relational Database Services in Azure*.

In all database scenarios, we will have different access requirements, and it is important (as in the example) to accurately delimit the access level needs of each profile.

Describing a data solution

There are two types of database solutions: transactional solutions and analytical solutions. In the following sections, we will understand in detail what these solutions are and the requirements for choosing between them.

Transactional databases

Transactional databases are used by systems for basic operations: creating, reading, updating, and deleting. Transactional systems are considered the core of the informatization of business processes. With these basic operations, we can create entities such as customers, products, stores, and sales transactions, among others, to store important data.

A transactional database is commonly known as **online transaction processing** (OLTP) considering that this type of database serves online transactional operations between the application and the database.

For an organization, transactional databases usually have their data segmented into entities, which can be tables (or not), with or without a relationship between these entities to facilitate the correlation between this data.

For example, an e-commerce database can be structured with a table called `Shopping_Cart`, which represents the products that are being selected in the store during user navigation, and another called `Purchases` with the completed transaction records.

The process of segmenting entities in a database is called **normalization**, which will be covered in *Chapter 3, Working with Relational Data*.

The format of a normalized transactional database is optimized for transactional operations, but it is not the best format for data exploration and analysis.

The following is an example of a relational transactional database:

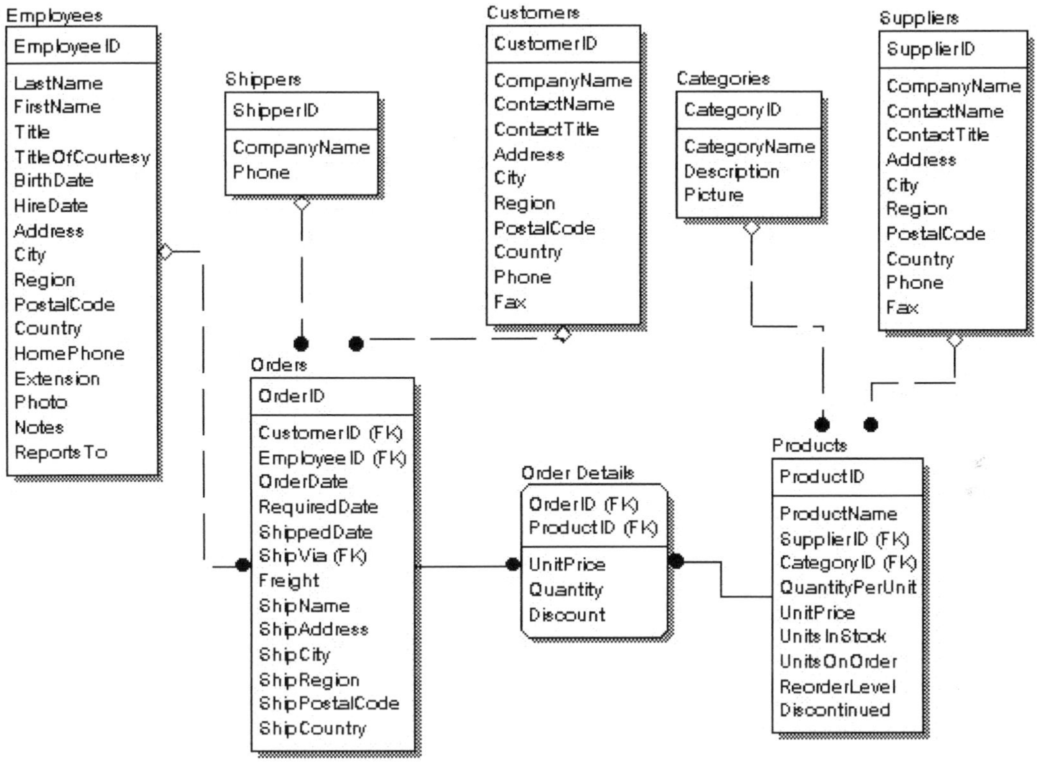

Figure 1.4 – Example of a relational transactional database

The preceding figure demonstrates a relational database of transactional workloads in a sales and delivery system. We can see the main entity, **Orders**, joined to **Employees**, **Shippers**, **Customers**, and **Order Details**, which then detail all products of this order in the relationship with the **Products entity**, which looks for information in the **Categories** and **Suppliers entities**.

Analytical databases

When the data solution requires a good interface for queries, explorations, and data analysis, the data storage organization is different from transactional databases. To meet this requirement, we prioritize the data aggregations and relationships for data consumption and exploration; this specialized data storage is called an **analytical database**.

Analytical databases use a process called **online analytical processing (OLAP)** and have undergone a great evolution in recent years with the emergence of data warehouses and big data platforms.

Analytical databases are constituted through a process of data ingestion, and they are responsible for processing and transforming the data into insights and information and then making this processed information available for consumption. The following steps describe this process:

1. **Data ingestion** – The process responsible for connecting to transactional databases or other data sources to collect raw transaction information and include it in the analytical database

2. **Data processing** – The process performed by the OLAP platform to create a data model, organize entities, perform indicator calculations, and define metrics for data consumption

3. **Data query** – After the data model is loaded with the proper organization for querying, data manipulation and reporting tools can connect to the OLAP platform to perform your queries

The following diagram is an example of a structured data model in an OLAP database:

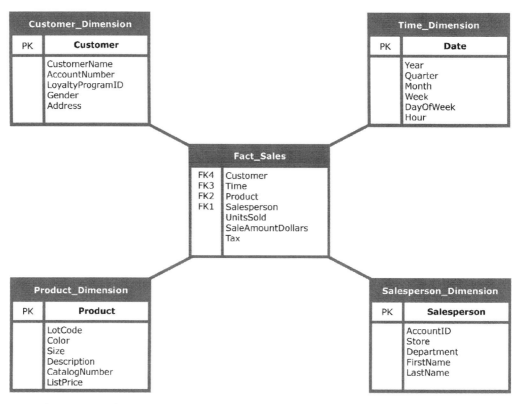

Legend: PK = primary key, FK = foreign key

Figure 1.5 – Example of an analytical relationship

The following diagram is a simple comparison of OLTP and OLAP databases:

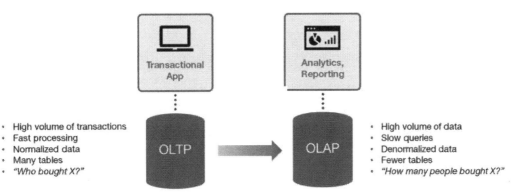

Figure 1.6 – Data flow between OLTP and OLAP

The preceding figure demonstrates the traditional flow of data, which is sourced and stored in transactional OLTP databases and then moved to OLAP analytical databases for data intelligence generation.

> **Important note**
>
> There are modern data storage platforms that aim to unite OLTP and OLAP on the same platform, but these databases, often called NewSQL, still need to mature their structures to deliver the best of transactional and analytical worlds in the same database. The industry standard is to keep transactional and analytical data structures separate.

In this section, we defined what transactional and analytical data solutions are and the characteristics of each solution. In the next section, we will detail the recommended data types and storage for each of these types.

Defining the data type and proper storage

Categorizing the data to identify its types and best solutions for your storage is an important process for a data solution, and not just for evaluating whether it is structured, unstructured, or semi-structured. In this section, you will learn about the characteristics of different types of data.

Characteristics of relational and non-relational databases

Relational databases are the most traditional and used database format, as they have an easy-to-understand design and a simple tabular data model like other simple platforms such as Excel spreadsheets. Relational databases have predefined schemas, which are the structures of their tables, containing columns, the data type of each column, and other parameters such as primary and secondary keys used in relationships.

However, relational databases with these rigid schemas can pose challenges, as presented in the following example.

Your CRM system has a database structure with a CUSTOMER table, where you intend to store customer data: CUSTOMER_ID, CUSTOMER_NAME, ADDRESS, MOBILE_PHONE, and ZIP_CODE. To do this, you start by creating a CUSTOMER table with five fields:

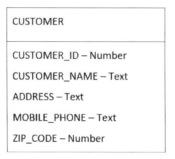

Figure 1.7 – Example of a CUSTOMER table in a relational database

However, after setting up this table, you realize that you have clients that have more than one address and zip code, and even more than one mobile phone number. How can you solve this issue?

To face problems like this one, we can use *normalization* one more time. Normalization is done when there is a need to split a table (CUSTOMER, in this example) into more child tables that are correlated to the initial table.

Therefore, we can change the CUSTOMER table as follows:

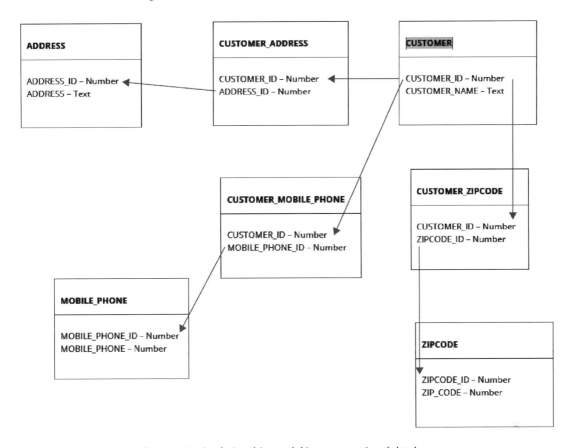

Figure 1.8 – A relationship model in a transactional database

Non-relational databases allow you to store data in its original format without having a predefined schema as in relational databases. The most common non-relational storage format is document storage, where each record in the database is an independent file. The benefit is that each file can have different and unique attributes.

On the other hand, the files being independent can present a challenge: **data duplication**.

Going back to our CUSTOMER entity example in a relational database, when two or more customers live at one address, the database records that relationship, and the normalized database only keeps one address record. But in a non-relational database, if two customers live at the same address, this address will be presented in the records of the first customer and the second customer as well, independently.

Let's now analyze how this storage could be structured in a relational database, using the concept of normalization:

CUSTOMER	
CUSTOMER_ID	CUSTOMER_NAME
0001	MARK HUGGS
0002	KRISTI LAMP

CUSTOMER_ADDRESS	
CUSTOMER_ID	ADDRESS_ID
0001	0001
0002	0001

ADDRESS	
ADDRESS_ID	ADDRESS
0001	1200, Harper Str
0002	585, Hampton Ave

Figure 1.9 – Example of data structured into tables

The preceding figure exemplifies the data stored within the relational model tables with the CUSTOMER, CUSTOMER_ADDRESS, and ADDRESS entities to understand the structure of a normalized table.

Now let's analyze the same data in a CUSTOMER table, but in the format of a non-relational database:

```
## JSON FILE - CUSTOMER ##
{
  "CUSTOMER_ID": "0001",
  " CUSTOMER_NAME":
  {
    "FIRST_NAME": " MARK",
    "LAST_NAME": " HUGGS"
  },
  "ADDRESS":
  {
    "STREET": "1200, Harper Str"
  }
}
## JSON FILE - CUSTOMER2 ##
{
  "CUSTOMER_ID": "0002",
  " CUSTOMER_NAME":
  {
    "FIRST_NAME": " KRISTI",
    "LAST_NAME": " LAMP"
  },
```

```
  "ADDRESS":
  {
    "STREET": "1200, Harper Str"
  }
}
```

In the preceding example, we can see two records in a CUSTOMER table, with each record being a JSON document structured with the attributes of each customer.

Thus, we can observe that the same data can be stored in relational and non-relational structures.

Therefore, to decide between a relational or non-relational data storage solution, you must evaluate the behavior of the application or the user that will use that database, the relationships between the entities, and possible normalization processes.

Both relational and non-relational databases should be used primarily for transactional workloads. In the upcoming sections, we will understand the differences between these transactional workloads and analytical workloads.

A transactional workload

Relational and non-relational databases can be used as solutions for transactional workloads, which are the databases used to perform basic data storage operations: **create, read, update, and delete (CRUD)**. Transactional operations must be done in sequence, with a transaction control that only confirms the conclusion of this transaction (a process called a **commit**) when the entire operation is successfully executed. If this does not occur, the transaction is canceled, and all processes are not performed, thus generating a process called **rollback**.

An important idea to help understand the difference between relational and non-relational databases is ACID, present in most database technologies. These properties are as follows:

- **Atomicity**: This is the property that controls the transaction and defines whether it was successfully performed completely to commit or must be canceled by performing a rollback. Database technology should ensure atomicity.

- **Consistency**: For a running transaction, it is important to evaluate consistency between the database state *before* receiving the data and the database state *after* receiving the data. For example, in a bank transfer, when funds are added to an account, those funds must have a source. Therefore, it is important to know this source and whether the fund's source exit process has already been performed before confirming the inclusion in this new account.

- **Isolation**: This property evaluates whether there are multiple executions of transactions similar to the current one and if so, it keeps the database in the same state. It then evaluates whether the execution of transactions was sequential. In the bank transfer example, if multiple transactions are sent simultaneously, it checks whether the amounts have already left the source for all transactions, or you need to review one by one, transaction per transaction.

- **Durability**: This is responsible for evaluating whether a transaction remains in the committed database even if there is a failure during the process, such as a power outage or latency at the time of recording the record.

ACID properties are not unique to transactional databases; they are also found in analytic databases. At this point, the most important thing is to understand that these settings exist, and you can adjust them as per the requirements of your data solution use case.

Since we are talking about databases, let's understand an acronym that is widely used to represent database software: DBMS.

Database management systems

Database management systems (**DBMSs**), which are database software, have ACID properties within their architecture, and in addition to performing these controls, they need to manage several complex situations. For example, if multiple users or systems try to access or modify database records, the database systems need to isolate transactions, perform all necessary validations quickly, and maintain the consistency of the data stored after the transaction is committed. For this, some DBMS technologies work with temporary transaction locks, so that actions are done sequentially. This lock is done during the process of an action executing in that record; for example, in an edit of a field in a table, the lock ends as soon as the commit is executed, confirming that transaction.

Some DBMSs are called **distributed databases**. These databases have their architecture distributed in different storage and processing locations, which can be on-premises in the company's data center or a different data center in the cloud. Distributed database solutions are widely used to maintain consistency in databases that will serve applications in different geographic locations, but this consistency doesn't need to be synchronous. For example, a mobile game can be played in the United States and Brazil, and the database of this game has some entities (categories, game modes, and so on) that must be shared among all players. But the transactions from the United States player do not necessarily need to appear to the player in Brazil in a real-time way; this transactional data will be synchronized from the United States to Brazil, but in an asynchronous process. Let's understand this process next.

Eventual consistency

All transactions in distributed databases take longer to process than in undistributed databases because it is necessary to replicate the data across all nodes in this distributed system. So, to maintain an adequate replication speed, the distributed databases only synchronize the data that is needed. This is the concept of *eventual consistency*, which configures ACID to perform replication between the distributed nodes asynchronously, after the confirmation of the transaction on the main node of the database is created. This technique can lead to temporary inconsistencies between database nodes. Ideally, the application connected to a distributed database does not require a guarantee of data ordering. It means that the data relating to this eventual consistency may appear to users with an eventual delay as well. Distributed databases are widely used by social media platforms, for news feeds, likes, and shares, among other features.

Let's use the following figure to understand the behavior of a database with eventual consistency:

Figure 1.10 – Diagram of an eventual consistency database

The preceding diagram shows behavior that we can observe when querying information in a database with eventual consistency. Instead of fetching the ball in a sequential way, the hero who retrieved it made the query of the ball in a future frame, generating a momentary duplication of the ball. In the end, only one ball was retrieved, after the sync was done.

This is an analogy for an eventual consistency database, where queries do not need to be made on entities that are already synchronized between all replicas of the database, and sometimes, this momentary duplication happens until the asynchronous process data update is complete.

In addition to transactional, relational, or non-relational databases, we also have another data workload, the analytical workload, which we will address in the next section.

An analytical workload

The second category of data solutions is the analytical workloads. These analytical solutions are based on high-volume data processing platforms, optimized for querying and exploring, and not for CRUD transactions or with ACID properties. In analytical databases, we aggregate various data sources, such as more than one transactional database, as well as logs, files, images, videos, and everything that can generate information for a business analyst.

This raw data is processed and aggregated, thus generating summaries, trends, and predictions that can support decision-making.

An analytical workload can be based on a specific time or a sequence of dated events. In these workloads, it's common to evaluate only the data that is relevant to the analysis. For example, if you have a sales system with a transactional database (source) with several tables recording all sales, products, categories, and customers, among others, it is important to evaluate which of these tables can be used for the analytical database (destination) and then perform the data connections.

To create an analytical database, it is necessary to perform data ingestion, a process of copying data from sources to the analytical base. For this, a technique called **extract, transform, and load (ETL)**, or the more recent **extract, load, and transform (ELT)**, is used. The following figure demonstrates this process with an example of a transactional database as the data source and the analytical database as the destination:

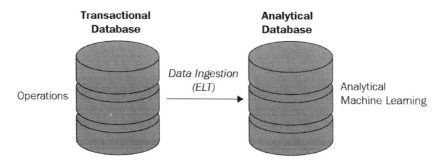

Figure 1.11 – Data flow between a transactional database and an analytical database

In the preceding diagram, we can see that transactional databases are storages of information systems that automate business processes. Analytical databases act on simple and advanced data analysis, using, for example, statistical models with the application of machine learning, a branch of artificial intelligence. The data ingestion process is an important process for assembling an analytical database that meets the data solution. In the next section, we will understand what data ingestion is and the different types of this ingestion.

Understanding data ingestion

Data ingestion is the process of copying operational data from data sources to organize it in an analytical database. There are two different techniques for performing this copy: batching data and online data streaming.

It is important to identify latency requirements between the time when the data is generated in the source database and the data availability in the analytical database.

Understanding batch load

When batching the data, the operation is offline. You must define the periodicity for creating the data batch load, collecting data in the data source, and then inserting it into the analytical database.

The periodicity can be hourly, daily, or even monthly, if the requirement of analysis of this data is met. Events that can trigger a batch load can be a new record on a table entity in the database, an action triggered by a user in an application, a manual trigger, and more.

An example of batch processing might be the way we get vote counts in elections. The votes are not counted one by one the moment after the voter has voted, but they are inserted in lots that are processed during election day until the completion of all charges and the definition of the results.

Advantages of batch load

Batch loads can be heavily used in data solutions, but they do not meet all requirements for data solutions. The following are two of the advantages of this ingestion technique:

- It is the most used method by companies that have multiple transactional systems with large volumes of data. This is because due to scheduling loads, it can be made at the most convenient time, such as outside business hours when transactional servers are in lower demand.

- You can monitor the loads to verify where you need to optimize a script or a method independently, so if you need to prioritize one specific load performance, you can manipulate your computing resources to prioritize that load.

Constraints of batch load

To continue the evaluation of the technique, it is important to understand the constraints of adopting batch loads as well:

- There is a delay between the time of data generation on the transactional database and the availability of this data on the analytical database, which sometimes makes it impossible to follow up and immediately make a decision based on the numbers

- The full batch of data must be completed to then begin copying, and if there is any data unavailability, inconsistent data, or network latency between transactional and analytical bases, among other situations, the batch load will fail

Batch loads can be our default data consumption for legacy databases, file repositories, and other types of data sources. But there are business requirements to consume some data in near real time, for monitoring and quick decision-making. And to meet these needs, we have another technique, called data streaming, which loads data online.

Understanding data streaming

In data-streaming-based data ingestion, there is an online connection between the data source and the analytical database, and the pieces of data are processed one by one, in events, right after their generation at this source. For example, for a sales tracking monitoring solution, sales managers need to track sales data in *near real time* on a dashboard for immediate decision-making. The sales transaction database is linked through a streaming load to the analytical database that receives this data, processes it, and demonstrates it on a monitoring dashboard.

Another example could be a stock exchange and its real-time stock tracking panels. These dashboards receive processed information from purchase and sale transaction data for stock papers in a data stream. See the following figure with the data flow in this scenario:

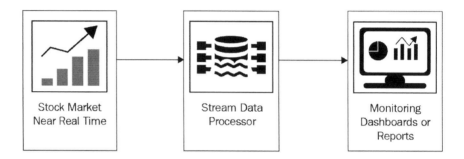

Figure 1.12 – Stock market example diagram

The load on data streaming is not always done online; it can also be done at intervals that load a portion of data. Data streaming is a continuous window of data ingestion between the source and the destination, while in the batch load, each batch opens and closes the connection to the process.

Let us now evaluate the advantages and disadvantages of the data streaming technique.

Advantages of data streaming

The advantages are listed as follows:

- The delay between data creation and analytical processing can be minimal
- The latency between the source and the target in the order of seconds or milliseconds
- Analytical solutions can demonstrate both past data and performance trends, which assists in immediate decision-making while events are happening

Constraints of streaming data load

The disadvantages are listed as follows:

- Most transactional database technologies do not have a native streaming data export technology, so you need to implement this technique through manual control of what has already been ingested and what has not yet been ingested. This generates great complexity.

- The size of each event is usually small to avoid having a very robust infrastructure to maintain this event's queue during the streaming. This makes it impossible to ingest large files, videos, audio, and photos, among others. These loads are often best implemented in batch loads.

In summary, we typically use batch data loads for the most of the structuring operations of the analytical base, the ingestion of the largest volumes of data, and unstructured data.

To understand in practice how these concepts are applied, let's now evaluate a case study of a complete data solution.

Case study

Webshoes is a fictitious sales company of shoes and accessories that is being created. The company's business areas have defined that Webshoes will have an online store and that the store will need to have personalized experiences. The requirements that the business areas have passed to the project development team are as follows:

- **Online store** – The online store should have a simple catalog with the 12 different products of the brand

- **Smart banner** – If the customer clicks on a product, similar products should appear in a **Recommended** banner, with products that have the same characteristics as the one selected, but only products that the customer has not purchased yet

- **Sales conversion messages** – If the customer does not complete the sale and has logged into the portal, the online store should contact the customer via email and a message on their cell phone later, with the triggering of a few messages created for conversion of the sale

By analyzing these business requirements, we can do the following *technical decomposition* to select the appropriate data storage:

- **Online store** – A repository to store the product catalog, a repository to register the sales through the shopping cart, and a repository to store customer login

- **Smart banner** – Depending on the customer and product selected, a near real-time interaction of banner customization

- **Sales conversion messages** – Will be processed after the customer leaves the online store (closing their login session) and depends on their actions while browsing the website and purchase history

Now, with the knowledge gained in this chapter, can you help me to select suitable storage types for each requirement?

Come on, let's go! Here are the solutions:

- **Online store** – *Transactional workload*. A SQL relational or NoSQL database can assist in this scenario very well, as it will have product entities, customers, login information, and shopping carts, among others, already related in the database.

- **Smart banner** – *Analytical workload*. For near real-time processing, data streaming is required, capturing the behavior of the client and crossing it with the other historical data. In this case, an analytical base can process the information and return the application/banner to the appropriate message for customization.

- **Sales conversion messages** – *Analytical workload*. In this case, the customer will have left the store, and we do not need to work with data streaming but rather a batch load of data. It is important to evaluate with the business area how long it is optimal to send messages to target customers, and the analytical base will process the information, generating the message list to be fired.

Therefore, each use case can define a different data workload type, which influences our database decision. In the next chapters, we will detail the Azure solutions for SQL transactional databases, NoSQL, and analytical databases, and the understanding of the different use cases will be simpler for sure.

Summary

In this chapter, we reviewed the core data concepts about data storage and processing, the different data types, and data solutions. We went through the explanation of relational, non-relatable, transactional, and analytical data, their particularities, and application cases.

Now you know how to differentiate a transactional database from an application and an analytical database. In the following chapters, we will go into the details of each of these workloads and of the Azure services that are implemented for this. But before we detail these structures, in the next chapter, we will understand the different roles and responsibilities in a data domain.

Sample questions and answers

Let's evaluate some sample questions related to the content of this chapter:

1. What type of workload is an OLAP model?

    A. Analytical workload

    B. Transactional workload

    C. Relational database

2. How is data in a relational table organized?

    A. Rows and columns

    B. Header and footer

    C. Pages and paragraphs

    D. Connections and arrows

3. Which of the following is an example of unstructured data?

    A. Audio and video files

    B. An `Employee` table with `EmployeeID`, `EmployeeName`, and `EmployeeDesignation` columns

    C. A table within a relational database

    D. A stored procedure in a database

4. What type of cloud service is a database deployed in a virtual machine?

    A. PaaS

    B. IaaS

    C. SaaS

    D. DaaS

Answer key

1-A 2-A 3-A 4-B

2
Exploring the Roles and Responsibilities in Data Domain

In this chapter, you will learn about the different professional profiles in a data organization. We will explore the different responsibilities from the data creation, storage and consumption.

In the DP-900 exam, we can find some questions related to roles and responsibilities in data organization, but this knowledge is interesting and important as well for anyone who wants to work in a data organization.

By the end of this chapter, you will be able to do the following:

- Understand the different profiles and responsibilities in a data team
- Explore the different tools and activities of these profiles

Different workforces in a data domain

Roles with technical activities and other process-oriented roles in business coexist in a modern data team. These complementary roles are important for developing solutions, not only for storing data properly but also for data analysis and generating insights connected to business needs.

Most common roles in a data domain

The basic roles of a data domain, found in most organizations, are as follows:

1. **Database Administrator (DBA)**: This is the administrator of database platforms. Being a technical profile, they are responsible for keeping platforms available, secure, and with adequate access control.

2. **Data engineer**: Being a technical profile, the data engineer is responsible for working with data, performing integrations, aggregations, calculations, modeling, and so on that are necessary for information and insights generation.

3. **Data analyst**: The data analyst is necessary for establishing the connection of a data team with the business side. They are responsible for generating indicators, reports, and dashboards, and supporting data-driven business decisions.

Now, let's understand the details of each of the profiles in a data domain.

Database Administrator

The DBA is responsible for designing transactional database solutions, choosing between relational and non-relational databases, and defining the processes of *monitoring and administering* these solutions. This profile is commonly responsible for managing analytical databases at the infrastructure, access control, and monitoring routine layers. Database administration includes keeping databases performing adequately with application and user needs, supportable backup and data restore continuity plans, disaster recovery plans, and data security (encryption, masking, access control, and so on).

Data engineer

The data engineer is responsible for planning and implementing data structures. These frameworks involve *data ingestion* pipelines, *data processing* frameworks, and *data modeling* for business intelligence consumption.

The data engineer works with DBAs and business areas of the organization to understand the behavior of database entities, and data analysts to understand the requirements of how data will be consumed.

Data analyst

Responsible for generating intelligence based on data, data analysts are the professionals who consume the models organized by data engineers to create reports, indicators, and insights for business areas. This role has the important responsibility of connecting the needs and requirements from business areas, and the solutions to implement on that, working with the *DBAs* and *data engineers* to define technical solutions and implement the data visualization *layers*. The following diagram identifies the data flow that starts in the infrastructure provided and maintained by the DBA, the data pipelines developed by the data engineer, and then the data analyst modeling and creating reports with the data:

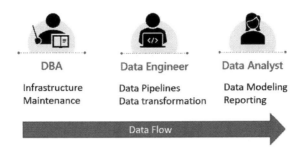

Figure 2.1 – A data flow showing the different roles in a data domain

When we are setting up our data strategy, we must pay attention to these profiles to see whether they serve our entire organization, or whether we have to define other roles.

In complex organizations, there are profiles of complementary professionals such as data scientists and data stewards, but for the DP-900 certification exam, a basic knowledge of the DBA, data engineer, and data analyst profiles is sufficient.

After planning a team and evaluating who will have each of these profiles, let's understand the *tools and tasks* of each of them in a data domain.

Tasks and tools for database administration profiles

To support database administration activities, which can be plentiful, it is necessary to have the appropriate tools for each operation, ensuring scalability, security, and productivity in the administration.

Tasks of the DBA

The tasks performed by the DBA vary greatly from organization to organization, and in the different database solutions being used. The following are some examples of the key tasks:

- Choosing the best data storage options based on the project requirements

- Defining a database capacity plan

- Installing and configuring databases and database tools

- Defining and implementing a data model (normalizing tables, primary and secondary keys definition, indexes in tables, and so on)

- Defining database access roles and managing these accesses

- Defining database availability requirements and defining/implementing high availability, load balancing, backup and restore strategies, and disaster recovery, among other management tasks

- Managing contracts with database vendors and managing support for this software

The tasks of the DBA are important, but what are the tools that this profile uses on a daily basis using Azure?

Tools for the DBA

The DBA's tools also vary, depending on the solutions being used by an organization. There are specialized tools for each database solution. In this section, we will cover the basic tools required for the DBA in Azure.

Azure Data Studio

Azure Data Studio is the primary tool for a data professional working with Azure. It offers functions for DBAs, data engineers, and data analysts, with base administration modules, modeling, exploration, and even simple visualization layers.

In *Chapter 8*, *Querying Relational Data in Azure*, we will use Azure Data Studio to run queries against Azure databases.

The following is a screenshot from Azure Data Studio:

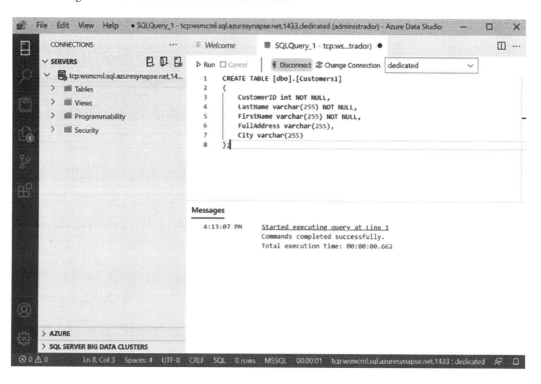

Figure 2.2 – Azure Data Studio

In the preceding figure, we can see a table creation SQL statement running a database in Azure. As we can see, the interface is very simple and allows you to navigate the database structures (on the left side), write SQL queries, and follow execution results.

At this point, don't worry about understanding the SQL instructions in the preceding screenshot; just focus on knowing that we will execute SQL queries in tools such as Azure Data Studio and SQL Server Management Studio. Queries will be explored deeper in *Chapter 8*, *Querying Relational Data in Azure*, and *Chapter 13*, *Working with Power BI*. Azure Data Studio can connect to SQL Server databases (in Azure or another host), Azure SQL Database, Azure Storage, PostgreSQL databases, Azure Synapse Analytics databases, and even Oracle databases, among others. With an easy and powerful query editor with IntelliSense for these platforms, Azure Data Studio enables integration with DevOps, source code version control platforms, and code snippets, among other functions.

SQL Server Management Studio

A traditional tool for SQL Server database administrators and users, SQL Server Management Studio has modernized in recent years, with roles for database administrators and other profiles. The manageability experience can be a hybrid between SQL Server databases on-premises and databases in Azure:

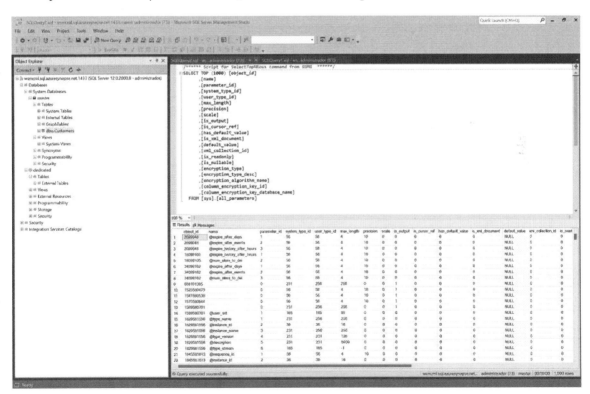

Figure 2.3 – A SQL Server Management Studio screenshot

SQL Server Management Studio is a tool that greatly supports the creation of Transact-SQL scripts to assemble its databases. These scripts can be used to automate the creation of these databases, control the versions of tables, and so on.

> **Important note**
>
> Transact-SQL is an enhanced version of the **Structured Query Language** (**SQL**), developed by Microsoft, which includes specific functions for working with the SQL Server database, among other differentials. When we use Transact-SQL in *Chapter 8*, *Querying Relational Data in Azure*, we will learn about some of these differentials.

The Azure portal

Part of database administration is available through the Azure portal interface, or through the Azure **Command-Line Interface** (**CLI**). The administration tasks you can perform on Azure Portal include provisioning a new database instance, from configuring serves from provisioning a new database instance from configuring its size to setting health and monitoring routines, such as health checks, auto backups, auto replication, and access controls.

The Azure portal has administration capabilities not only for Azure-managed databases (platform-as-a-service databases) but also for SQL servers that are deployed to infrastructure-as-a-service virtual machines, through the SQL Server IaaS Agent extension. The SQL Server IaaS Agent extension informs Azure that a virtual machine has a SQL Server installation.

You can find the benefits and features of the SQL Server IaaS Agent extension in the official Microsoft documentation on the topic:

```
https://docs.microsoft.com/en-us/azure/azure-sql/virtual-machines/
windows/sql-server-iaas-agent-extension-automate-management
```

The DBA is often a professional who works within the IT department, managing database environments.

Let's now analyze other profile, the data engineer, and their tasks and tools.

Tasks and tools for data engineer profiles

Data engineers have a key role in a modern data organization. It is a multidisciplinary role, so it needs knowledge of programming, data transformation, and mathematics, among other areas. To support these important activities, there are several open source and Azure-native tools to help data engineers perform their day-to-day operations.

Tasks of the data engineer

The following are some examples of tasks that are the responsibility of the data engineer:

- Developing data ingestion pipelines
- Setting connectivity standards in data sources with proper security and latency
- Maintaining data pipelines creating scripts for data structures with versioning control
- Applying modern data exploration languages and libraries to generate insights
- Supporting database administrators in the necessary analytical database maintenance routines
- Modeling and implementing data consumption structures aligned with the business area needs
- Supporting the automation of data analysis processes, model creation, and databases (DataOps)

This is just a short list of the responsibilities of the data engineer. This role is usually very flexible in most organizations, and more specialized in organizations that have more people and greater demand, where there is a need for assembling integration pipelines or data modeling. Now, let's get to know the data engineer tools on Azure.

Tools for the data engineer

The data engineer works with the same tools as the DBA, such as Azure Data Studio and SQL Server Management Studio, already mentioned in the previous section. However, they also typically use more complex and specialized tools for data exploration, such as Azure Databricks, Azure HDInsight, and Azure Synapse Analytics.

Synapse Analytics will be used in *Chapter 12, Provisioning and Configuring Large-Scale Data Analytics in Azure*, when we will be evaluating analytical data.

In addition to data exploration activities, the data engineer is responsible for building batch and stream data load pipelines to build analytical databases. These pipelines can be copies of data from source or involve a series of transformation steps, aggregations, calculations, and so on. Tools in Azure to perform these operations are Azure Data Factory, Azure Synapse pipelines, and Azure Stream Analytics, among others.

We will run some queries in Synapse Analytics Studio in *Chapter 12, Provisioning and Configuring Large-Scale Data Analytics in Azure*. The following is an example of data exploration done in Azure Synapse Analytics Studio:

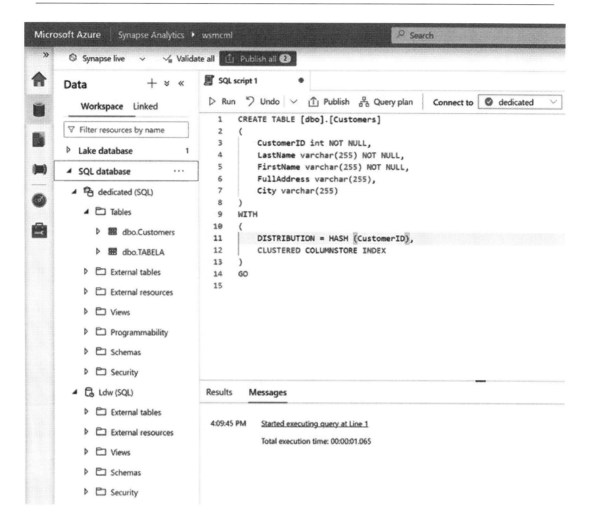

Figure 2.4 – An Azure Synapse Analytics Studio screenshot

In the preceding screenshot, you can clearly see the organization between the hierarchy of objects present in a data lake or a SQL database (on the left-hand side of the screen) and the workspace window (on the right-hand side of the screen), where the queries are written and executed. In the panel at the bottom, the results of executions help us to assess whether this execution was successful and how long it took.

Azure Synapse Analytics is a work suite for engineers, analysts, and data scientists. We have modules for ingesting, exploring, and presenting data, all in the same web interface. With Azure Synapse Analytics, in a single service suite, the data engineer can implement data pipelines, SQL analytics, and Spark analytics.

> **Note**
> Data engineers commonly use languages such as Python, R, Scala, and so on, in conjunction with the standard SQL language of databases, to increase the capabilities of modeling and processing data.

In addition to the more technical profiles of the DBA and data engineer, one of the main roles to generate results for an organization with a data strategy is the data analyst, which we will detail now.

Tasks and tools for the data analyst

Data analysts are responsible for generating insights from data models and integrations performed by the data engineer. They create analytical reports and dashboards that support the decision-making of companies.

The primary function of the data analyst is not to create reports but to analyze in detail the data visualization requirements of an organization, and then define the best way to present this data.

Tasks of the data analyst

The following are the key tasks of the data analyst:

- Creating reports related to the viewing needs of business areas
- Simplifying understanding of the data model in reports
- Supporting the data engineer in assembling the necessary data integrations, modeling, and organizations
- Creating prototypes and reports, charts, histograms, chart maps, and trend charts, and entering other representations of the data
- Exploring information with advanced techniques, always seeking the best information generated, based on raw data

The task list can be much longer, depending on the scope of the data analyst in an organization. However, there are many tools that support these analysts too; let's now get to know the most widely used tools in the Microsoft stack.

Tools for the data analyst

The key tools in the Microsoft portfolio for the data analyst to use are Power BI and SQL Server Reporting Services. Power BI is a market-leading self-service BI platform, and it has enough SaaS operations and connectors to consume data models in more than 90 types of data storage on the market. Other ways to explore data models are with traditional spreadsheet tools in Microsoft Excel.

The following is a screenshot of a dashboard created in Microsoft Power BI:

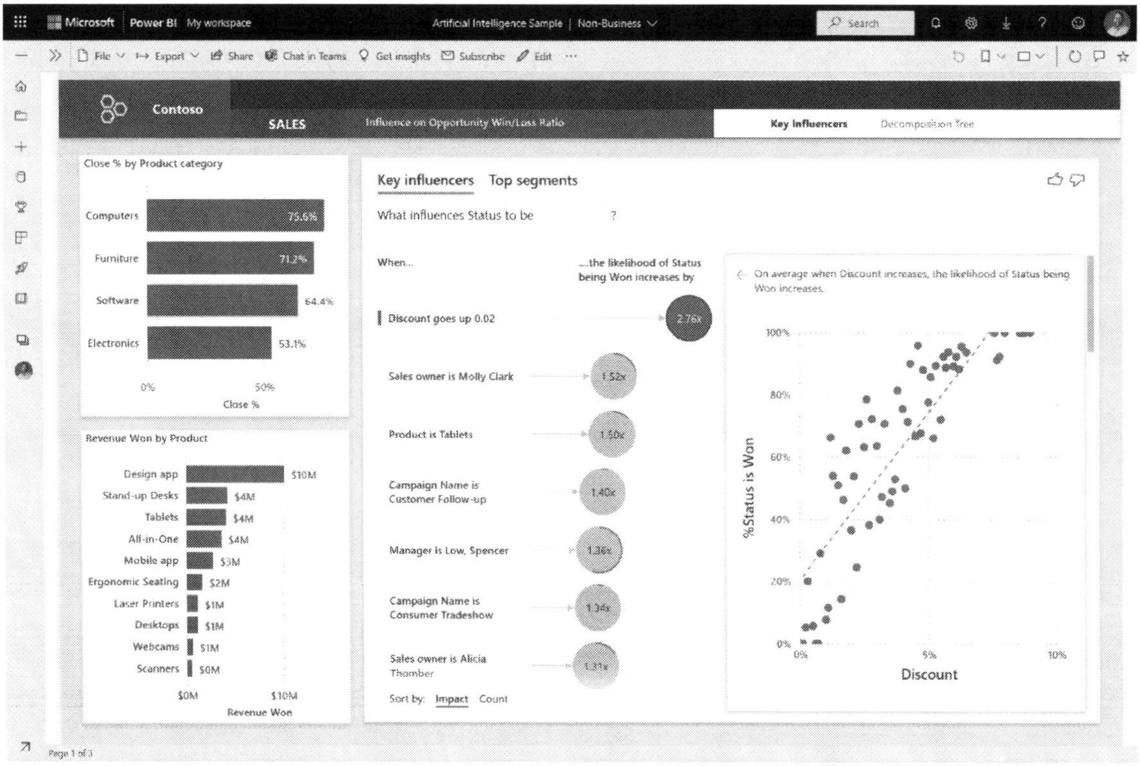

Figure 2.5 – A Power BI dashboard sample

In the preceding screenshot, we can see a sample dashboard created in Power BI, with visual elements and indicators that represent the data processed in an analytical model.

The dashboard object is one of the features of Power BI. In *Chapter 13*, *Working with Power BI*, we will explore the main objects of this very important platform for our data analysis strategy.

Now that we know the three basic profiles of domain data and which tools each one uses in their day-to-day working in Azure, let's evaluate a case study of a team implementing a data initiative.

Case study

You are responsible for setting up a data organization in your company, you are working with Azure as your cloud provider, and you are looking to select professional profiles to organize the data management and data analytics practices, as well as tools to support these professionals.

Your company has four main applications, a *Financial application* with controls for accounts payable and receivable, a **Customer Relationship Management** (**CRM**) application for managing customer data, an *e-commerce* operation (an online store), and an *HR team application* for managing employee information:

- *Professional one requirement*:

  You need a professional to manage the four application transactional databases, which are the following:

  - Two SQL servers on virtual machines
  - One Azure SQL database
  - One Azure Cosmos DB

- *Professional two requirement*:

  Create reports that demonstrate the financial reality of the company, merging e-commerce sales information with the profile and history of the customer present within the CRM, relating to the data of the sellers that are in the HR application.

  For this reason, you need a professional to create an analytical database, which brings together the relevant information from the four databases and forms the necessary relationships to create a data model for the reports.

What professional profiles should you have to meet the requirements listed previously, and what are the basic tools for each profile? Let's take a look at the answers:

- *Professional one* – the DBA:

  - *Tools*: **SQL Server Management Studio** (**SSMS**), Azure Data Studio, and the Azure portal
  - *Justification*: They will be responsible for defining the database (transactional and analytical) system that will store the CRM application data, in addition to monitoring and managing this database

- *Professional two* – the data analyst and the data engineer:

  - *Tools*

    - Data Analyst: Power BI
    - Data Engineer: SSMS, Azure Data Studio, and Azure Synapse Analytics

- *Justification*: In the data domain, we have two profiles to work on these requirements, the Data Analyst and the Data Engineer. The Data Analyst is responsible for creating reports that demonstrate the financial reality of the company, merging e-commerce sales information with the profile and history of the customer present within the CRM, relating to the data of the sellers that are in the HR application. However, to organize the data before that the data engineer will perform the data integration and modeling processes, joining the entities and creating the information consumption structure for the data analyst. These will all be done using the analytical database provided by the DBA.

Therefore, virtually all data use cases involving storage, transaction, and analysis will need to rely on these three basic profiles of professionals. Organizations that are more experienced in data exploration practices may have more specialization roles that complement these ones.

Summary

Managing and manipulating data are not simple operations, and it is necessary to define how data is organized, have specialized professionals in each role, and use the best tools to ensure success in a data strategy.

In this chapter, you learned some of the possible roles in a data team, as well as the common tasks and tools used by these roles in Azure implementations.

With basic knowledge about the different types of data solutions and the profiles of the professionals who make up a data team, we will dive into the details of relational databases in our next chapter.

Sample questions and answers

Try and answer the following questions:

1. Which one of the following tasks is the responsibility of the data engineer?

    A. Backing up and restoring databases

    B. Creating dashboards and report

    C. Creating pipelines to process data in a data lake

    D. Database maintenance

2. Which one of the following tasks is the responsibility of a database manager?

    A. Backing up and restoring databases

    B. Creating dashboards and reports

    C. Creating pipelines to process data in a data lake

    D. Machine learning development

3. Which role is most likely to use Azure Data Factory to define a data pipeline for an ETL process?

   A. Data engineer

   B. Data analyst

   C. Database manager

   D. Data scientist

4. Which single service would you use to implement data pipelines, SQL analytics, and Spark analytics?

   A. Azure Synapse Analytics

   B. Azure SQL Database

   C. Microsoft Power BI

   D. SQL Server

5. Which single service would you use to manage backups and restores on a SQL Server?

   A. SQL Server Management Studio

   B. Visual Studio

   C. A third-party vendor

   D. SQL backups

Answer key

1-C 2-A 3-A 4-A 5-A

3
Working with Relational Data

In this chapter, you will learn the concepts of relational databases and the SQL language, which is widely used by relational database management systems.

We will explore the relational model for databases, how tables are structured, how you can use database objects such as indexes to improve query performance, and views to simplify complex queries.

The purpose of this chapter is to explore the concepts of relational databases and how SQL is used. For this reason, we will not run the scripts yet, as the result is not important right now; understanding the logic is our target.

In *Chapter 8, Querying Relational Data in Azure*, we will run the SQL scripts and evaluate their returns.

By the end of this chapter, you will be able to understand the following:

- The characteristics of relational data
- How to build a relational model
- Normalization and SQL language concepts
- Relational database components

Exploring the characteristics of relational data

Relational data is data that can be organized into a relational model, based on tables and their relationships.

Created in 1985 by Edgar Frank Codd, the relational model is a data storage format that models tables and the relationships between them before a database begins to receive data.

Let's start by understanding the relational data characteristics, the basic objects that make up this approach, and the most common usage scenarios.

Tables and entities

A **table** is a materialized structure of an entity for storing structured data in *columns* and *rows*.

Entity is anything you want to store data on. They usually represent people, things, actions, processes, and so on. For example, CUSTOMER, PRODUCTS, SALES, and OFFICES entities can be materialized in tables within a relational database.

These *columns are* predetermined and configured to receive specific data types, while the rows will be the records or data present in the table. A column can be set to be required or not, which is an important setting to maintain the quality of records. Another relevant setting is *data entry masks*. For example, an EMAIL column should contain a *text+@+an extension*. These data masks help standardize your data in columns, making the database have better organization and data quality.

Also, in the aforementioned examples, in a CUSTOMERS table, each *row* represents a customer; in PRODUCTS, each row represents a product; and in SALES, each row represents a sales record, each of which has a unique registry identifier in the database. When, in a record row, there is a column that has no required padding and is left blank, the record in this column is called NULL.

Data types configured by columns can vary between **Database Management Systems** (**DBMs**)but generally use the standard set by the **American National Standards Institute** (**ANSI**).

Relationship between entities

Relational databases have a connection between one or more tables; these are called *relationships*, so the organization and consumption of the data of this database are done optimally. In the next section, we will explore these relational database structures.

Exploring relational data structures

Database schema is a table and column model that is designed and implemented before we start using a relational database.

To begin to understand the details of the relationships between tables in a relational database, let's evaluate the process created to troubleshoot data duplication, a process called *normalization*.

Data normalization

Normalization is used to develop the *database schema* to minimize data duplication. Data duplication occurs when we need to write more than one piece of data for a single record.

Let's look at an example with a table called SALES, with the following columns and records:

SALES					
ORDER_ID	ORDER_DATE	CUSTOMER	PRODUCT	QUANTITY	PRICE
00034	3/26/22	Matt Dunst	Laptop XPTO	0001	$320
00034	3/26/22	Matt Dunst	Mouse Pad	0001	$12
00034	3/26/22	Matt Dunst	Bluetooth Keyboard	0001	$28
00035	3/26/22	Ryan Philips	Laptop XPTO	0001	$320
00035	3/26/22	Ryan Philips	Laptop Case	0001	$32

Figure 3.1 – A sales table example

As we can observe, in the same single sales record, we had more than one product purchased by customers. With only one table representing the SALES entity, the data related to ORDER_ID, ORDER_DATE, and CUSTOMER needs to be duplicated to maintain the integrity of each of the orders. To avoid this duplication, we can work with normalization by segmenting this table into auxiliary tables for distributed data storage, as shown in the following example:

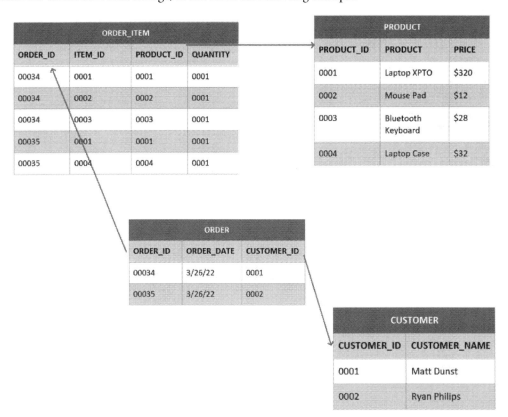

Figure 3.2 – An example of a relational database with normalization applied

In normalized databases, each table has a reference ID or other key field for relationships; these are called *primary keys*. These primary keys are used to reference a record from a table in other tables, and how much this occurs and how many of these keys are written to another table, depends on whether they have *foreign key* names.

Relational Database Management Systems (**RDBMSs**) ensure the integrity of these keys – that is, deleting a record from a table that has its foreign key referenced in another table is not allowed to ensure integrity between relationships.

The relationship example presented in the previous diagram is simple, but imagine a scenario with a big database schema, with tables containing multiple columns/attributes. If all these columns were duplicated multiple times, the data store would be very redundant. It is exactly this type of duplication that is avoided with normalization.

Continuing the example, in the CUSTOMER table, we could have attributes such as ADDRESS, AGE, and GENDER. If you wanted to change one of these attributes, you would only need to edit a single record in the CUSTOMER table and not all the records for that customer in the initial SALES table, as shown in *Figure 3.1*. To take advantage of these relationships and perform query operations in relational databases, in addition to other write, edit, and delegate operations, we use the *SQL language*, which will be covered in the next section.

Introducing SQL

Structured Query Language (**SQL**) is the most widely used language in relational database platforms for recording, editing, re-editing, and querying operations. SQL was created by Donald D. Chamberlin and Raymond F. Boyce in 1974 in an innovation lab at IBM and has since evolved with DBMSs that use it with Microsoft SQL Server, Oracle Database, MySQL, PostgreSQL, and MariaDB.

SQL has been standardized by ANSI and the **International Organization for Standardization** (**ISO**), but each of the RDBMS has some exclusive extended SQL standard instructions, primarily for administration, monitoring, and other operations unique to that RDM.

These unique patterns have names such as the following:

- T-SQL or Transact-SQL is the version used by Microsoft SQL Server and Azure SQL versions
- pgSQL is the default of PostgreSQL databases

We will now list some of the additional advantages that made the SQL language the standard used in relational databases.

Key advantages of SQL

The list of advantages is very long, but the main points are as follows:

- **Standardization**: As mentioned, SQL has been standardized by *ANSI* and is still used in many database systems. This is why SQL is one of the most documented languages today, easier to learn, and useful for day-to-day activities.

- **Simplicity with scalability**: SQL is an easy-to-understand language with simple syntax fundamentals, answering high-scalability database scenarios by processing millions of pieces of data.

- **Portability**: Because it is standard in several *DBMSs*, SQL is portable between these different types of database managers, even though there are some particularities in the SQL of each.

- **Multiple data views**: With SQL, it is possible to define different views of the database structure for different user needs. For example, you might have users who are only allowed to explore the data and perform SELECT commands, whereas other users can add columns in tables but cannot delete any columns. This granularity of permissions makes databases more fully configurable.

Key disadvantages of SQL

Of course, we can find more disadvantages when we know about NoSQL databases, but the disadvantages most encountered by data architects to justify an analysis of other databases are these:

- **Database processing cost**: In general, the cost of processing a database that uses the SQL language is high compared to more modern database languages. This means that the database needs a robust infrastructure for data processing. Compared to a NoSQL database, a SQL database uses compute power, RAM, and storage speed more intensively.

- **Pre-build and fixed schema**: A SQL database must be planned and implemented (the creation of tables, columns, relationships, and so on) before implementing the software. Your schema should be created and, once created, only changed upon a general impact analysis of the database.

This generates a lack of flexibility and more time spent at the beginning of a project in the planning and implementation of the database.

> **Important note**
> As this book prepares you for the Azure DP-900 certification, we will address transact-SQL-based commands, the default in the relational databases of the Microsoft portfolio.

Let's now get to know the categories of SQL commands.

Understanding the categories of SQL commands

To understand the structure of SQL, it is subdivided into five categories of commands:

- **Data Query Language** (**DQL**): Defines the command used so that we can query (SELECT) the data stored in the database

- **Data Manipulation Language** (**DML**): Defines the commands used for manipulating data in the database (INSERT, UPDATE, and DELETE)

- **Data Definition Language** (**DDL**): Defines the commands used for creating tables, views, and indexes, updating these structures (ALTER), as well as removal (DROP)

- **Data Control Language** (**DCL**): Defines the commands used to control access to database data by adding (GRANT) and removing (REVOKE) access permissions

- **Data Transaction Language** (**DTL**): Defines the commands used to manage transactions executed in the database, such as starting a transaction (BEGIN), confirming it (COMMIT), or undoing it (ROLLBACK)

The following diagram demonstrates the categories of the SQL language and their main commands for quick reference:

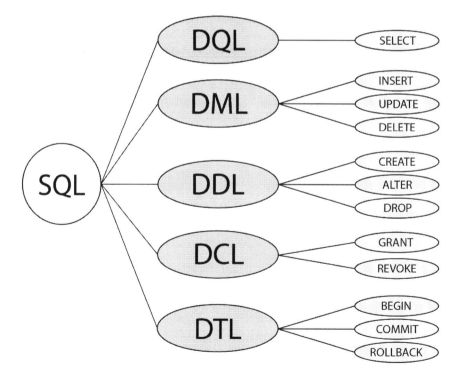

Figure 3.3 – SQL language categories

These five categories contain all the necessary syntaxes of SQL commands for operations in a database. In the next sections, we will learn more about the main categories and their commands.

In this chapter, we will cover DDL, DML, and DQL, the latter also in *Chapter 8, Querying Relational Data in Azure*. These are the most important categories of SQL commands for anyone starting to use SQL databases, and they are also required for the DP-900 certification.

DDL

DDL, as its name suggests, is used to define the creation or editing of the schema of your database, considering the tables, visualizations, procedures, and all other objects in the database.

The following are the standard DDL instructions for Microsoft databases:

Instruction	Objective	Example
CREATE	Create objects in the database	CREATE TABLE Customers (CustomerID int, LastName varchar(255), FirstName varchar(255), Address varchar(255), City varchar(255));
ALTER	Change objects in the database	ALTER TABLE Customers ADD Country varchar(255);
DROP	Delete objects in the database	DROP TABLE Customers;

Figure 3.4 – DDL Instructions

To understand this further, we will create examples of these instructions when applied to a table called Customers.

The first step is to create the table:

```
CREATE TABLE Customers (
    CustomerID int,
    Name varchar(255),
    Celphone varchar(255),
    City varchar(255)
);
```

In the preceding example, we are creating a `Customers` table and defining that it will receive four fields, `CustomerID`, `Name`, `Cellphone`, and `City`, none of which are mandatory.

Now, with our `Customers` table created, we can use commands from the SQL DML category to insert data.

DML and DQL

The following is a list of commands that we can use in the SQL DQL and DML categories:

Instruction	Objective	Example
SELECT	Query data from one or more tables	SELECT * FROM Customers WHERE ID=4;
INSERT	Insert new data	INSERT INTO Customers (ID, NAME, AGE) VALUES (4, "Jason", 33);
UPDATE	Edit existing data	UPDATE Customers SET AGE=35 WHERE ID=4;
DELETE	Delete data	DELETE FROM Customers WHERE ID=4;

Figure 3.5 – DML and DQL instructions

In this example, we will add the customer `Jason` data:

```
INSERT INTO Customers (CustomerID, Name, Cellphone, City)
VALUES (1, 'Jason', '+1 (424) 919-2387', 'Stavanger');
Applying the command above, we are creating a record in the
Customers table, with data from customer Jason.
```

Remember the CRUD we talked about in *Chapter 1, Understanding the Core Data Terminologies*?

To implement the basic operations of `CREATE`, we use the `INSERT` instruction, and to read is `SELECT`, to edit a record is `UPDATE`, and to delete is `DELETE`.

> **Important note**
> The CREATE statement is used to create objects such as tables and databases, not to create data. The data is inserted into the tables, so the INSERT statement is used.

The SELECT statement is the one that has the greatest possibility of being structured because it is responsible not only for performing queries in tables, with the appropriate filters using the WHERE add-on, but also for performing operations using the relationships between these entities or tables, using the JOIN statement.

Here is an example of the SELECT instruction, using WHERE and JOIN between two tables:

```
SELECT o.ID, o.Date, o.TotalValue, c.Name, c.Celphone
FROM Orders AS o
JOIN Customers AS c
ON o.CustomerID = c.ID
WHERE o.Date="3/30/2022")
ORDER BY c.Name;
```

In the preceding example, there are two tables: one called Orders, with all the sales orders, and another called Customers, with customer data. In this SELECT sentence, the goal is to create a list of the resultant data with the Sales Order ID fields, the total value of that order, the customer's name, and the mobile phone of that customer.

We also use the supplementary WHERE clause so that the result is filtered when the order date is 3/30/2022 and that a result list is ordered by the customer's name, using the ORDER BY clause.

The WHERE clause can also be used to delimit the execution of an UPDATE or DELETE command by updating and deselecting records from a specific filter table.

> **Important note**
> Operations on a database do not have confirmations before committing, which means that if you start a DELETE operation, the records will be deleted. Therefore, whenever you run a SQL command of operations such as UPDATE and DELETE, evaluate the use of a WHERE clause to delimit this execution and ensure a proper backup of your data.

Another important concept in SQL is the NULL value in some columns. NULL means that the column has no value.

It is common to find NULL values in databases, as it is possible to create records in tables with some columns without data as long as that column is an optional one.

When creating a table or when editing a table's schema, it is possible to include the NOT NULL clause in a column, and this will ensure this column has to accept values, and not accept NULL, in a record.

We will exercise more SQL in *Chapter 8* of this book, where we'll use the top SQL commands in Azure relational databases.

In addition to tables, database systems have important components for their operations. In the next session, we will understand these components.

Describing the database components

There are components in a relational database that are important to maintain the organization and productivity. The four most common components among database systems are as follows:

- **Views**
- **Stored Procedures**
- **Triggers**
- **Indexes**

Let's take a look at each of them in detail in the following sections.

Views

A *view* can be considered a virtual table because it is composed of rows and columns of data, the results of a SELECT SQL instruction in one or more database tables. Views are great resources for organizing information from different tables to create reports.

The following is a *view* example, with the name High_price_products, which is constructed with a SELECT statement in the PRODUCTS table, filtering the Price field by the average greater than that of the other products in the table:

```
CREATE VIEW [High_price_products] AS
SELECT Product_Name, Product_Price
FROM Products
WHERE Product_Price > (SELECT AVG(Product_Price) FROM
Products);
```

Views are important features, especially for generating reports. But another object that's also widely used in SQL databases, and which can help in the development of solutions, is a stored procedure, which we'll look at in the following section.

Stored procedures

A *stored procedure* is a set of SQL statements stored in a database. These statements can request data entry parameters, which are used as variables during execution, and can constitute a data output.

In the following example, we can see the creation of a *stored SQL procedure* called `All_Customers`, which requests two variables, `City` and `PostalCode`, to filter the results in the query:

```
CREATE PROCEDURE All_Customers
@City nvarchar(30), @PostalCode nvarchar(10)
AS
SELECT * FROM Customers WHERE City = @City AND PostalCode = @
PostalCode
GO;
```

Objects in a database need a trigger to be called and start executing. For this reason, there is an object in relational databases called a *trigger*. Let's analyze it now.

Triggers

Triggers are a type of stored procedure, configured to call whenever an event occurs. This trigger can be used, for example, to signalize the execution of some statements whenever new data is included in a table, or a record is edited in the table.

Many *trigger* use cases are about creating transaction audit tables and maintaining data consistency, by reviewing relationships before confirming any type of transaction. We can use a trigger in the data definition and for data manipulation instructions.

In the following, we will use the `DDL CREATE` statement, which we have already seen in this chapter to create tables, but now we will use it to create a `TRIGGER`:

```
CREATE TRIGGER LOG_PRICE_HISTORY before update
on PRODUCTS_SERVICES
for each row
insert into PRICE_HISTORY
values(old.PRODUCTID, old.BASEPRICE, old.DISCOUNT, old.
FINALPRICE, old.DATELASTUPDATE);
```

Executing this command, the `LOG_PRICE_HISTORY` trigger will be created and linked to the `PRODUCTS_SERVICES` table, with the following condition: whenever an item is edited in this table, a new record will be created in the `PRICE_HISTORY` table with the data from this table before the change.

This makes it possible for you to keep a history of this table and know exactly the changes that were made.

Sometimes, tables become very large, with thousands and even millions of records. This size can cause performance problems in database operations, and one of the methods used to mitigate these problems was indexes, which we are going to look at now.

Indexes

An *index* is created by a table or view to define a field that can be used to optimize queries.

The best way to understand an *index* is to observe the index section typically present in a book. This section summarizes the main topics in the book and references the page each topic begins on. This is exactly what an index does in a database table or view.

Some database platforms have an *auto index*; others use the primary key of the tables to create their indexes.

You can create multiple *indexes* in each table. Each *index* generates a record in an internal database table, with a copy of the data in order and pointers that indicate the fastest way to get to the information, which help the database search system find that record.

To create an *index* in a table, the SQL statement is very simple:

```
CREATE INDEX IDX_CUSTOMERNAME
ON CUSTOMERS(Name);
```

This way, we create an index called IDX_CUSTOMERNAME in the CUSTOMERS table, using the Name field to help the database organize queries for customer names.

So, we close the main SQL commands used in relational databases. Of course, all commands are used in a large database, but by understanding the statement and how they work, you will surely be able to implement your commands at the right time.

Now, to finish, let's evaluate a complete case study based on SQL language.

Case study

In this case study, we will analyze the creation of a relational database for a simple bank checking account system.

To start structuring the database, we will perform the DDL of database creation and tables, with the proper types of data in each column, its primary keys, and indexes:

1. The first sentence will create a database called CRM:

    ```
    CREATE DATABASE CRM;
    ```

2. We continue to create the `Customers` table; in it, we will put the fields that will store the attributes of this client, which show the type of data in SQL, which of the fields cannot be NULL, and the primary key:

```
CREATE TABLE Customers(
    CustomerID int NOT NULL PRIMARY KEY,
    LastName varchar(255) NOT NULL,
    FirstName varchar(255) NOT NULL,
    FullAddress varchar(255),
    City varchar(255)
);
```

3. Now, let's create an index in the `LastName` field of this table:

```
CREATE INDEX idx_lastname
ON Customers(LastName);
```

Great! This way, we have already created the *schema* from our database.

4. Now, let's explore data operations by inserting two records into the `Customers` table:

```
INSERT INTO Customers (CustomerID, LastName, FirstName,
FullAddress, City)
VALUES ('001536', 'Malcom', 'Thomas', '1156 Congress
Avenue', 'Dallas');
INSERT INTO Customers (CustomerID, LastName, FirstName,
FullAddress, City)
VALUES ('001537', 'Diaz', 'Matt', '7373 Sunrise Street',
'Miami');
```

5. To evaluate whether the records were written correctly to the database, let's do a SELECT statement:

```
SELECT * FROM Customers;
```

If your table has only the two records, the result will be like this:

CustomerID	LastName	FirstName	FullAddress	City
001536	Malcom	Thomas	1156 Congress Avenue	Dallas
001537	Diaz	Matt	7373 Sunrise Street	Miami

Figure 3.6 – The SELECT statement results

6. The customer `Matt` has just reported a change of address, which you can update with the UPDATE command:

```
UPDATE Customers
SET FullAddress = '3877 Arlington Avenue', City=
'Arlington'
WHERE CustomerID = 1537;
SELECT * FROM Customers;
```

Let's look at the result:

CustomerID	LastName	FirstName	FullAddress	City
001536	Malcom	Thomas	1156 Congress Avenue	Dallas
001537	Diaz	Matt	3877 Arlington Avenue	Arlington

Figure 3.7 – The new SELECT statement results after UPDATE

With that, we can analyze a use case of the SQL language for table creation, data inclusion, editing, and data selection. The important thing is to understand the sequence of events required to create and use a database.

A simple database like this can already store very valuable information for individual entrepreneurs and small companies, organizing customer data and guaranteeing its history in the database.

An extension of this case would be to include tables of products and sales, correlating with the table customers to understand which products have already been purchased by these customers. This way, we would already have a simple sales system in the database.

In the next chapters, we will undergo more exercises about SQL and more real use cases, and you will have the chance to explore them by yourself.

> **Important note**
>
> These commands could be used in various relational databases that use SQL because they are base commands of the language. The only concern is about the differences in column data types, which are usually different between one platform and another.

Summary

As we have observed, SQL commands are simple and intuitive but very scalable. Based on this, relational databases are the most used database format on the market.

In this chapter, we learned about the fundamentals of relational databases, table normalization, and the basics of SQL.

In the next chapter, we will address non-relational databases, considering so-called **NoSQL** (**Not Only SQL**).

Sample questions and answers

Let's evaluate some sample questions and answers about relational databases for the DP-900 certification:

1. Which of the following statements is characteristic of a relational database?

    A. A row in a table represents a data type.

    B. Rows in the same table can contain different columns.

    C. A table has columns (attributes) and rows (records).

    D. All columns in a table should have the same data type.

2. Which SQL statement is used to create new rows in a table?

    A. CREATE ROW

    B. CREATE

    C. INSERT

    D. NEW ROW

3. What is an index?

    A. A structure that enables queries to locate rows in a table quickly

    B. A virtual table based on the results of a query

    C. A pre-defined SQL statement that modifies data

    D. A type of primary key column

4. Which statement is an example of DDL?

    A. SELECT

    B. INSERT

    C. DELETE

    D. DROP

Answer key

1-C 2-C 3-B 4-D

4

Working with
Non-Relational Data

With the evolution of applications, new database formats were required, and several open source projects began a new group of database specialization, not only using the SQL standard but also creating the NoSQL concept for non-relational databases.

In this chapter, you will learn about non-relational and NoSQL databases, and understand the different types of non-relational databases and their common applications.

This is the fundamental information needed for the *Describe how to work with non-relational data on Azure* item in the *Skills measured* section of the exam's syllabus.

By the end of this chapter, you will be able to understand the concepts of NoSQL databases, including the following:

- Characteristics of non-relational data
- Understanding the types of non-relational data
- NoSQL databases
- Identifying non-relational database use cases

Exploring the characteristics of non-relational data

The relational database that we discussed in the previous chapter is widely used, but it does not fit some types of existing data. This data is related to transaction logs, audio files, videos, images, and formatted files such as JSON and XML, among others.

For this reason, specific databases have been created for non-relational data.

Generated data needs to be stored, some of it temporarily and some permanently. Some types of data files are **structured** and prepared to be stored in a relational database, and others are **semi-structured** or **unstructured**, as we already discovered in *Chapter 1, Understanding the Core Data Terminologies*. This data is called **non-relational data**. Let's better understand these structures and how we can store each type of unstructured or semi-structured data.

The characteristics of non-relational data are as follows:

- They are usually files
- They have different organization schema formats, and these formats are mutable to any new record
- They do not have primary key flagging or indexers
- They have different query format needs

For example, a video file might have the basic need only to reproduce the video when needed. A JSON file might need to be queried in a chain of relationships with other JSON files, which is a **Graph** format that we will address shortly in this chapter. Therefore, due to the flexible characteristics of this data, storage systems need to respect these characteristics and maintain interfaces for basic **create, read, update, and delete** (**CRUD**) operations.

In the next section, we will understand the types of non-relational data and how to make the best decision to store them.

Understanding the types of non-relational data

Non-relational data is all types of data that we can store in an entity, and is not relationally structured data. This means that any type of document, event, log, photo, or video, among others, can be stored in a non-relational database.

Now, let's look at the different types of non-relational data.

Non-structured data

Non-structured data is data that does not have **queryable** formatting and can be from log files without header structures, image files, videos, and audio, among other binary formats. These files are not easily interpreted by query indexing tools, so they are called **unstructured**.

Before this data becomes information and can assist in decision-making, it is necessary to go through systems that organize the data of these files in a way that facilitates their understanding by the query tools.

Here are two examples of categories of data transcription processes from unstructured files:

- **Speech-to-Text** (**STT**) – Audio-to-text transcription
- **Optical Character Recognition** (**OCR**) – Text extraction in images

These processes are responsible for transcribing data from files into structured text. In most cases, the result of the data transcription platforms used in non-structured data is stored in JSON files, which are considered semi-structured data.

Here are some examples of Azure Cognitive Services tools that can perform data transcription from unstructured files:

- **Azure Computer Vision** – OCR capability in images
- **Azure Speech service** – Audio transcription capability from audio or video files
- **Azure Video Analyzer for Media** – Video-to-text transcription

Therefore, files containing unstructured data can generate semi-structured data files and can then be stored in databases.

Semi-structured data

Semi-structured data is generally JSON, CSV, XML, or other files that contain some kind of metadata for an organization but are not simple to insert into a predefined tabular structure, such as in a relational database.

These files, despite having a structure of attributes and data, need to be organized and optimized for queries.

Non-relational data basic storage

Before we start to explore non-relational databases, some types of data files don't need to be in a database system because they need to be stored only for querying and editing controls of the files.

In cloud environments, it is very common for these files to be stored in object stores; in Azure, the service is called **Azure Blob Storage**.

This storage is an object store optimized for storing very large volumes of unstructured data, with access control and versioning to evaluate whether file binaries have changed.

However, these object stores do not have a database structure to process queries and should not be used to perform CRUD transactional operations, only to store files securely and work with Download and Upload operations.

Important note

When Azure Blob Storage is configured as Azure Data Lake Storage Gen2, it can be used as a document store for big data and data analytics workloads. In this configuration, CRUD operations are performed by the big data and data analytics platform, while the data continues to be stored in the repository.

So, if your non-relational data needs to perform CRUD operations, you should opt for NoSQL databases, which we will address in the next section.

Exploring NoSQL databases

To store non-structured and semi-structured data in an organized manner and perform CRUD operations, NoSQL database projects were started by the open source community. The main characteristic of NoSQL databases are flexibility the database schema, accepting different types of data insertion because the data will be organized at the time of the query. That is, these databases have the schema defined in the data query and not when the data is inserted into the database.

What is a NoSQL database?

NoSQL means **Not Only SQL**, thus it is a database that can accept standard SQL language statements but can also have other interfaces to perform operations on the database.

NoSQL databases are flexible and have multiple forms of operation, not just using the SQL language, based on the open source projects to specialize the database for some use cases.

You should know the different formats of NoSQL databases for the DP-900 certification, and this knowledge helps to meet the needs of querying the data. For each of these formats, there are different types of technology solutions, which will also be exemplified in the next sections.

Key-value store

In this type of NoSQL database, the data is stored in a very simple way, in a two-column tabular organization:

- **Key** – A unique identifier of that record
- **Value** – All data from that record

Despite the simplicity, the key-value type of NoSQL database is scalable and partitionable, being suitable for **high-volume** data storage, which, in many scenarios, becomes a challenge for SQL language databases.

In the Value field, you can store several attributes from that record. This causes the Key field to be used for indexing and querying, and the Value field to keep all the details of the record.

> **Important note**
> In key-value databases, it is common to have big records in the Value column. But this large volume of data in the Value column (with more attributes or very long data) does not impact the query speed of this database because of the keys.

Some usage cases for key-value databases can be found in games, marketing databases, and **Internet of Things (IoT)** solutions.

One of the most well-known key-value database systems on the market is the open source database, **Cassandra**. In Azure, you have two possibilities for key-value databases, the Azure Cosmos DB Cassandra API and the new Azure SQL Managed Instance for Apache Cassandra, which will be covered in detail in *Chapter 9, Exploring Non-Relational Data Offerings in Azure*.

The following is a key-value database example using a phone directory:

Phone directory

Key	Value
Paul	(091) 9786453778
Greg	(091) 9686154559
Marco	(091) 9868564334

Figure 4.1 – Key-value database example

In the preceding figure, we can observe that the key-value database is formed of only two columns, and the *key* is indexed for queries and the *value* contains the details of that record. Now that we understand the key-value database, let's evaluate one of the most widely used NoSQL patterns on the market, the **document** database.

Document database

A document database (sometimes called a document store or a document-oriented database) is a NoSQL database that stores data in documents.

Document-type databases accept JSON files, which for many developers becomes simple because they can structure these files within their source code and work with the files being stored and integrated between the different NoSQL databases in the document database format.

Some of the benefits of a document database are as follows:

- An intuitive data model that developers can work with quickly and easily
- A flexible schema that permits the data model to adapt as the demands of the application change
- The ability to scale out horizontally
- Document databases are general-purpose databases that may be employed in several use cases and sectors due to these benefits

The following is a one-document database record sample. This document stores information about Ryan that could be added to a `Customers` collection:

```
## JSON FILE - Customer Ryan ##
  {
      "_id": 345,
      "first_name": "Ryan",
      "email": "ryan@email.com",
      "spouse": "Marie",
      "likes": [
          "soccer",
          "baseball",
          "workout"
      ],
      "businesses": [
          {
              "name": "Pro Consulting",
              "status": "Ongoing",
              "date_founded": {
                  "$date": "2011-02-11T01:00:00Z"
              }
          }
      ]
  }
```

In this example, we can look at the attributes on the left side, preceded by " " :, and the contents of this record.

The difference with a table, with columns and rows, is that the document is created by individual records and maintains a hierarchy of attributes as we can see by the `businesses` attribute; this makes the bank have its data model flexible at the time of insertion of a new record.

Column family database

A **column family database** is a type of NoSQL database that uses a column-oriented model to store data.

A **keyspace** is a notion used in column family databases. In the relational paradigm, a keyspace is like a schema. All the column families (such as tables in the relational model) that contain rows and columns are contained in the keyspace.

The following figure demonstrates this keyspace involving different column families:

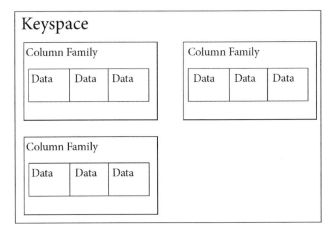

Figure 4.2 – The keyspace structure column families

In the following figure, we can observe the detailing of each of the **Data** boxes in *Figure 4.2*, and it represents a record recorded in the database :

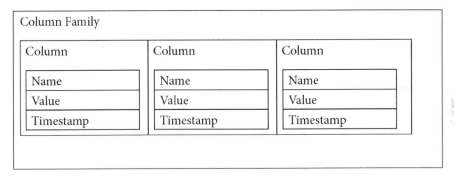

Figure 4.3 – Details of the Data records in the column family

Let's understand these elements:

- **Column** – A name, a value, and a timestamp appear in each column.
- **Name** – This is the name of the name/value pair.
- **Value** – This is the name/value pair's value.
- **Timestamp** – This information includes the date and time the data was entered. This can be used to find the most recent data version.

Let's take look at a column family database example with sample data:

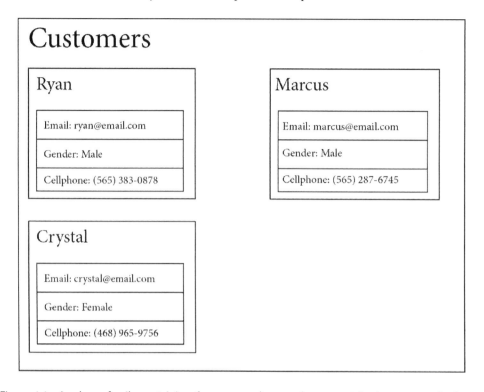

Figure 4.4 – A column family containing three rows, where each row contains its own set of columns

The column family database has a different architecture, but it is a very simple database to use in practice, and I hope that with the preceding example, the layout of the records in this database has become clear.

Two of the most well-known databases in this format are **Cassandra** and **HBase**.

Now that we understand the column family database, let's meet one that has a different architecture: the graph database.

Graph database

Instead of tables or documents, a graph database maintains nodes and relationships.

A graph database is a database that represents and stores data as graph structures containing **nodes**, **edges**, and characteristics for semantic queries.

The graph connects the store's data items to a set of nodes and edges, with the edges signifying the connections between the nodes.

Because relationships are permanently kept in the database and can be easily seen using graph databases, they are advantageous for highly interconnected data.

Relationships are stored in a much more flexible style alongside the data pieces (nodes). Everything in the system is designed to go through data quickly; each core can handle millions of connections per second.

Graph databases handle major issues that many of us face regularly when we try to explore the data visually. These are the main use cases for graph databases:

- Navigate through complex structures

- Find hidden connections between items that are far apart

- Find out how products are related to one another

One of the major graph database use cases is social networks, to connect different users in the network based on interests and behaviors. Look at the following sample:

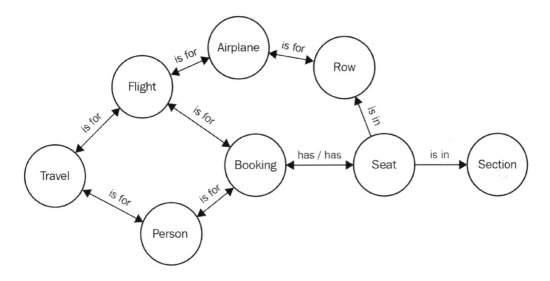

Figure 4.5 – A graph database with a social network implementation

As shown in the preceding figure, data interconnections are clear and facilitate the exploration of these relationships through queries.

Now that we've evaluated the types of NoSQL databases, let's evaluate the top use cases for non-relational databases.

Identifying non-relational database use cases

You must be wondering how we decide between a relational or non-relational database in a new application.

The following are a few characteristics of a non-relational database:

- **Flexibility during development** – Although the type of data matters in the decision, many companies and applications adopt NoSQL databases because the development team needs flexibility and speed, choosing not to draw the relational database schema before starting coding.

- **Modern software architecture (microservices)** – Modern applications are typically developed in the concept of microservices, which are small independent applications that interact to generate the complete application. These services have different storage needs and query formats, and NoSQL solutions often best suit these multi-database scenarios. For example, a document type of storage to store orders in a sales system, or a key-value simple table to store information about the active session of the application, and so on, are use cases for NoSQL databases.

- **Hybrid data storage** – How do we store structured, semi-structured, and unstructured data in the same database? This is only possible with NoSQL. You can store transactional data, such as customer records, customer photos, and sales transaction logs, all in the same database. This hybrid storage can facilitate organization and related queries in this data.

- **High scalability** – A relational database needs to be planned because there are table size, number of columns, and other limitations. In NoSQL databases, the idea is that they have no limits, or at least the writing is not prevented by capacity outages. Queries are responsible for interpreting the different formats of data and organizing the data, aggregating the data, and creating the ResultSet data as a return.

- **Near real-time solutions** – NoSQL database solutions have greater integration with data streaming technologies. For use cases where data is written within the database and needs to be processed to generate some feedback, NoSQL databases can better address these integrations and give quick results.

Therefore, if you have any of the usage scenarios explained in the preceding points, you should consider a NoSQL database adoption analysis.

Case study

To understand how a NoSQL database works, let's explore two possible use cases and understand the most appropriate requirements, solutions, and NoSQL database format for them.

A 360-degree customer view

It is common for organizations to find customer data spread across multiple control systems, separated into departments and verticals, and stored in **data silos**.

For example, imagine the phone support in a company. This company has a customer behavior analysis procedure in place when browsing its websites, sales interaction history, and basic customer registration.

These behaviors have important customer data, and we can use a graph database to connect all these data into a single view and explore it:

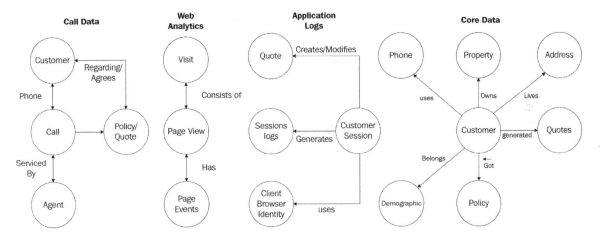

FOUR ISOLATED CUSTOMER VIEWS

Figure 4.6 – Four isolated customer data silos

To create a **consolidated view** of customer data, we copy this information to a NoSQL graph database:

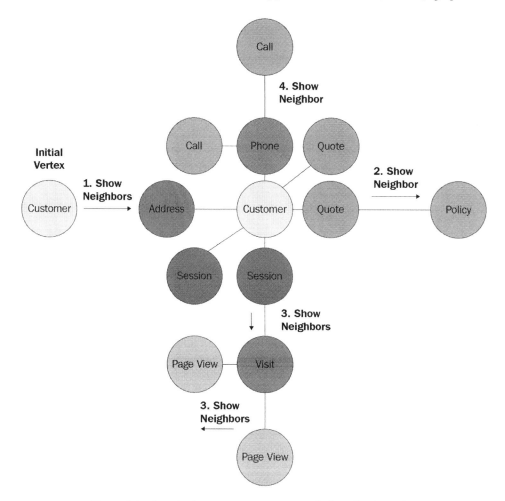

Figure 4.7 – One single customer structure excluding the data silos

With this new basis, you can see a customer diagram view with its vertices demonstrating the data and relationships between them.

Fraud detection – financial institutions

One of the biggest challenges for financial institutions is detecting **fraud**.

These financial institutions have distributed systems that record the behavior of their products' use by customers and record historical fraud operations that occurred. Let's evaluate three different solutions to support fraud with NoSQL in this use case:

- With these two pieces of information: the product use behavior and historical fraud operations records, you can use a NoSQL **graph** database that stores the behavior of a fraudulent transaction.

- A NoSQL **document** database can be used to receive data from a transaction, and as soon as that file is generated, perform a graph base query to define the transaction's fraud risk percentage.

- A NoSQL **key-value** database can still be used to store the results of fraud tests for easy querying and definition of the next steps by the software that is calling these databases.

Therefore, in this example we use three different types of NoSQL databases for semi-structured data storage, thus creating a high-speed and scalability database solution.

Summary

NoSQL non-relational databases are designed for specialized data storage and management in use cases that relational databases were not optimized for, but we should always reflect on these possibilities, requirements, and objectives before deciding on which database will be used.

In this chapter, we looked at the characteristics of non-relational databases, created the different types of data and NoSQL databases, and evaluated use cases for NoSQL database solutions.

But not all databases are for transactional operations. In the next chapter, we will enter the analytical world, evaluating the important aspects of decision-making for an analytical database.

Sample questions and answers

Try answering the following questions to test your knowledge:

1. Which of the following is a document's unique identifier, which is often hashed for even data distribution and helps in data retrieval from the document in the document data store?

    A. Primary key

    B. Hash key

    C. Secondary key

    D. Document key

2. The object data values and named string fields in documents are managed by a document data store. The document key is a unique identifier for the document that is frequently hashed to ensure that data is distributed evenly. It facilitates data retrieval from the document. The document key is established automatically in certain document databases, while in others, you must set a property of the document and use it as the document key. Select the correct statement:

    A. A document data store's document does not have a primary key. The data is obtained using a document key, which is a unique identifier.

    B. In the document data storage, there is no hash key. The data is obtained using a document key, which is a unique identifier.

    C. There is no secondary key in the document of a document data store. The data is retrieved with the help of a unique identifier, the document key.

    D. The document key is a unique identifier for the document, often hashed for the even distribution of data. It helps in the retrieval of data from the document.

3. Non-relational data systems, often known as NoSQL databases, are well suited to managing vast amounts of unconnected and frequently changing data, making them an excellent choice for database migration. Select the correct statement:

    A. Inventory management systems necessitate a certain structure, as well as the necessity for constant database and system synchronization.

    B. For dealing with enormous volumes of unconnected, constantly fluctuating, and ambiguous data, database migration systems can use Azure's non-relational data solutions.

    C. Accounting systems are often associated with legacy systems that are designed for relational structures, undermining the importance of non-relational data.

    D. Complex querying requirements and the necessity for multi-row transactions are common in transaction management systems. As a result, Azure's non-relational data products may not be a good fit.

4. Which of the following are unstructured data examples?

    A. Binary data files and audio files

    B. JSON files

    C. Tables in a SQL Server database

    D. Excel spreadsheets

5. Structured data is data that has a predefined structure. In a relational database, structured data is often tabular data represented by rows and columns. Unstructured data is data that lacks a specific structure. Semi-structured data does not reside in a relational database but still has some structure. Which of these statements is incorrect?

    A. Audio and video files, as well as binary data files, are structured data since they have a specific structure

    B. Because it has predefined columns and structure, a table in a SQL Server database is an example of structured data

    C. Structured data is exemplified by a student table with a defined set of rows

    D. Semi-structured data includes documents in the **JavaScript Object Notation (JSON)** format

Answer key

1-D 2-D 3-B 4-A 5-A

5
Exploring Data Analytics Concepts

Now that we understand how to store our transactional data in databases, in this chapter, we will address generating intelligence with that data through **data analytics**. In modern software architecture, analytical workloads are important for processing data in near-real-time and creating smarter solutions based on that data.

These concepts are important for understanding the logic behind Azure Data Analytics services, which are evaluated in the DP-900 test and can be used in your projects.

By the end of this chapter, you will understand data ingestion, processing, modeling, and visualization concepts, which make up the end-to-end data flow for data analytics.

In this chapter, we will cover the following topics:

- Data ingestion and processing
- Analytical data store
- Analytical data model
- Data visualization

Exploring data ingestion and processing

The process of obtaining and importing **raw data** for immediate use, processing, or storage is known as **data ingestion**.

To build an analytical environment, we use data ingestion techniques to copy data from sources and store it within a **data lake** or an **analytical database**; this process is called a **data pipeline**.

Data ingestion pipelines are composed of one or more steps of data processing, that is, a dataset of the data source is captured and processed, and then the output dataset is generated.

Data pipelines

Data pipelines load and process data through connected services, allowing you to select the best technology for each phase of the workflow.

For example, in Azure, you can use a SQL Server as a data source, then use Azure SQL Database to run a store procedure that searches for data values, and then run a processing routine with Azure Databricks by applying a custom data model. All of these are steps in a data pipeline.

Data pipelines can also have built-in activities that do not need to be linked to a service, such as a filter, aggregation, calculation, and so on.

> **Important note**
> Analytical workloads should not be implemented directly in transactional databases. For example, if your application is running on a SQL Server, it is not recommended to connect a business intelligence tool such as Power BI directly to that database. Transactional and analytical processes are concurrent in the performance usage of resources, so the approach needs to be separated.

A few years ago, there was a lot of talk about **extract, transform, and load** (ETL) pipelines. This means that at the time of data extraction, the data engineer has already created the transformation routines necessary for the analysis of this data and then performed the load of the result in an analytical database.

With the advent of big data and the concept of data lakes, a variation of this acronym was created called **ELT**, which stands for **extract, load, and transform**. This sequence change between the letters means that the data will be copied in its raw format to the data lake, and then modeling routines are performed so that this data is prepared for consumption.

Currently, we favor data ingestion for this process, and the role responsible for planning and implementing the data pipelines is that of the data engineer.

To understand the complete data flow from ingestion to data consumption by data analysts, let's understand the following diagram:

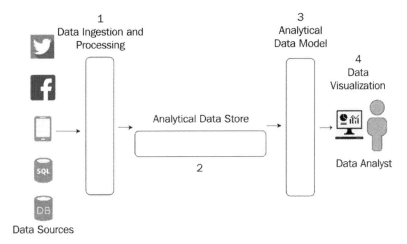

Figure 5.1 – Data flow in an analytical environment

Let's discuss the components of the diagram:

1. **Data ingestion and processing** – The process begins with the ingestion of data sources, which, in this example, is data generated on social networks, mobile device data, and system databases. At this stage, the processing used for filtering and data transformation is the ETL and ELT techniques, before being loaded in the analytical data store.

2. **Analytical data store** – The data is stored in an analytical data store. This store can be an **object store** or a relational table in an **analytical database**.

3. **Analytical data model** – Modeling consists of creating the aggregations, calculations, **key performance indicators** (**KPIs**), and relationships, based on a data modeling technique, so that this data becomes information prepared to be consumed by data analysts. Often, these models are called **data cubes** because they demonstrate a particular subject (called a **fact**) in various perspectives (called **dimensions**), thus allowing data analysts to consume this data and drill down to understand the details of the information. We'll drill down further into this concept in the *Exploring an analytical data model* section later in this chapter.

4. **Data visualization** – Data analysts consume modeled data and generate reports based on **business area** requirements. These reports may contain calculations, filters, and aggregations, but it is not ideal for data to be transformed so that data governance remains active.

> **Important note**
>
> Databases called **NewSQL** have the proposition of eliminating the need for the data copying process of data ingestion. Also, the data is written transactionally in these databases and this data would already be available for analytical purposes. But these technologies are new and still have some limitations, which makes data ingestion the predominant standard in the data analytics market.

Now, let's look at the different types of data ingestion performed in analytical workloads.

Data ingestion types

Data ingestion pipelines can be processed in two ways:

- **Batch processing** – The ingestion layer receives data from sources sequentially and sends it to the application in batches. To define incremental loads, the data can be classified according to a set of rules or criteria, such as whether specific conditions are met. This method is suitable for applications that do not necessitate real-time data.

- **Stream or real-time processing** – Stream processing does not categorize data in any way. Instead, each piece of data is loaded as an event and processed as a separate object as soon as it is recognized by the ingestion layer. This strategy should be used by applications that demand real-time data analysis.

Now that you have understood the different techniques of data ingestion, let's analyze a super important point in this process—how to connect to our data sources.

Data source connectors

Choosing the right method of connection to the data source and the target can be the success factor for implementing your data ingestion pipeline.

On Azure, we have tools such as **Azure Synapse Pipelines** and **Azure Data Factory**, which have more than 90 different standard connectors for batch loads.

To work with **stream data** ingestion, the most used options are **Azure Event Hubs** and **Azure Stream Analytics**, but there are also specialized solutions such as **Azure IoT Hub** and **Azure Logic Apps**, among others.

In the following figure, we can look at the list of connectors that are available in Azure Synapse Pipelines. Connectors are for SaaS solutions such as Salesforce, Marketo, SAP Cloud, and Dynamics 365, and for databases such as Oracle DB, DB2, SQL Server, files, and API connections:

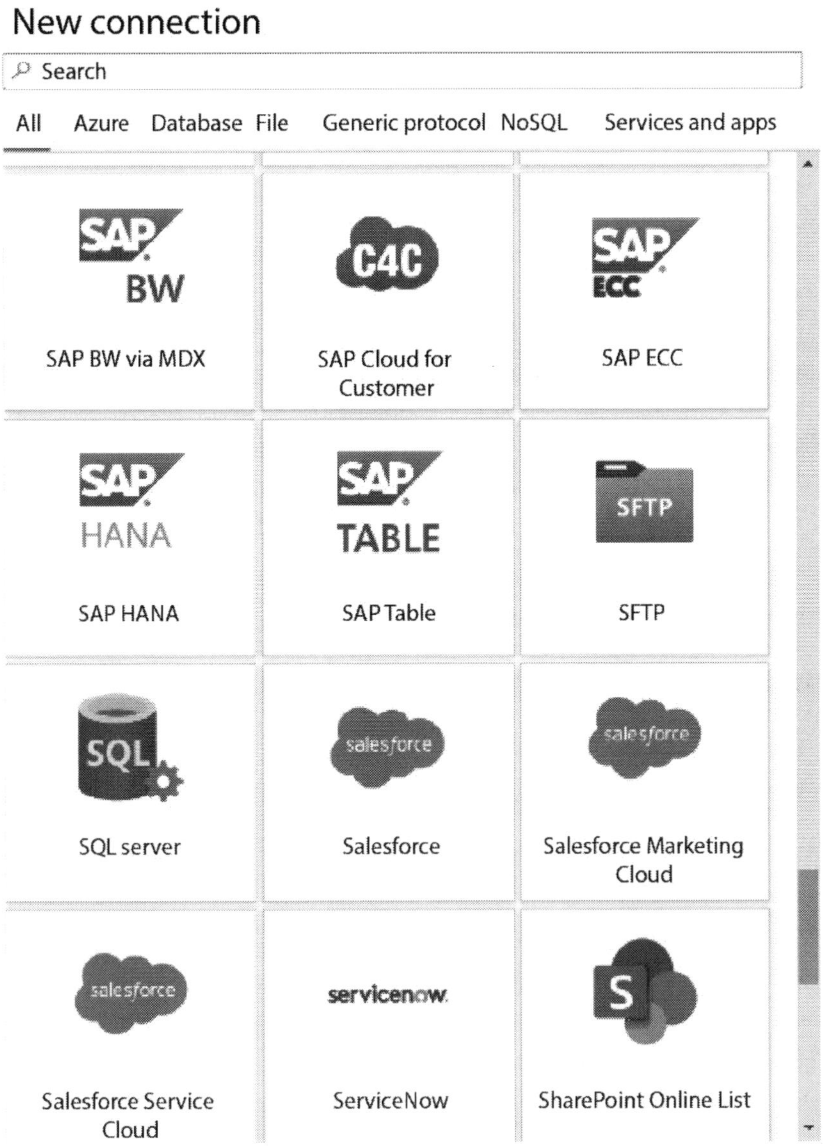

New connection

🔍 Search

All   Azure   Database   File   Generic protocol   NoSQL   Services and apps

SAP BW	**C4C**	**SAP ECC**
SAP BW via MDX	SAP Cloud for Customer	SAP ECC
SAP HANA	**SAP TABLE**	**SFTP**
SAP HANA	SAP Table	SFTP
SQL	**salesforce**	**salesforce**
SQL server	Salesforce	Salesforce Marketing Cloud
salesforce	**servicenow.**	**S**
Salesforce Service Cloud	ServiceNow	SharePoint Online List

Figure 5.2 – Azure Synapse Pipelines – list of connectors

After the data source connection, you can perform some filtering or selection operations, and then you generate your result set to target the destination, which will be the analytical data store. In the next section, we will discuss this type of storage; we're going to exercise these operations in *Chapter 12, Provisioning and Configuring Large-Scale Data Analytics in Azure.*

Exploring the analytical data store

After the ingestion process, the **result set** is stored in an analytical data store, which can be a relational database (the default in data warehouse solutions) or a standard object store in **big data** lakes.

It is important to evaluate these two types of storage. Let's discuss them in detail.

Data warehouse

A data warehouse is a relational database with a **predefined schema**, designed for data analysis purposes rather than transactional workloads.

Analytics databases are typically **denormalized** in a scheme in which numeric values are stored in central fact tables, which are linked to one or more dimension tables that represent entities that can be aggregated.

A fact table can, for example, contain sales order data that can be grouped by customer, product, store, and time (allowing you, for example, to easily find the total monthly sales revenue per product for each store).

The **star schema** is a type of fact and dimension table schema that is often developed in a **snowflake schema** by adding extra tables connected to dimension tables to describe dimensional hierarchies (for example, *product* may be related to *product categories*).

When you only have transactional data that can be organized into a structured schema of tables and you want to query it using SQL, a data warehouse is an excellent option.

Data lake

A data lake is a repository of files for access to high-performance data, typically in a distributed filesystem. This is ideal for accepting not only structured data in our data loads but also semi-structured and unstructured data.

To process queries in stored files and return data for **reports** and **analysis**, technologies such as **Spark** or **Hadoop** are often employed.

These systems often use a schema technique in reading to create **tabular schemas** in semi-structured data files as they are ready for analysis, rather than imposing limitations when data is saved.

Data lakes are ideal for storing and analyzing a variety of structured, semi-structured, and unstructured data without the need for schema application when data is written to storage.

Hybrid approaches

In a **lake database** or **data lakehouse**, you can employ a hybrid solution that combines elements of data lakes and data warehouses.

Raw data is stored as files in a data lake, and a relational storage layer abstracts the underlying files and exposes them as tables, which can be queried using SQL.

Data lakehouses are a relatively new approach to Spark-based systems and are enabled by technologies such as **Delta Lake**, which adds relational storage capabilities to Spark, allowing you to define tables that enforce schemas and transactional consistency, support batch loading, and streaming and query data sources using a SQL API.

The concept of data analytics architecture will become clearer when we exercise the implementation of a modern data warehouse in *Chapter 12, Provisioning and Configuring Large-Scale Data Analytics in Azure*.

Closing the analytical flow, we will now detail the concepts of an analytical data model.

Exploring an analytical data model

Analytical data models allow you to organize the data so that it can be analyzed.

Models are defined by the quantitative values that you want to analyze or report (known as **measures**) and the entities by which you want to aggregate them and are based on connected data tables (known as **dimensions**).

A model can, for example, include a table with numerical sales measures (such as revenue or quantity), as well as dimensions for products, customers, and time. This would combine sales data of one or more dimensions (for example, to identify total revenue per customer or total items sold per product per month).

The model is conceptually a **multidimensional** structure known as a **cube**, where each location in which the dimensions meet represents an added value.

To understand this cubed data organization, let's look at the following figure:

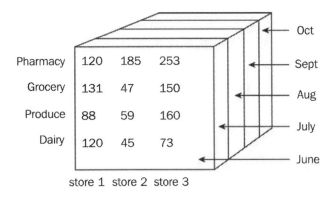

Figure 5.3 – Cube data model

In the example, we are analyzing a fact (*Sales*) and we have the following dimensions:

- Premises for sale – store 1, store 2, and store 3

- Sale value – 120, 185, 47, and so on

- Product category - Pharmacy, Grocery, Produce, and Dairy

- Sale months – June, July, Aug, Sept, and Oct

With this data organization, the generation of information can be very granular, generating all the intelligence necessary for decision-making.

But what are facts and dimensions? Let's look at these concepts now.

Facts and dimensions

Dimension tables are the entities that you want to use to aggregate numeric metrics, such as products or customers. A row with a unique **key value** represents each entity.

The remaining columns include properties of an entity, such as `names` and `categories` for `Product`, or `addresses` and `gender` for `Customer`. Most analytical models include a `Time` dimension so that number measures related to occurrences can be aggregated over time.

In the following figure, we can observe a table called `Fact_Sales`, which has dimensions based on `Store`, `Date`, and `Product` in other tables:

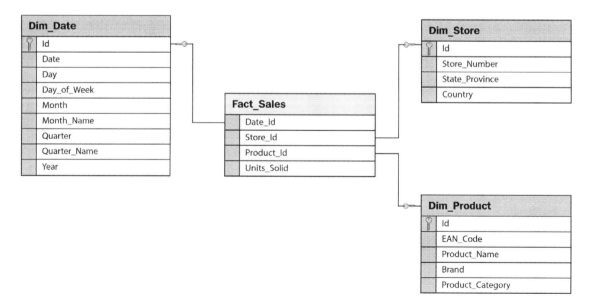

Figure 5.4 – Fact and dimension table sample

These dimensions are connected to the fact table, which is the central entity of analysis and makes connections and aggregations with the other dimension tables. It provides us granularity for data exploration around the different dimensions of this data model.

> **Important note**
> The data modeling theme is extensive, but the concepts presented in this book are sufficient for you to start a data warehouse project and to be prepared for the DP-900 certification issues.

Now that we understand the process of ingestion, processing, and storing the data, let's talk about the visualization layer.

Exploring data visualization

Modern data analysis systems serve **business intelligence (BI)** workloads that include **data modeling** and **visualization**. Essentially, data visualization enables data-driven decisions to be made in organizations.

We will explore data visualization in detail in *Chapter 13, Working with Power BI*.

Data analysts can use a variety of data visualization tools. For example, charting support in productivity tools such as Microsoft Excel and built-in data visualization widgets on notebooks are used to explore data on services such as Azure Synapse Analytics and Azure Databricks, to visually explore data and summarize **insights**.

Enterprise-scale business analytics, on the other hand, often require an integrated system that can enable complex data modeling, interactive reporting, and secure sharing.

The following is an example of data modeling in Power BI Desktop:

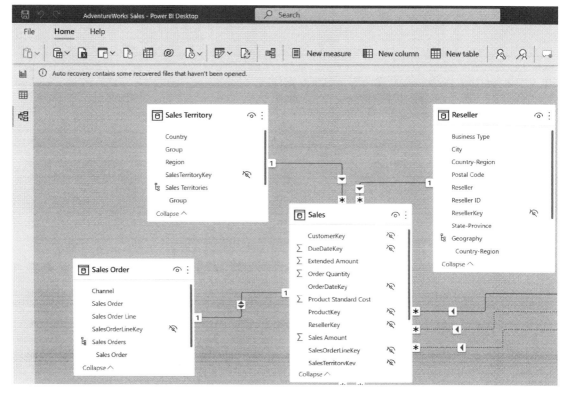

Figure 5.5 – Data modeling in Power BI

As we can see, Power BI Desktop allows you to create an analytical model using data tables imported from one or more data sources. You can create relationships between fact tables and dimension tables by defining hierarchies, renaming table columns, changing data types, and other transformation activities.

> **Important note**
>
> Data visualization tools are not the only data target processed in a data analytics environment. In modern applications, it is common to have a data exposure layer modeled via APIs to return applications' results.

Now, with the concepts of data ingestion, storage, modeling, and visualization, we've completed all the data flow items in an analytical environment.

Case study

Data analytics is today one of the main topics within companies. With it, the use cases are endless, depending on the industry of the organization and the department that is working on the data.

In this chapter, we will discuss a case study of a global food company, a leader in its field, detailing its journey of implementing a data analytics strategy.

Data-driven culture

In a large and complex organization, the ability to balance continuity and change has been key to its success. The enterprise realized that in order to react rapidly to the market, its staff required improved access to data and to create a **data-driven culture**.

These building blocks are used as the foundation for analytical solutions for an organization in business areas such as financial management, marketing, sales, and HR.

This organization is utilizing innovative technologies, including blockchain, IoT, and cloud computing, to make shopping even more frictionless and personalized, for more than 100 million customers monthly. *Figure 5.6* demonstrates the interaction between the person (customer) and the coffee shop, which runs data analytics in the cloud:

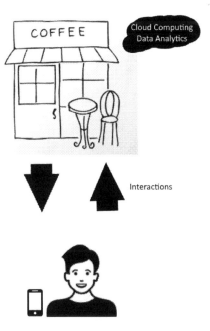

Figure 5.6 – The interaction between the person (customer) and the coffee shop

To give users of the company's app a better-tailored experience, they have been utilizing reinforcement learning technology, a sort of machine learning in which a system learns to make judgments in complicated, unexpected contexts based on external feedback.

Customers receive personalized order suggestions within the app, which is powered by a reinforcement learning platform created and hosted in Azure. The members with active rewards receive intelligent recommendations for food and drinks via the app based on local store inventory, popular choices, weather, time of day, community preferences, and past orders thanks to this technology and the expertise of internal data scientists.

Customers are more likely to receive ideas for goods they'll like thanks to personalization. For instance, if the customer often purchases dairy-free beverages, the platform can deduce that the customer prefers non-dairy products, so avoid recommending items that include dairy and instead, propose dairy-free meals and beverages.

Reinforcement learning essentially enables the program to learn more about each user. The final goal is an interpersonal connection, even though a machine is what drives the recommendations.

The organization enabled all users worldwide to access the data, using a data analytics structure based on Azure and Power BI. The organization has implemented its self-service BI approach in stages, starting with department systems and integrating their **Enterprise Resource Planning** (**ERP**) based on SAP.

Summary

A data analytics workload involves a **data flow**, which starts with the **data ingestion** and **processing** technique, through to **storing** and **modeling**, until it is prepared to be consumed by **visualization** tools.

The most important knowledge of this chapter sits on the concepts behind this analytical process because when we get to future chapters (which are more hands-on), you will have the proper knowledge to implement the data analytics concept using Azure Synapse Analytics and Power BI.

This knowledge is a foundation for the preparation for the DP-900 test because part of the questions is based on concepts and not only on specific configurations.

In the next chapter, we begin Part 2 of our book, which will be more technical and provide more details about Azure tools for relational databases.

Sample questions and answers

In this section, you will see sample questions about Microsoft tools. Do not be alarmed; we will cover them in the next chapters, but usually, the data analytics concepts are evaluated in DP-900 asking questions or analyzing implementation scenarios in Microsoft analytics platforms.

Here are some questions:

1. You've gathered data in a variety of formats from a variety of sources. Now, you must convert the data into a single, consistent format. Which of the following processes would you use?

   A. Data ingestion

   B. Data modeling

   C. Data storage

   D. Dataset

2. The process of transforming and translating raw data into a more useable format for analysis is known as _____:

   A. Data cleaning

   B. Data ingestion

   C. Data modeling

   D. Data analysis

3. Choose the best sequence for putting the ELT process into action on Azure:

   A. Prepare the data for loading by extracting the source data into text files. Use PolyBase or the COPY command to load the data into staging tables. Transform the data and insert it into production tables by storing it in Azure Blob storage or Azure Data Lake Storage.

   B. Extract the data from the source into text files. Place the information in Azure Data Lake Storage or Azure Blob storage. Make sure the data is ready to be loaded. Using PolyBase or the COPY command, load the data into staging tables, transform the data, then insert the data into production tables.

   C. Extract the data from the source into text files. Place the data in Azure Blob storage or Azure Data Lake Storage, as appropriate. Make sure the data is ready to be loaded. Use PolyBase or the COPY command to load the data into staging tables. Fill in the blanks in the production tables with the data and then transform the information.

   D. Prepare the data for loading by extracting the source data into text files. Use PolyBase or the COPY command to load the data into staging tables. Place the data in Azure Blob storage or Azure Data Lake Storage, as appropriate. Fill in the blanks in the production tables with the data and then transform the information.

4. Consider the following statements:

   • S1: Make dashboards available to others, particularly those who are on the go

   • S2: Use Power BI mobile apps to view and interact with shared dashboards and results

- S3: Import data and produce a report in Power BI Desktop

- S4: Upload to the Power BI service, where you can create new dashboards and visualizations

The common flow of activities in Power BI is represented by which of the following sequences of the preceding statements?

A. S1-S2-S4-S3

B. S2-S1-S3-S4

C. S3-S4-S2-S1

D. S2-S3-S1-S4

5. In a data warehouse analytical database, which of the following languages is used to create, read, update, and delete data?

A. SQL

B. C#

C. U-SQL

D. PL/SQL

Answer key

1-A 2-D 3-B 4-C 5-A

Part 2:
Relational Data in Azure

This part will provide complete coverage of the knowledge and skills required for the *Skills measured* under the *Describe how to work with relational data on Azure* section of the exam syllabus.

In this part, you will learn about the concepts and services in Azure for implementing relational databases in the cloud. You'll explore service options, the provisioning and basic configuration of these services, and how to query the data using SQL.

This part comprises the following chapters:

- *Chapter 6, Integrating Relational Data in Azure*
- *Chapter 7, Provisioning and Configuring Relational Database Services in Azure*
- *Chapter 8, Querying Relational Data in Azure*

6

Integrating Relational Data on Azure

In this chapter, we will explore scenarios for using **relational database management systems** (**RDBMSs**) to store transactional data on Azure in services like Azure SQL Database, Azure Database for PostgreSQL, Azure Database for MySQL, and Azure Database for MariaDB.

Many databases currently in operation are relational, based on SQL Server, PostgreSQL, MySQL, and others, and in general, many of them are still running in local data centers (on-premises). This chapter will provide the fundamental knowledge you need to plan to modernize these databases for Azure and prepare for DP-900 certification questions related to these technologies.

By the end of this chapter, you will understand the different Azure data services for relational databases, the use case for each one, and how to choose the right relational database for your Azure project.

In this chapter, we will cover the following topics:

- Exploring relational Azure data services
- Understanding Azure databases offers

Exploring relational Azure data services

In this section, we'll understand the characteristics of Azure relational databases, the differences between the services that are offered, and the most common usage scenarios for each. Several database services are supported by Azure, allowing you to run common RDBMSs in the cloud, such as SQL Server, PostgreSQL, and MySQL.

Most Azure database services are fully managed services, allowing you to spend less time managing your database, delivered as **Platform as a Service** (**PaaS**).

You can quickly scale an infrastructure or distribute your database across structures around the world, without worrying about downtime, deployment, and maintenance of that entire infrastructure.

Azure database services already have advanced security controls, with automatic monitoring and threat detection, auto-scaling for increased performance if needed, automated backup, and built-in high availability.

All these benefits are provided by database services through a **Service-Level Agreement (SLA)**, which defines the commitment to deliver this entire infrastructure by the cloud provider, in this case, Microsoft Azure.

> **Important note**
>
> The cost of Azure database services is very varied, from free databases where the only cost is storage to very large capacities with high cost. Understanding the cost metrics and pricing of services is not a relevant topic for the DP-900 exam, but as this is an important subject for your projects, I suggest you better understand the cost composition of the services by referring directly to the pricing by product area of the Azure website:
>
> `https://azure.microsoft.com/en-us/pricing/#product-pricing`

Let's now understand the different relational database services in Azure and how to choose between these different options.

Azure SQL

Azure offers three types of SQL Server databases. They are as follows:

Service	Offer	Use Case
Azure SQL Database	PaaS	Suitable for new applications, cloud-native applications, or applications that may have their interaction behavior with the database reviewed.
Azure SQL Managed Instance	PaaS	Suitable for legacy SQL Server migration to Azure. It has more than 95% similarity with traditional versions of SQL Server, but with the benefits of a PaaS database.
SQL Server on virtual machines	**Infrastructure as a Service (IaaS)**	The traditional SQL Server deployed on virtual machines in Azure. It is fully compatible with legacy SQL Server databases that are in operation in on-premises environments.

Table 6.1 – Types of Azure SQL Server databases

Let's discuss the main differences between these offers now.

Azure SQL Database

Azure SQL Database is a PaaS service. You establish a cloud-based managed database server and then deploy your databases to it.

> **Important note**
> An Azure SQL Database server is a logical entity that serves as an administrative hub for multiple, single, or grouped SQL databases, user logins, firewall rules, audit rules, threat detection policies, and failover groups.

Azure SQL Database can be used as a *single database* or as part of an *elastic pool*.

Single database

When you enable an Azure SQL Database single database, you configure a standalone SQL Server PaaS and start using it simply and directly. All you need to do is provision the service, create your tables, and populate them with your data, because Azure will manage all the server-side infrastructure.

If you need more storage space, memory, or compute power, you can increase these resources without any downtime. Resources are pre-allocated by default, and you'll be billed by the hour for those you requested.

There is also an Azure SQL Database single database *serverless* option, with similar behavior, but in this option, you will be sharing the physical server with other Azure clients, with Azure managing the confidentiality and security side.

> **Important note**
> Serverless database options should always be carefully evaluated to identify whether requirements are met by service resource limits. In the case of Azure SQL Database serverless, considering the resource sharing, you may have some resources that generate latency in your database responses. As with every serverless option, the benefit is that the database is scaled and automatically tuned.

Elastic pool

An Azure SQL Database elastic pool is a service where you can have multiple databases, sharing the same resources such as memory, data storage space, and computing power.

Pool is a term used to describe a collection of resources, in this context, a collection of databases that share the same Azure SQL Database cluster.

A pool is created by you in your account and can only be used by your databases, such infrastructure being dedicated to a single customer and not shared with other Azure customers.

If you have databases with resource requirements that change over time, this strategy can help you save money.

For example, your payroll system database, uses a lot of CPU capacity on a specific date when processing payroll for the month's accounts closing operation. But during the rest of the month, the database has normal behavior, with a small number of transactions.

An elastic pool allows you to use the pool resources during the processing of this heavier workload and release them as soon as processing is finished to be used by the other databases in the pool.

Azure SQL Database is Azure's best cost-benefit solution. It has minimal administration and is suitable for all cloud-native solutions that will be developed from scratch in Azure. It is not fully compatible with SQL Server on-premises deployments, so it is not usually the best option for migrations, and these should be accommodated in Azure SQL Managed Instance, which we will look at in the next section.

Advantages of using Azure SQL database

Here are the key advantages of Azure SQL Database:

- Azure SQL Database is **updated** and **fixed** automatically to ensure that you are always using the latest and most secure version of the service.

- With the **scalability** capabilities of Azure SQL Database, you can increase the resources available to store and process data, without having to perform an expensive manual upgrade.

- **High availability** guarantees are provided by the service, ensuring that your databases are available at least 99.99% of the time.

- **Point-in-time restore** in Azure SQL Database allows you to restore a database to the state it was in at any point in the past. Databases can be duplicated in many locations to increase resiliency and disaster recovery.

- **Advanced threat prevention** includes advanced security features, including vulnerability assessments that can help you detect and fix potential database security issues.

- **Anomaly detection** is a security feature that detects anomalous behavior in database access. This means this feature can prevent your database from being accessed by users or apps without the proper permission. **Database auditing logs** can help us to investigate an event, using the history of logs generated and stored automatically on Azure.

- **Azure SQL Database** protects your data while it is kept in the database (at rest) and while being transported (in transit) over the network using *encryption*.

The Azure databases explained in this chapter, except for Azure Database for MySQL (MySQL has a specialized open source tool called MySQL Workbench), can be managed through **Azure Data Studio**, which we discussed in *Chapter 2, Exploring Roles and Responsibilities in Data Domain*.

In the following screenshot, we see an example of access to Azure SQL Database, opening databases and tables and performing a query:

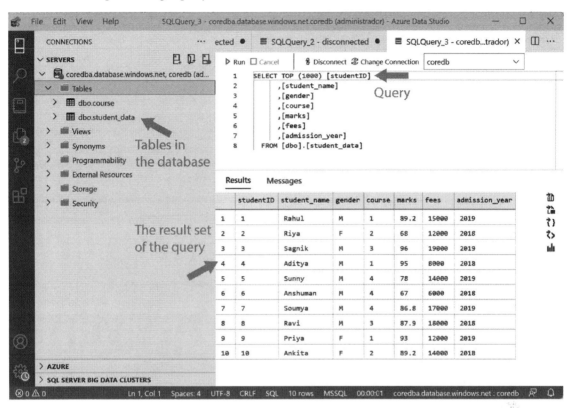

Figure 6.1 – Azure Data Studio querying Azure SQL Database

Azure Data Studio is a free and very intuitive tool for accessing Azure databases. It works with most database services and helps a lot in the organization and governance of these records.

With it, you can configure access, perform ad hoc queries in the database, and build your objects.

Much like SQL Database's service, but recommended for legacy SQL Server migrations, is **Azure SQL Managed Instance**. Let's look at that.

Azure SQL Managed Instance

Azure SQL Managed Instance is a PaaS version of a self-managed, intelligent, and scalable SQL Server database of Azure. It can be configured using **capability mode** from older versions of SQL Server, such as 2005, 2008, and later. This makes the service almost *99% compatible* with these legacy versions of SQL Server, ideal for existing database migrations.

To maintain all PaaS administrations of the service, some limitations are found, especially in the customization and management layers of the system operator and services of the SQL Server installation. The *limits are found* because the user of this service does not have access to the virtual machine server that SQL Server will be installed on, as in a traditional SQL Server installation.

Advantages of using Azure SQL Managed Instance

The main benefits of the Azure SQL Managed Instance service are as follows:

- The **SQL Server version** of Azure SQL Managed Instance is compatible with legacy SQL Server versions since 2005

- Azure SQL Managed Instance is based on the latest version of the SQL Server software, so it always has all the newest features of the SQL Server Enterprise version

- It provides a native private **Virtual Network** (**VNet**) implementation that addresses common security concerns, such as network isolation and a private IP for the database

- Existing SQL Server users can use Azure SQL Managed Instance to migrate their on-the-go applications to the cloud with *minimal changes* to the application and database

- It has *PaaS features*, such as automated fixes and version upgrades, automated backups, and built-in high availability

Due to the capability mode of older versions of SQL Server, the main use case of Azure SQL Managed Instance is existing SQL Server migration.

Now that we know about these two PaaS formats, let's evaluate the Azure IaaS offering of SQL Server on virtual machines.

SQL Server on virtual machines

Azure offers virtual machine images with SQL Server already installed and configured, in different versions and architectures (Always-On cluster, Windows Server, Linux, and so on) and supports customized installation of SQL Server environments.

When SQL Server is deployed on a virtual machine in Azure, it's in IaaS format, meaning Azure management is limited on the hardware and operating system infrastructure layers, and all configuration, monitoring, updates, and customizations are the user's responsibility.

Advantages of using SQL Server on virtual machines

Although not the most recommended format for Azure, there are some benefits to using SQL Server for virtual machines:

- There is 100% **compatibility** with legacy applications for migrations that Azure Managed Instance doesn't support.

- **Customizations** can be made at the operating system and/or SQL Server installation level, for example, using local users created in the operating system.

- There is an Azure benefits package called **SQL Server IaaS Agent Registration** that enables this virtual machine to have some administration features similar to PaaS, such as automated backup, Azure Defender for SQL Server, and SQL assessment. You can find a list of all the benefits available at this link:

  ```
  https://docs.microsoft.com/en-us/azure/azure-sql/virtual-machines/
  windows/sql-server-iaas-agent-extension-automate-management
  ```

- There is *portability* between on-premises and other cloud platforms.

Since this option has more manual configurations and manageability tasks for DBAs, it should be used if Azure SQL Database and Azure SQL Managed Instance do not meet your project requirements.

> **Important note**
> Azure still has **Azure SQL Edge** options, which is a version of SQL Server for offline data storage on a cloud-connected device. This is a very specialized version, so it is unlikely there will be questions about it in the DP-900 exam.

Now that we know about the different versions of SQL in Azure, let's evaluate the open source options that Azure also offers for relational databases.

Azure Database for MySQL

Based on **MySQL Community Edition**, Azure Database for MySQL is a PaaS implementation of MySQL in the Azure cloud.

Figure 6.2 – Azure Database for MySQL is similar to MySQL Community Edition

Like Azure SQL Database, in Azure Database for MySQL, the *security* of a database connection is provided by the server, which enforces restrictions via a firewall and optionally requires SSL connections. The user can configure server settings, such as lock modes, the maximum number of connections, and timeouts, using various server parameters.

High availability and *scalability* are included in the Azure Database for MySQL service at no additional cost. You only pay for the services you use. Backups are done automatically and can be restored at a specific time.

Most popular applications are built on top of the concept of **LAMP** (which stands for **Linux, Apache, MySQL, PHP/Perl/Python**). For those applications, on Azure, the best option for a database is Azure Database for MySQL.

Azure Database for MySQL is a worldwide database solution that lets you scale up huge databases without having to worry about managing hardware, network components, virtual servers, software patches, or other underlying components.

Because Azure Database for MySQL is a PaaS solution, some common open source *customizations in MySQL* are not available in the service. On the other hand, security and management tasks—which are the main concerns when we are planning a new database—are all managed by Azure in Azure Database for MySQL.

> **Important note**
>
> Burstable virtual machines are a family of Azure virtual machines that have bandwidth shared by multiple users. They're ideal for workloads that don't need a dedicated resource for performance and are a good way to have a database that is more cost-effective. Burstable machines will be discussed later in this chapter.

There are two deployment options for Azure Database for MySQL: **Single Server** and **Flexible Server**.

Azure Database for MySQL – Flexible Server

Azure Database for MySQL Flexible Server is an interesting option for those who want to have flexibility in configuring database capacity. With this option, you can configure how the data distribution for the high availability of data will work, in a single or multiple availability zones, and have efficient controls to work with virtual machines such as servers in start/stop mode in burstable and dedicated formats (General Purpose and Business Critical formats).

Azure Database for MySQL – Single Server

Azure Database for MySQL Single Server is a fully managed service database with predictable performance and scalability and is ideal for applications that are already running on a single server.

Azure Database for MySQL comes with the following important features:

- Built-in **high availability**
- **Performance** can be predicted
- **Scalability** is simple and demand is met quickly

- Data is protected at rest and in transit with **encryption**

- Automatic **backups** and point-in-time **restores** are kept for the last 35 days

- There is **security** and legal compliance at the corporate level

- The **pay-as-you-go** pricing model ensures that you pay only for what you use

- The **monitoring** feature is available for Azure Database for MySQL, including the ability to create alarms and view metrics and logs

In addition to MySQL, another open source database often found in relational applications is PostgreSQL. For this reason, Azure has also prepared a managed service for it. Let's learn about it now.

Azure Database for PostgreSQL

If you prefer PostgreSQL, you can run a PaaS implementation of PostgreSQL in the Azure cloud using Azure Database for PostgreSQL. This service has the same MySQL capabilities in terms of availability, performance, scale, security, and administration.

Figure 6.3 – Azure Database for PostgreSQL is similar to PostgreSQL

Some features of PostgreSQL databases in custom installations are not available in Azure Database for PostgreSQL, so it is important to evaluate the impacts of a possible *migration* before considering the service for your project.

These features are primarily based on extensions that users can install in a database to perform specific activities, such as writing storage procedures in various programming languages (in addition to existing **pgSQL**, the native language of PostgreSQL) and communicating directly with the operating system. These extensions are very common in legacy PostgreSQL databases, such as **TimescaleDB** for time-series implementations on PostgreSQL or **PostGIS** for spatial database needs.

The good news is that there is support for a main set of the most used extensions and the list of accessible extensions is updated regularly by Azure. In the following link, you can find all the extensions available on Azure Database for PostgreSQL:

```
https://docs.microsoft.com/en-us/azure/postgresql/single-server/
concepts-extensions
```

There are three deployment options for Azure Database for PostgreSQL:

- **Single Server**
- **Flexible Server**
- **Hyperscale**

Let's learn about each of them now.

Azure Database for PostgreSQL – Single Server

The Azure Database for PostgreSQL Single Server deployment option offers PaaS managed infrastructure advantages like Azure Database for MySQL. **Basic**, **General Purpose**, and **Memory Optimized** are the three types of prices available. Each layer has a varied number of CPUs, RAM, and storage sizes; you choose one based on the expected load.

Azure Database for PostgreSQL – Flexible Server

A fully managed database service is available with the PostgreSQL Flexible Server deployment option. It offers more power and flexibility in server configuration as well as superior cost-cutting controls.

In general, the service offers greater flexibility and server configuration adjustments based on the needs of the user.

You can collocate the database engine with the client tier for better latency and choose high availability inside a single availability zone or across many availability zones thanks to the Flexible Server architecture.

With the option to *stop/start* your server and a burstable virtual machine, flexible servers offer superior cost optimization controls.

The PostgreSQL 11, 12, and 13 Community versions are now supported by Azure Database for PostgreSQL – Flexible Server.

Flexible Server is ideal when the following are required:

- **Better control** and adaptations, which are required for application development
- **High availability** zone redundancy
- **Maintenance windows** that are well managed

Azure Database for PostgreSQL – Hyperscale (Citus)

Hyperscale (Citus) is a deployment option for large database loads that scales queries across multiple server nodes. Your database is distributed across multiple nodes. The value of a partition key is used to divide the data into parts. You can consider using this deployment option for the large PostgreSQL database deployments of the Azure cloud.

The Azure PostgreSQL service has some very interesting points that can justify its use:

- The **SLA is 99.99%,** with built-in high availability.

- It has integrated **failover and fault detection** methods.

- The **pgAdmin** tool, which can be used to manage and monitor a PostgreSQL database, is familiar to PostgreSQL users.

- Azure Database for PostgreSQL saves information about queries that run on the server databases in the **azure_sys database**. You can see this information by querying the `store.qs` query view, which can be used to track queries that users are executing.

A newer database, but one that has been considered in some modern application scenarios, is **MariaDB**. Let's evaluate the Azure Database for MariaDB service now.

Azure Database for MariaDB

Azure Database for MariaDB is a MariaDB database management system that has been converted to run on Azure. It uses MariaDB Community Server as the foundation, but has all the benefits of a PaaS database on Azure.

MariaDB is a very scalable database and has architectural similarities to MySQL. This means that migration between these two databases is simple, and you can choose what will be suitable for your use case.

Figure 6.4 – Azure Database for MariaDB and the MariaDB open source

The primary use case for this service is database migrations to Azure, from on-premises MariaDB, PostgreSQL, or Oracle Database.

Azure manages and controls the database completely. The system requires almost no additional administration after you provision the service and transfer your data.

Azure Database for MariaDB provides the following features:

- **High availability** is incorporated at no extra cost

- Predictable results can be obtained with all-in-one **pay-as-you-go** prices

- In seconds, you can **increase or decrease** the compute resources as needed

- **Sensitive data** is protected both at rest and in transit

- Up to 35 days of automatic **backups** and point-in-time **restore** can be configured

- There are **security** and **compliance** controls at the enterprise level

Now we've listed all the relational databases available in Azure. In the next chapter, we'll start provisioning jobs in Azure, so get ready.

To finish up this chapter, we will evaluate use cases for the databases we have covered thus far in this chapter.

Use cases

An RDBMS uses SQL as its default language. In general, use cases that can be applied to Azure SQL Database can also be applied to Azure Database for MySQL, PostgreSQL, and MariaDB, depending on which technology you want to use or what your application has already been developed on.

Therefore, instead of showing use cases of each of these technologies, in this section, I will present the reasons for opting for Azure SQL Database.

> **Important note**
> Whether you use a SQL or NoSQL database for a particular use case is one of the most important questions for a data architect. You will complete your knowledge in *Chapter 9, Exploring Non-Relational Data Offerings in Azure*, where we will discuss Azure NoSQL databases and list the main reasons for using a NoSQL database.

The big difference between a relational database and a non-relational database is the schema definition, which is defined at the beginning of the project on the relational database.

Before you start using `INSERT` statements on your database tables, it is necessary to run a `CREATE TABLE` query, with columns set to the appropriate data type, and then that database will be prepared to stop receiving the data.

Defining this schema at the beginning of the project enables relational databases to be more easily documented and governed in an enterprise structure.

But that's not the only reason why they are the most widely used databases on the market. We can also list the following advantages:

- A few years ago, they were **unique in the market**, with the large presence of Microsoft SQL Server, Oracle Database, MySQL, and PostgreSQL, which means that many applications were created using these databases and continue to work only with these systems

- They are highly **reliable** and **stable**, and this is proven by critical business applications such as large ERPs and CRMs, among other applications

- They follow a standard that works well with major software stacks, such as LAMP

- They've been in use for over 40 years, making many professionals specialized in this type of database and **SQL**, facilitating implementation and support

- They are **ACID** compliant by default

- They provide the best **support** options for enterprise-level projects

Now, let's evaluate the disadvantages, which may sway your choice in favor of using a NoSQL database:

- There are **sharding** and **scalability** challenges because they are databases that have several routines that run even before database transaction operations begin. This causes these databases to initially consume more resources than a NoSQL database.

- There is **low efficiency with blob**. Even for databases that have this data type, it is much better to store a JSON document, for example, in a NoSQL database than in a binary or BLOB column.

With this knowledge, you are prepared to start configuring relational databases in Azure and exploring the capabilities of the SQL language. This will be our focus in *Chapter 8, Querying Relational Data in Azure*, but first, we will review what we learned in this chapter and evaluate a few simulated questions from the DP-900 test.

Summary

In this chapter, we learned that Azure offers great options for relational databases in the *PaaS format*, such as Azure SQL, Azure Database for MySQL, Azure Database for PostgreSQL, and Azure Database for MariaDB, and enables custom installation of other types of databases in *IaaS format*.

We understood the key differentials of Azure relational databases and features that are common in all offerings, such as *built-in high availability*, high scalability, *auto-backup* and point-in-time restore, and encryption of data at rest and in transit, among others.

It's important to evaluate your project requirements, primarily in the migration of existing applications, to identify the best service option in Azure.

In the next chapter, we'll work through the provisioning and basic settings of a relational database in Azure.

Sample questions and answers

The following are some questions and answers that simulate the DP-900 test on Azure relational database services:

1. Which of the following is a built-in feature of SQL databases?

    A. Cross-cluster copies

    B. Dashboards and reports

    C. High availability

    D. Analytical database

2. Which of the following systems is not an Azure database type?

    A. MongoDB

    B. MariaDB

    C. MySQL

    D. PostgreSQL

3. Which version of Azure PostgreSQL best fits an 80 TB database?

    A. Hyperscale

    B. Single Server

    C. Flexible Server

    D. Serverless

4. You must migrate a legacy application running SQL Server 2008 on-premises to Azure. Which Azure service will you analyze first for this migration?

    A. Azure SQL Managed Instance

    B. SQL Server on virtual machines

    C. Azure SQL Database

    D. Azure Database for MySQL

Answer key

1-C, 2-A, 3-A, 4-A

7

Provisioning and Configuring Relational Database Services in Azure

Now that we've met Azure relational database services in the previous chapter, let's explore how to provision and configure the Azure relational database services: Azure SQL Database, Azure Database for PostgreSQL, and Azure Database for MySQL.

This is the chapter where we begin the action! We are going to delve into the implementation in Azure, so it's time to sit in front of the computer, put your book on the table, and follow the steps.

By the end of this chapter, you will be able to understand how to provision the Azure relational database services and the basic configurations around these databases.

In this chapter, we will cover the following topics:

- Provisioning relational data services
- Configuring relational data services

Technical requirements

This is your first chapter with hands-on exercises. To explore the services in this chapter, the following is required:

- A computer with Windows 10 (or a newer OS) and internet access
- An active Azure account (`http://www.azure.com`)
- Access to the book's code repository on GitHub (`https://github.com/PacktPublishing/Microsoft-Certified-Azure-Data-Fundamentals-Exam-DP-900-Certification-Guide`)

> **Important note**
>
> At this time, if you don't already have an Azure account, you can create a free account that will give you $200 of Azure credits to run your tests for 30 days. After this period, you still have access to more than 40 free services, some without a certain deadline, some for 12 months. Among these services are some of the databases seen in this chapter. You can read the complete list of free Azure services that you get here: `https://azure.microsoft.com/en-us/free/search/`.

If this is your first interaction with a cloud computing environment, follow these tips to avoid incurring costs that you have not planned for:

- All services we will use must be instantiated in their smaller formats, thereby maximizing the number of Azure credits we will use.

- Everything in cloud computing has some kind of billing metric – after all, it is an on-demand computing service.

- While not using a service, go to the settings of this service and look for and select the **Stop** or **Pause** option, and when you need to use it again, click **Run**. This way, you will only consume credit for the time that you are doing your exercises.

- When we create our free trial account, we need to add a credit card to validate the account, but Azure won't automatically charge your credit card for your Azure consumption. When your free credits run out, you'll receive a message asking whether you plan to activate credit card payment or not.

With your Azure environment ready, let's start our hands-on exercises.

Provisioning relational Azure data services

In this section, we'll explore the characteristics of *Azure relational databases*, the differences between the services that are offered, and the most common usage scenarios for each.

First of all, let's access the Azure portal: `http://portal.azure.com`.

Now let's look at the provisioning of the main Azure relational database services.

Provisioning Azure SQL Database

The following is the home page of the Azure portal, and in it, we already have access to the category of products such as SQL databases, SQL servers, and Azure Synapse Analytics, among others:

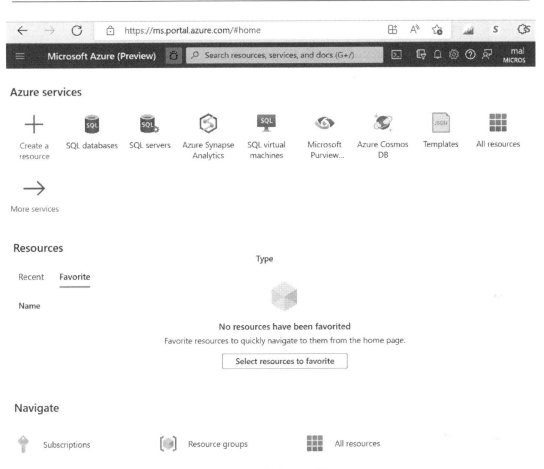

Figure 7.1 – Azure admin portal home page

Let's move on to the step-by-step Azure SQL Database provisioning:

1. In the Azure portal, go to the **Azure SQL** session, which you will find in the hidden menu on the left-hand side (click on the three dashes in the top-left corner for the menu to appear) or by searching in the top bar of the portal or shortcut, which by default, is present on the home page. After accessing it, a page will open as follows:

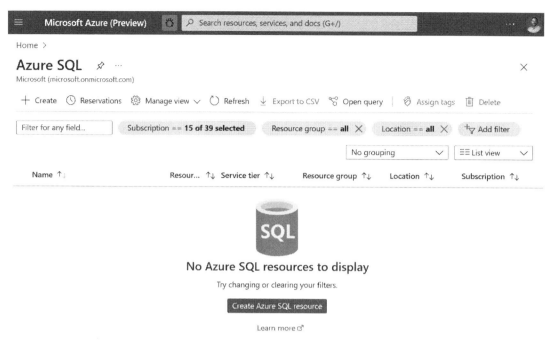

Figure 7.2 – The Azure SQL page on the Azure admin portal

2.   Then, click +**Create** to open the SQL database type selection page you would like to create:

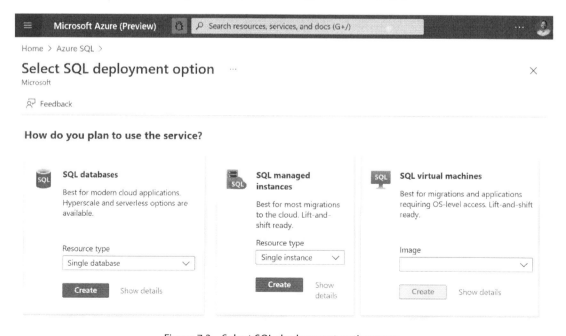

Figure 7.3 – Select SQL deployment option page

> **Note**
>
> On this page, you can create SQL databases and SQL-managed instances; two Azure database-managed services – in the **Platform-as-a-Service (PaaS)** format – and virtual SQL machines, which are virtual machines running SQL Server – in the **Infrastructure-as-a-Service (IaaS)** format.

For this exercise, we will choose **SQL databases | Single database** and then click **Create** to go to the following page:

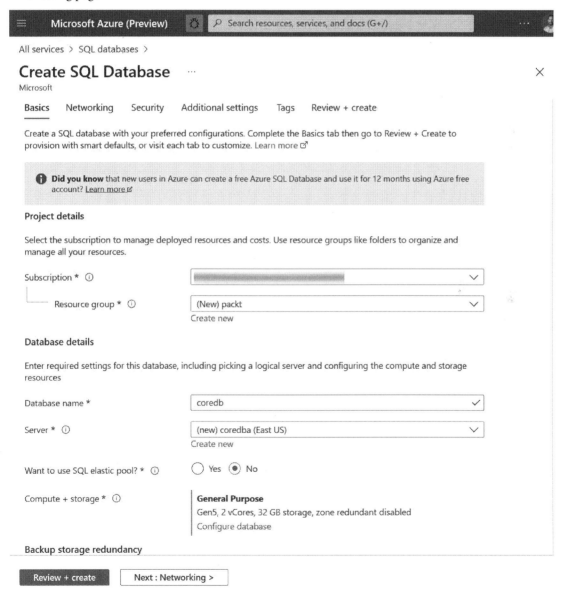

Figure 7.4 – Create SQL database page

3.   Fill out the form as follows:

- **Subscription**: Select your subscription name

- **Resource group**: You can create a resource group or use one that you already have in this subscription

- **Database name**: `coredb`

- **Server**: In this section, use the **Create new** button to open the following page:

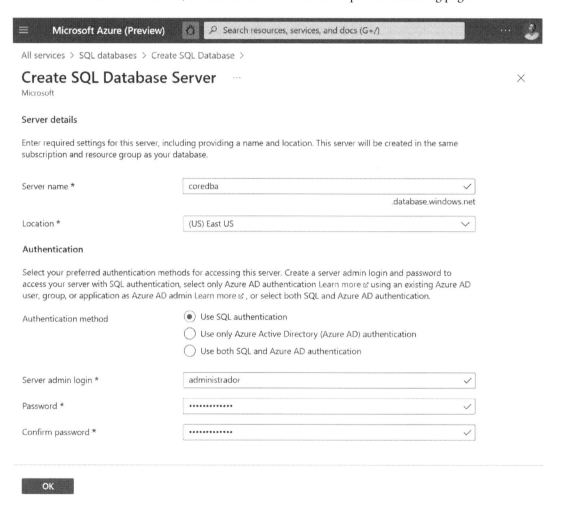

Figure 7.5 – Create SQL Database Server page

The following are the database settings. We will use these settings in later chapters to connect and explore this database:

- **Server name**: `coredba`

- **Location**: `(US) East US`

- **Authentication method**: **Use SQL authentication**

- **Server admin login**: `administrador`

> **Important note**
>
> Azure reserves some words, such as administrator, admin, and others, to avoid security issues. That's why I have used **administrador** (which is the word for administrator in Portuguese). In your projects, you can use something such as **admin2022** and similar variations for creating the admin login, but to make sure you follow all the exercise steps, please use **administrador** for this example.

- **Password**: `Pass@word#123`

When you confirm your settings, the page will return the following:

- **Want to use SQL elastic pool?**: `No`

- **Compute + storage**: `Gen5, 2 vCores, 32 Gb storage, zone redundant disabled`

- **Backup storage redundancy**: `Locally redundant backup storage`

After you finish, click **Next: Networking >**.

4. To give your computer access to this server, you need to configure the following settings in the **Networking** tab:

- **Connectivity method**: `Public Endpoint`

- **Add current client IP address**: `Yes`

> **Important note**
>
> All Azure databases have firewalls that control user and system access to the database's instances. This setting will add your personal computer's IP to a firewall rule.

Move on by clicking the **Next: Security >** button.

5. In the **Security** session, we will only adjust one item:

   • **Enable Microsoft Defender for SQL**: Not now

   Then, click **Next: Additional settings >**.

   In the **Additional settings** session, we will not change any items, but it is interesting to note that Azure SQL Database provides options to automatically restore an existing Backup or to populate a database with Sample or None data (as in, an empty database).

   Another important session is the *collation* configuration, which can also be done on this screen.

   Click the **Next: Tags >** button.

6. We won't add tags now using this feature, so we can already move on and click **Next: Review + create >**. The portal will summarize all our settings, validate whether anything is missing, and then allow us to click on the **Create** button.

   Now, just wait for the Azure processes page that shows us the execution process and informs us when it's available to use!

Important note

We won't cover all the details of Azure SQL Database settings in this book because they are not required for the DP-900 certification, but if you're building a production environment on Azure, it's important to evaluate each of the settings for a better service usage experience, especially network and security items.

After finishing the creation, click **Go to resource** to be directed to the settings page of the new SQL database:

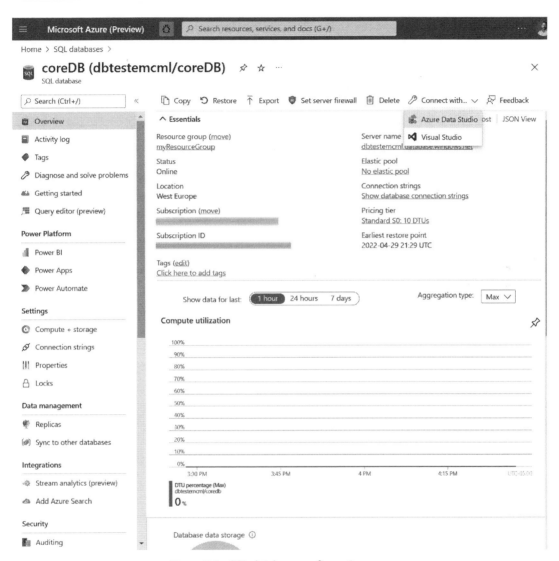

Figure 7.6 – SQL database configuration page

It's ready. Your SQL database is already provisioned, and you can now start configuring access to this new database.

Now, let's look at the other possibilities for transactional databases. Let's evaluate Azure database provisioning for PostgreSQL and MySQL.

Provisioning Azure Database for PostgreSQL and MySQL

Azure Database for PostgreSQL and *Azure Database for MySQL* provisioning work similar to Azure SQL Database. For this reason, this provisioning will be less detailed. Let's move on to provisioning Azure Database for PostgreSQL:

1. In the Azure portal, look for the **Azure Database for PostgreSQL servers** button. You might have to use the search bar at the top or browse the items in the **All services** pane until you find the following page:

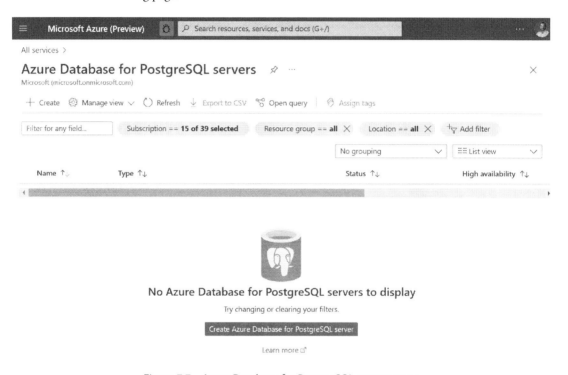

Figure 7.7 – Azure Database for PostgreSQL servers page

2. After clicking **+Create** in the Azure Database for PostgreSQL service, you are redirected to the deployment options page as follows:

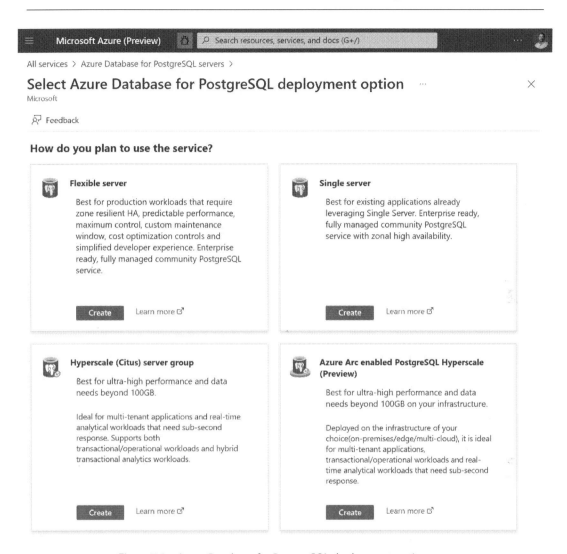

Figure 7.8 – Azure Database for PostgreSQL deployment option page

3.   In this step, you can select from the four options that we discussed in *the previous chapter*:

 • **Flexible server**

 • **Single server**

 • **Hyperscale (Citrus) server group**

 • **Azure Arc enabled PostgreSQL Hyperscale (Preview)**

Let's select **Flexible server** and click **Create**:

> **Important note**
>
> **Azure Arc enabled PostgreSQL Hyperscale (Preview)** will not be covered in this book, as this is a service that is not yet in its final version (GA – General Availability) and is therefore not recommended for Azure productive environments and is not required in certification tests such as the DP-900.

4. In the creation form, use the following settings:

    - **Subscription**: Select your subscription name.

    - **Resource group**: You can create a resource group or use one that you already have in this subscription.

    - **Database name**: pgdbflex

    - **Region**: East US

    - **PostgreSQL version**: 13

    - **Workload type**: Development.

    - **Compute + storage**: We don't need to change it. Because **Workload type** is Development, Azure already understands that it will be a small configuration for testing.

    - **Availability zone**: No preference

    - **Enable high availability**: No

    - **Admin username**: coredb

    - **Password**: Pass@word#123

    - **Confirm password**: Pass@word#123.

This page has a real-time cost estimation feature, depending on your settings, which helps a lot with decision-making. The following is a screenshot:

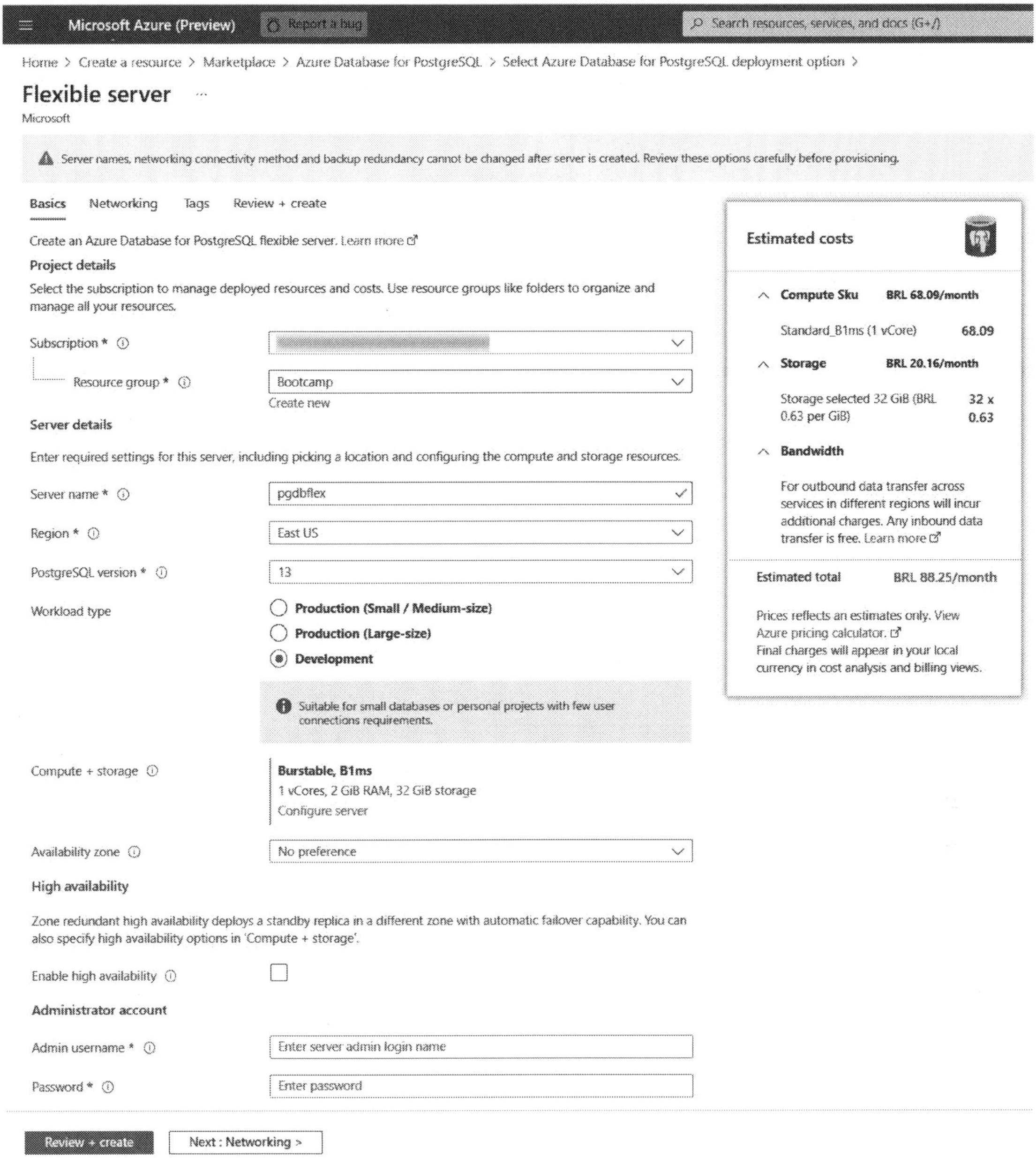

Figure 7.9 – Azure Database for PostgreSQL deployment configuration page – estimated costs

Now, you can click **Next: Networking >**.

5. In **Networking**, the only change needed is to add your IP in a release rule in the firewall. For this, the page already suggests a + **Add current client IP address** link. Click this link to add it and then you can go straight to the **Review + create** button.

After reviewing your configurations, you are ready to click **Create** and wait a few minutes.

Creating Azure Database for MySQL follows exactly the same pattern, only swapping PostgreSQL for MySQL.

However, in *step 2* of this walkthrough, you will only have the **Flexible server** and **Single server** options as follows:

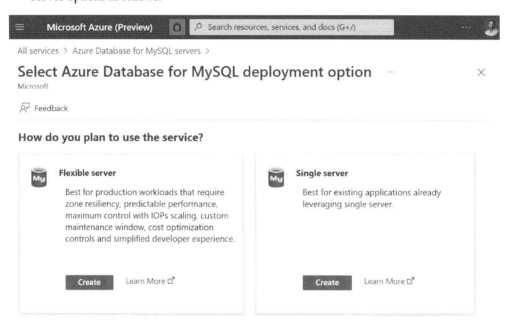

Figure 7.10 – Azure Database for MySQL deployment option page

The other steps are very similar to *Azure Database for PostgreSQL* provisioning, but I invite you to do an *Azure Database for MySQL* deployment as well, so you can experience that and are able to use it in future projects.

Now that we've created relational databases in Azure, let's explore the most important settings for each of these databases.

Configuring relational databases on Azure

After provisioning Azure database services, some basic configuration operations must be performed before starting database usage.

In this section, we will evaluate the PaaS features of Azure databases that assist us in these configurations. To do this, we will use the Azure SQL Database instance provisioned from this chapter, but we have similar features on Azure Database for PostgreSQL and MySQL.

Configuring Azure SQL Database

To follow along, return to the Azure portal and search for the **Azure SQL Database** service instance provisioned at the beginning of this chapter.

As soon as you access the service, you will see a side menu with all the settings for this Azure SQL Database service instance, plus a summary with the most relevant information and graphics that demonstrate its behavior, as shown in the following screenshot:

Figure 7.11 – SQL database configuration page

Let's evaluate the basic settings that must be performed in databases in Azure step by step.

Access Control – Access control to your database is one of the first settings to configure and this setting always raises questions. Do you remember that we added a rule to the firewall so that your computer could access the service? This is a prerequisite, but your user may not have access to the database. Another relevant fact is that user access is not configured at the `coredb` database level but the server level.

To access the server, you can click the **coredba.database.windows.net** link below **Server Name** and the **coredba** server settings page will open:

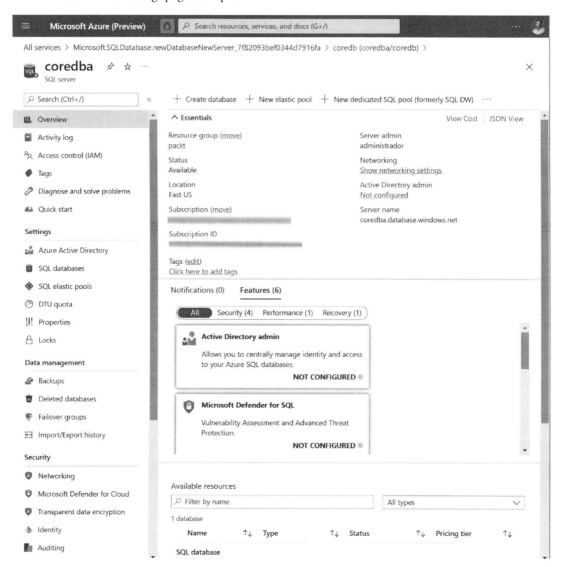

Figure 7.12 – SQL database – SQL server configuration page

This page contains some properties at the SQL server level, one of which is **Access Control (IAM)** in the left-hand menu on the screen, as seen in *Figure 7.13*. On this page, you can add users from your corporate network (if it is connected to Azure) to access this database and create and configure custom access roles, among other features:

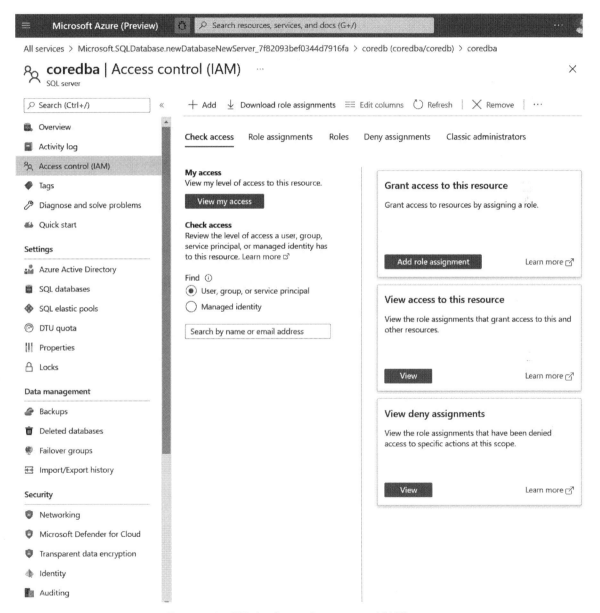

Figure 7.13 – SQL database – Access control (IAM) page

Backups – Another super important configuration at the beginning of using this service is the configuration of the **Available backups** and **Retention policies** routines for your databases, as seen in *Figure 7.14*. Access **Backups** from the left-hand menu and evaluate these settings before you start using the database:

Figure 7.14 – SQL database – Backups page

As you can see in the preceding screenshot, you have control over when each of the *backups* is performed, whether it is scheduled correctly, or whether you need some extra settings.

These are some of the most important Azure database configuration operations at the beginning of your Azure project and for the DP-900 certification test. Other settings you should explore a bit more are as follows:

- **Security > Networking** – Primarily, access release settings are only for internal networks or public networks, and firewall rules settings are for releasing the connection to IPs

- **Security > Microsoft Defender for Cloud** – A security tool that helps you perform the best security risk mitigation settings

Now that we know the particularities of Azure SQL Database, let's understand the details of the Azure Database for PostgreSQL and MySQL settings in the next section.

Configuring and managing Azure Database for PostgreSQL and MySQL

The configurations and administrative operations of Azure Database for PostgreSQL and Azure Database for MySQL are almost the same. What differs most from Azure SQL Database is that in these services, the Server object is *not logically separated* in Azure – that is, you configure and administer each instance in the Azure Database for MySQL and Azure Database for PostgreSQL sessions.

To follow these explanations, it is recommended that you go back to the Azure Database for PostgreSQL or Azure Database for MySQL created in *Chapter 6, Integrating Relational Data on Azure*, to identify the most important sections explained here and the extra configuration possibilities.

Backups – The **Backups** feature has a different look and feel, but the functionality is very similar to that of Azure SQL Database. You can configure your automated backup in the **Compute + storage** section as shown in the following figure, and during your configurations, you can estimate how much this backup will cost:

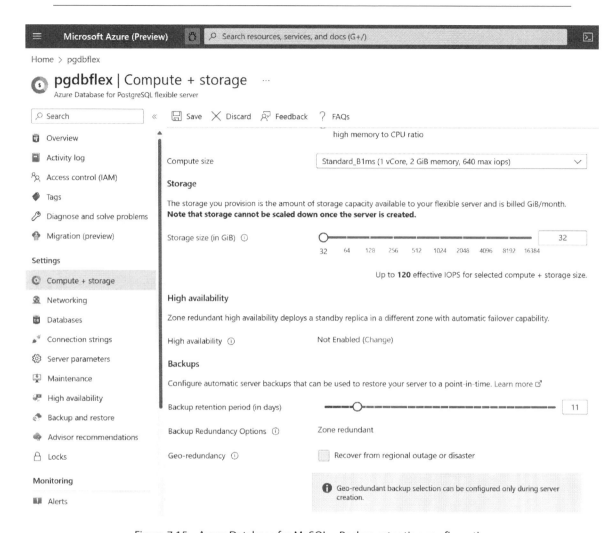

Figure 7.15 – Azure Database for MySQL – Backup retention configuration

With this knowledge, you are already prepared to start using relational databases in your Azure projects, but how to make the connection, create tables, and explore the data, among other operations? We'll look at all of this in the next chapter.

Summary

Azure databases, including *SQL*, *PostgreSQL*, and *MySQL*, are enterprise-scale managed database (or PaaS) infrastructures. They can be used in enterprise applications of any size.

In this chapter, we began to put our knowledge into practice by navigating the Azure services of relational databases and seeing how to provision and configure these services.

In our next chapter, we will connect these databases and perform the most important operations of the SQL language, but before that, we will evaluate some possible questions about this content in the *DP-900 certification*.

Sample questions and answers

Try answering the following questions to test your knowledge:

1. Which type of database is Azure Database for PostgreSQL?

    A. PaaS

    B. IaaS

    C. Microsoft SQL Server

    D. On-premises

2. Relational data is stored in…:

    A. A filesystem as unstructured data

    B. A hierarchal folder structure

    C. A tabular form of rows and columns

    D. Comma-separated value (CSV) files

3. Select the option that best completes the sentence:

    A(n) _____ contains keys built from one or more columns in the table or view.

    A. procedure

    B. field

    C. index

    D. view

4. You plan to deploy a PostgreSQL database to Azure. Which hosting model corresponds to the available deployment options?

    A. PostgreSQL on Azure VM (PaaS) and Azure Database for PostgreSQL (SaaS)

    B. PostgreSQL on Azure VM (SaaS) and Azure Database for PostgreSQL (PaaS)

    C. PostgreSQL on Azure VM (IaaS) and Azure Database for PostgreSQL (PaaS)

    D. PostgreSQL on Azure VM (PaaS) and Azure Database for PostgreSQL (IaaS)

5. Your Azure project will use an Azure Database for MySQL instance. The service has already been provisioned, but the DBA of the project is not able to access MySQL via MySQL Workbench, even after entering the username and password of the administrator of the database. What may be missing?

    A. Adding the DBA user to the database's access control

    B. Adding the DBA computer's IP to a rule in the firewall of Azure Database for MySQL Server

    C. Setting up a database access VPN to the local infrastructure of the DBA computer

    D. Enabling the user in Azure Active Directory

Answer key

1-A 2-C 3-C 4-C 5-B

8

Querying Relational Data in Azure

In this chapter, you'll learn more about **Structured Query Language** (**SQL**), and how you can use it to query, insert, update, and delete data in a relational database.

Now that we have touched on the provisioning of Azure relational databases in the previous chapter, we are ready to explore the structures and data using SQL in these relational databases. This chapter is important for all professionals who will work with data in the market because SQL is most commonly used in relational, non-relational, and analytical databases.

SQL is fundamental for data professionals, and in the DP-900 exam, there are some questions directly related to SQL performing operations.

By the end of this chapter, we will cover the following:

- Introducing SQL on Azure
- Querying relational data in Azure SQL Database
- Querying relational data in Azure Database for PostgreSQL

Technical requirements

The SQL commands are available in this book's GitHub repository for you to follow alongside this chapter: `https://github.com/PacktPublishing/Microsoft-Certified-Azure-Data-Fundamentals-Exam-DP-900-Certification-Guide`.

Introducing SQL on Azure

We established from the previous chapters that SQL is used in several types of databases in Azure. Of these, we will use **Azure SQL Database** and **Azure Database for PostgreSQL** in this chapter

SQL is used in other Azure database offerings, such as **Azure Cosmos DB** and **Synapse Analytics**, which we'll explore in *Chapters 10*, *12*, and *13* of this book on NoSQL and analytical databases. The knowledge generated by this chapter will be important for your projects with all databases on Azure.

> **Important note**
>
> This is a continuation of *Chapter 7, Provisioning and Configuring Relational Database Services in Azure*, where we'll use the databases that were deployed in it. You'd need to provision the databases from that chapter to follow the exercises in this chapter.

Let's now explore different SQL scenarios applied to Azure's core relational database services, starting with Azure SQL Database.

Querying relational data in Azure SQL Database

Let's now explore the Azure SQL Database created in *Chapter 7, Provisioning and Configuring Relational Database Services in Azure*, executing the SQL statements. To follow the exercise, you must follow these steps:

1. Navigate to the Azure portal in your browser using the following link: `https://portal.azure.com/`.

2. Browse to the **SQL databases** option, as shown in *Figure 8.1*:

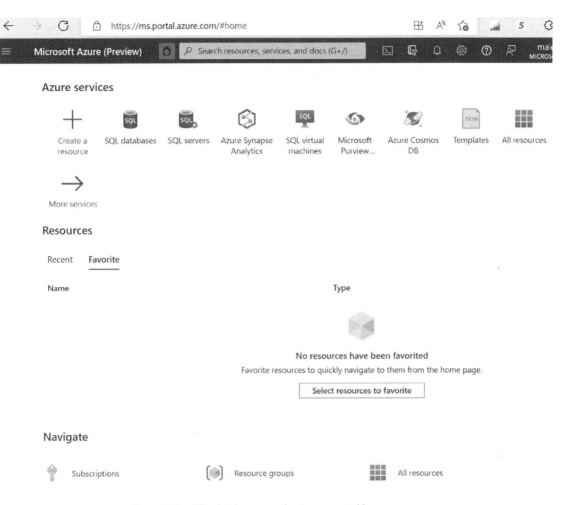

Figure 8.1 – SQL databases on the Azure portal home page

3.   Under the **Server** category, select the **coredb** database that we created in *Chapter 7, Provisioning and Configuring Relational Database Services in Azure*, as shown on the following screen:

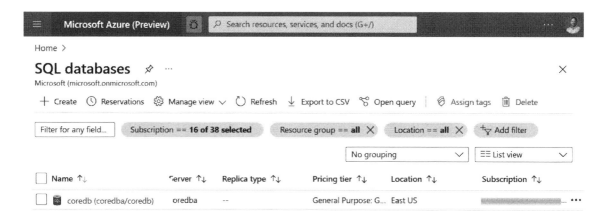

Figure 8.2 – SQL databases coredba configuration page

4. Next, you would need to select the **Connect with…** drop-down menu, as shown in *Figure 8.3*, and select **Azure Data Studio**:

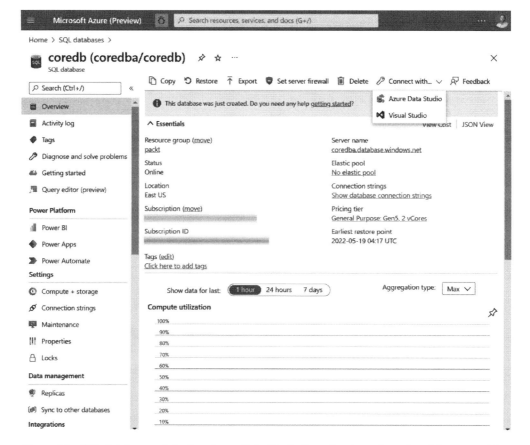

Figure 8.3 – SQL databases – Selecting Azure Data Studio from the drop-down list of Connect with…

5. At this point, the Azure portal will give you the option to open Azure Data Studio if you already have it installed on your computer, or to download it. If you do not already have it installed, I recommend that you download it and follow the installation instructions.

6. Once you have Azure Data Studio on your computer, go back to the portal and click **Launch it now**:

Start Modern Data Workflow in Azure Data Studio

Azure Data Studio is a new open source, cross-platform desktop environment for data professionals using the Azure Data family of on-premises and cloud data platforms. Learn more ☑

Download Azure Data Studio

Already have the app? Launch it now ☑

Figure 8.4 – The launch of Azure Data Studio

When Azure Data Studio opens, it will ask whether you want to establish this new connection. Next, confirm it and proceed to open the connection configuration setup page, as seen in the following screenshot:

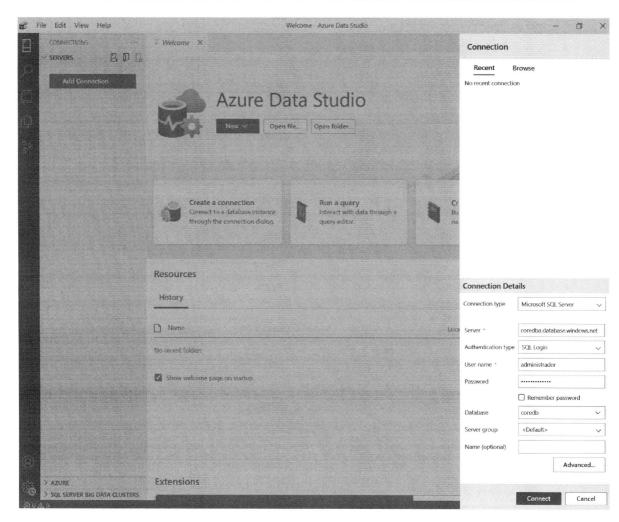

Figure 8.5 – Azure Data Studio connecting to coredb

> **Note**
>
> To open this new connection page from the home page of Azure Data Studio, you can click on the **New Connection** button.

7.   In the connection details, fill in the username with `administrador` and the password with `Pass@word#123`, as we set up in *Chapter 7, Provisioning and Configuring Relational Database Services in Azure*, and click **Connect**.

> **Important note**
>
> Azure reserves some words such as administrator, admin, and others, to avoid security issues. That's why I have used **administrador** (which means administrator in Portuguese). In your projects, you can use something such as `admin2022` and variations of this kind for creating this admin login, but to make sure you follow all the exercise steps mentioned in this book, use **administrador**.

In this step, you may have problems establishing your connection, so let's evaluate common connection issues with Azure databases.

Common connection issues

If you find a problem with this connection, the most normal causes are as follows:

- **Network restriction** – This is the most common problem! Make sure your IP is released in the **Azure SQL Database firewall** by reviewing the steps in the *Provisioning Azure SQL Database* section in *Chapter 7, Provisioning and Configuring Relational Database Services in Azure*. If the problem persists, it can be a restriction on your personal computer, such as a network proxy or some other type of connection filter.

- **Username and password** – If you have configured the service with another username and password, you will need to remember them at this time. If this occurred and you forgot them, you can delete your database and go back to the *Provisioning Azure SQL Database* section in *Chapter 7, Provisioning and Configuring Relational Database Services in Azure*, and revise the configurations of your Azure SQL Database. For security reasons, it is not possible to retrieve an administrator password, so if your authentication is not working and you don't know the exact username and password, it'll be better to delete this instance and create a new Azure SQL Database instance.

Okay, now we're connected, and we can already evaluate the objects that this database has. At the moment, all folders on the left side should be empty, as shown in the following screen:

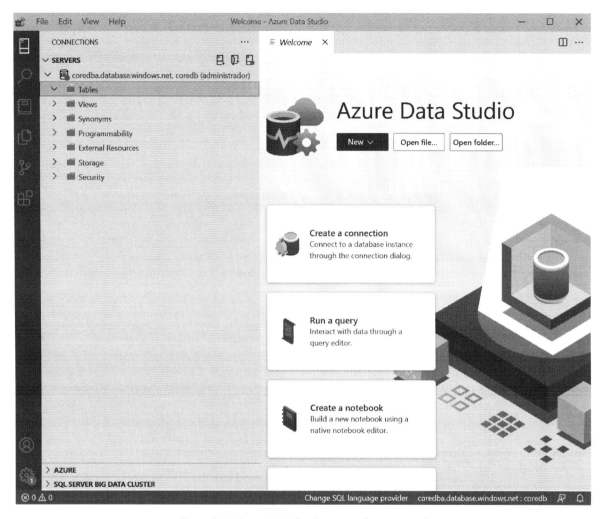

Figure 8.6 – Azure Data Studio – coredb connected

Now, it's time to start building our Azure SQL Database. To do this, let's use a schema from a student database.

This simple relational database will receive data from students enrolled in courses, relating to a table of courses.

Let's go step by step.

Creating tables in an Azure SQL Database

To start, click on **New** | **New Query** or use the *Ctrl + N* shortcut on your keyboard. A blank block of text will be created so that you can write your queries and execute them.

Go to the book's GitHub repository (`https://github.com/PacktPublishing/Microsoft-Certified-Azure-Data-Fundamentals-Exam-DP-900-Certification-Guide/tree/main/Chapter08`), open the `Chapter8.sql` file, and copy the SQL script under *//STEP 1* and click on the **Run** button, as follows:

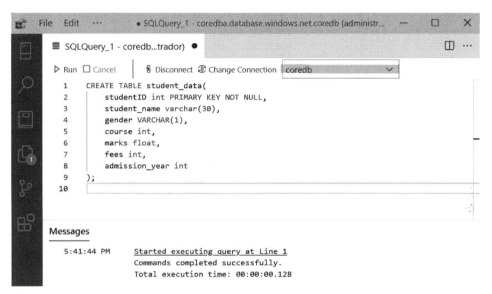

Figure 8.7 – Azure Data Studio – query execution

Let's discuss this action in detail:

- As we can see in the selection box at the top of the screen, we are connected to the `coredb` database (if it's not selected in your session, you can change the connection to **coreDB**).

- Our structure is creating a table called `student_data` in the database.

- Within this table, we will have seven columns:

  - `studentID` – The numeric (integer) data type (`int`) is the primary key of this table (`PRIMARY KEY`) and cannot accept null values (`NOT NULL`)

  - `student_name` – Text data type with a maximum of 30 characters (`varchar(30)`)

  - `gender` – Text data type with a maximum of one characteristic (`VARCHAR(1)`)

  - `course` – Data type: integer numeric values (`int`)

  - `marks` – Data type: floating numeric values (`float`)

  - `fees` – Data type: integer numeric values (`int`)

  - `admission_year` – Data type: integer numeric values (`int`)

This is the basis for creating any table in Azure SQL Database. You have several different data types to specialize the contents of each column.

For SQL Database, the available data types are as follows:

- **Exact numeric types** – bigint, numeric, bit, smallint, decimal, smallmoney, int, tinyint, money, and approximate numerics such as float and real

- **Date and time** – date, datetimeoffset, datetime2, smalldatetime, datetime, and time

- **Character strings** – char, varchar, and text

- **Unicode character strings** – nchar, nvarchar, and ntext

- **Binary strings** – binary, varbinary, and image

- **Other data types** – cursor, rowversion, hierarchyid, uniqueidentifier, sql_variant, xml, and spatial geometry types

> **Tip**
> The full list of available data types on Azure SQL Database is always up to date in the Microsoft Transact-SQL document: https://docs.microsoft.com/en-us/sql/t-sql/data-types/data-types-transact-sql.

Based on the same syntax, we will now create the second table in our database, the course table.

For the next step, from the same Chapter8.sql file, copy the SQL script //STEP 2, and click on **Run** to create our second table, course:

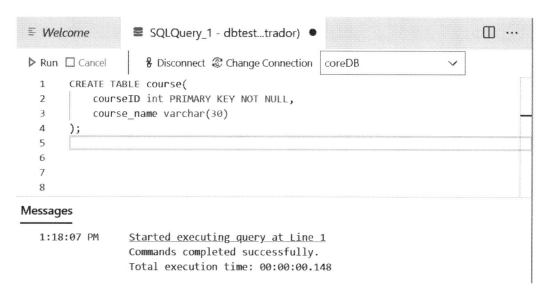

Figure 8.8 – Azure Data Studio – Execution message window

Altering table schemas in an Azure SQL Database

To explore more SQL commands, from the same `Chapter8.sql` file, copy the SQL script *//STEP 3*, paste it into Azure Data Studio, and click on the **Run** button.

The `ALTER TABLE` query is used to alter the schema of the table, including adding columns, removing columns, changing data types, and so on. After executing this command, the `course` table has one more column, called `course_startdate`.

You can see this new column navigating through the table structure in the left-hand menu of Azure Data Studio. If it doesn't appear, right-click on the connection of your Azure SQL Database and then **Refresh**.

Deleting table schemas in an Azure SQL Database

Next, we will copy the script under *//STEP 4* from the `Chapter8.sql` file and click on the **Run** button in Azure Data Studio.

The `DROP TABLE` statement is used to delete a table from an Azure SQL Database.

After this operation, check the left side menu of Azure Data Studio, refresh it, and the `course` table should no longer appear.

`DROP TABLE` is a widely used operation of a `CREATE TABLE` script, used to make sure that this table does not exist in the database in question.

But we're going to use our table to perform the next operations, so let's recopy the script under *//STEP 1* from the same `Chapter8.sql` file and click on the **Run** button.

Inserting data into Azure SQL Database

Now, let's add some data to the tables. To do this, copy the SQL script under *//STEP 5* from the `Chapter8.sql` file, as shown here, and click on the **Run** button:

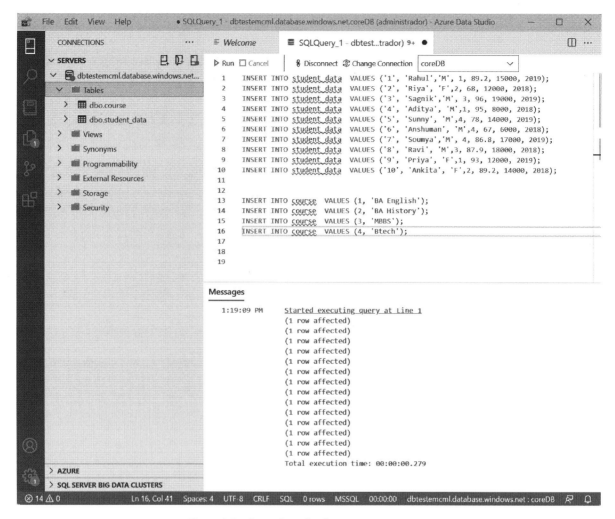

Figure 8.9 – Azure Data Studio – insert execution

Now that the tables have data, let's perform the queries on these entities.

Selecting data from Azure SQL Database

Now let's explore the data, using the SELECT statement to query the student_data table. To do this, you can write the complete statement, or right-click on the table name on Azure Data Studio and click on the **Select Top 1000** button to create the query automatically as follows, or copy the script under *//STEP 6* from the Chapter8.sql file:

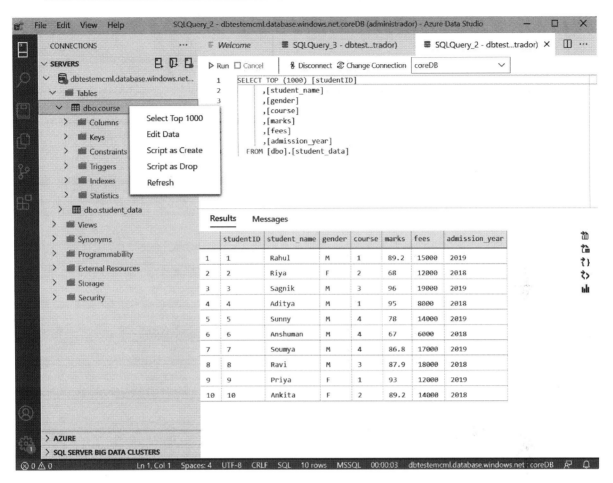

Figure 8.10 – Azure Data Studio – Select Top 1000 table execution

The **Select Top 1000** button will generate a SQL statement considering the **SELECT TOP (1000)** records in that table.

Now, let's extend this SELECT statement by joining both tables together. This will show us the relationship between these two tables using the SELECT and JOIN statements. We will join the student_data table, using its course ID in correlation with the course ID of the course table. To do this, we can complement the script with the INNER JOIN command, as you can copy from the script under //STEP 7 from the Chapter8.sql file:

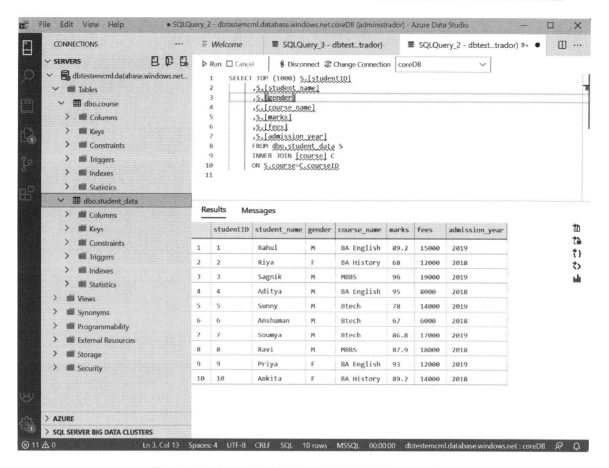

Figure 8.11 – Azure Data Studio – select joint tables execution

With this complete statement, your results will be connected, joining the records from `student_data` and `course` in a single table or result set.

> **Tip**
> The result set is the name used for the table generated by a query execution, considering the columns, records, and metadata related to this data.

So, in this way, you can explore more possibilities for creating tables, adding data, and selecting data relating to tables.

Now that we've explored Azure SQL Database, let's do our next exercise in **Azure Database for PostgreSQL**.

Querying relational data in Azure Database for PostgreSQL

To complement our exploration of Azure relational database offerings, in this section, we will use Azure Database for PostgreSQL to test some SQL scripts.

For the DP -900 exam, it is important to study not only Azure SQL Database but also Azure Database for PostgreSQL and Azure Database for MySQL, as both are included in the exam questions. As mentioned earlier, Azure Database for PostgreSQL and Azure Database for MySQL are Azure offerings that are very similar in configuration, and both use SQL, so it is important to examine at least one of these two options.

> **Note**
>
> If you're interested in developing your projects with Azure Database for MySQL, this chapter can help you, as the PostgreSQL configuration processes are the same as MySQL, except for the administration tool we use. In the case of PostgreSQL, the administration tool that we use is Azure Data Studio, and for MySQL, it is necessary to use the official MySQL tool, **Workbench**, which can be found at this link: `https://dev.mysql.com/downloads/workbench/`.

The first step to start our Azure Database for PostgreSQL exploration is to return to the Azure portal home page (`http://portal.azure.com`).

Now, let's search for the **Azure Database for PostgreSQL servers** section in the portal and access it, as follows:

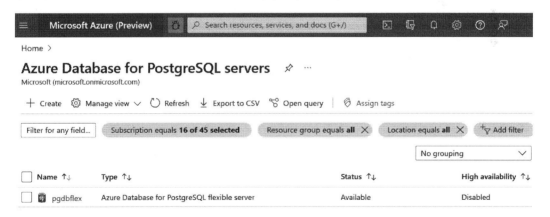

Figure 8.12 – Azure portal – Azure Database for PostgreSQL servers page

Connecting to Azure Database for PostgreSQL

Click on the `pgdbflex` database, created in *Chapter 7*, *Provisioning and Configuring Relational Database Services in Azure* of this book, to access its settings.

In this settings screen, you will not see the **Connect** button that Azure SQL Database has. To connect to Azure Database for PostgreSQL, you need to copy the *connection settings* present on this screen and then paste them into your administration tool:

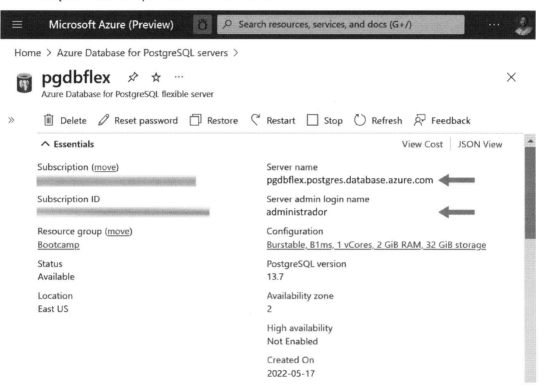

Figure 8.13 – Azure Database for PostgreSQL configuration page

The connection information is as follows:

- **Server name** – Can be found on the settings home page as shown in the preceding screenshot
- **Username and Password** – You need to remember the password of the admin login or other database user

> **Important note**
>
> To manage PostgreSQL databases on Azure Data Studio, you need to install a PostgreSQL extension, available for free on the Azure Data Studio documentation website.

Installing the Azure Data Studio extension for PostgreSQL is simple and can be found in this **EXTENSIONS** section in Azure Data Studio itself:

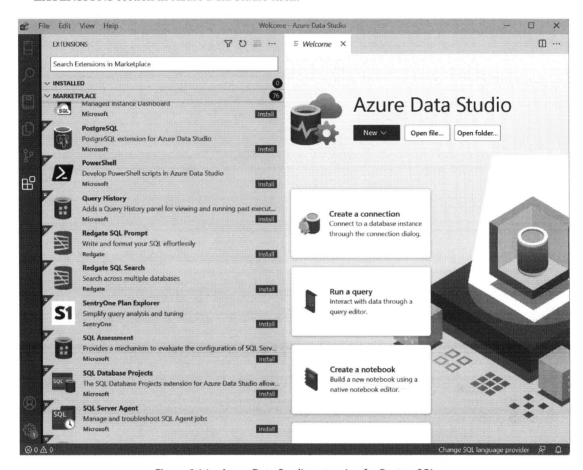

Figure 8.14 – Azure Data Studio extension for PostgreSQL

Install this extension to follow with the connection.

Navigate to the **CONNECTIONS** section and select the **New Connection** button. Once you sign in to **New Connection**, just fill in the information. As you can see, you have two options in **Connection type**: **SQL Server** or **PostgreSQL**.

The username is administrador and the password is Pass@word#123, as we set up in *Chapter 7, Provisioning and Configuring Relational Database Services in Azure*. When you have filled in the information, click on **Connect**, as follows:

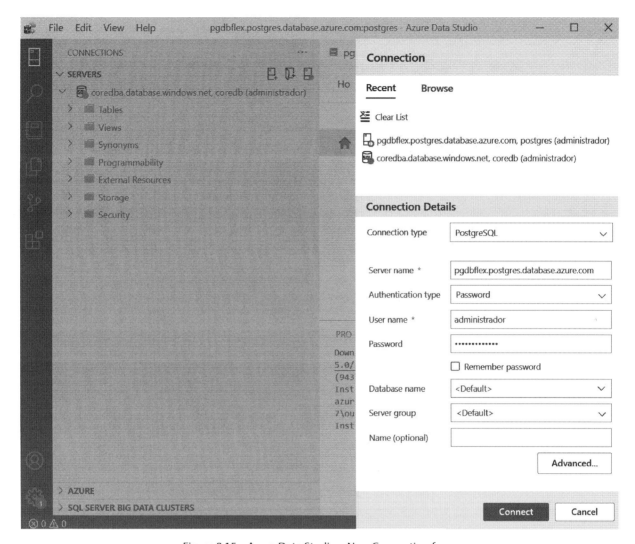

Figure 8.15 – Azure Data Studio – New Connection form

If you encounter an issue with this connection, return to the Azure SQL Database connection in the *Common connection issues* section of this chapter, where I gave some tips on the most common issues.

Querying Azure Database for PostgreSQL

Now, browse the objects of your PostgreSQL server, go to the `postgres` database, and right-click to find the **New Query** option:

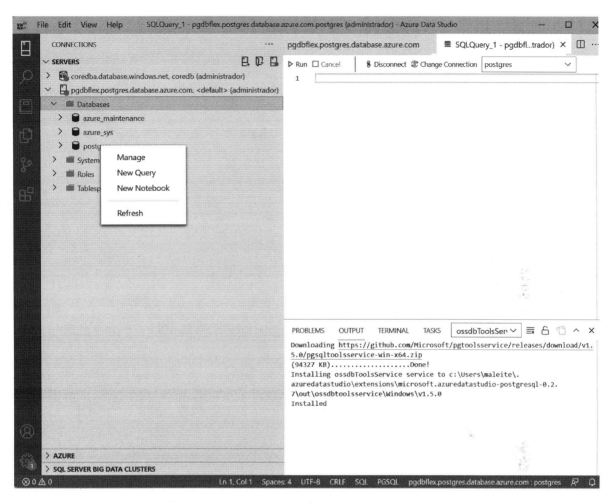

Figure 8.16 – Azure Data Studio – PostgreSQL New Query

The query window will open, and you can start writing your instructions as we did with Azure SQL Database.

Now, open again our source code available in this book's GitHub repository, and let's create the tables, insert data, and perform queries.

Open the Step 4 POSTGRESQL and Step 5 POSTGRESQL files, and copy the script to the Azure Data Studio notebook windows (on the right). After that, click on **Run**.

You are using a different file from the Azure SQL Database because the syntax of PostgreSQL is a little different from the SQL Server. It happens with all different SQL relational databases; they have the same logical basis but require some changes to the SQL syntax.

The query will give the following output:

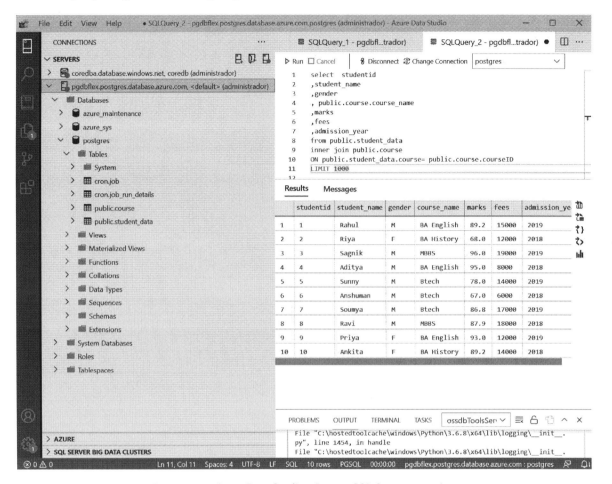

Figure 8.17 – Azure Data Studio – PostgreSQL Query execution

Now, we've already explored the use of the two main Azure relational databases, SQL Database and Database for PostgreSQL.

As I mentioned earlier, the scripts to use in Azure Database for MySQL are very similar to Azure Database for PostgreSQL scripts, but at the time of connection, you will use the open source tool MySQL Workbench to perform your SQL scripts, instead of Azure Data Studio.

Summary

Relational databases are most widely used in the market for transactional work. Mastering one of the services with Azure SQL Database will give you the basis to implement other formats, such as Azure Database for PostgreSQL and MySQL.

In this chapter, we have looked at the connection of these databases in a simplified but sufficient way for you to start your projects and for the **DP-900** certification questions.

In the next chapter, we will start *Part 3* of this book, and *Chapter 9, Exploring Non-Relational Data Offerings in Azure* will explore non-relational databases on Azure.

Sample questions and answers

Try answering the following questions to test your knowledge:

1. Which administrative tool is used in Azure Database for MySQL?

    A. MySQL Workbench

    B. Azure Data Studio

    C. SQL Management Studio

    D. The Azure CLI

2. Which database service is the simplest option for migrating a LAMP application to Azure?

    A. Azure SQL Database

    B. Azure Database for PostgreSQL

    C. Azure Database for MySQL

    D. Azure Cosmos DB

3. You need to modify a view in a relational database by adding a new column. Which statement should you use?

    A. MERGE

    B. ALTER

    C. INSERT

    D. UPDATE

4. Matching the SQL data processing objects to requirements, find the two wrong statements:

    A. Tables store instances of entities as rows

    B. Views create relationships

    C. Indexes improve the processing speed for data searches

    D. Keys display data from predefined queries

5. You need to create a relation between two different tables that have one related column. Which statement should you use?

    A. SELECT AND DROP

    B. SELECT AND JOIN

    C. SELECT AND CASE

    D. CREATE AND RELATION

Answer key

1-A 2-C 3-B, D 4-B 5-B

Part 3: Non-Relational Data in Azure

This part will provide complete coverage of the knowledge and skills required for the *Skills measured* under the *Describe how to work with non-relational data on Azure* section of the exam syllabus.

You will learn about the fundamentals of NoSQL database concepts in a cloud environment, get basic skills related to using cloud data services, and build your foundational knowledge of cloud data services within Microsoft Azure. You will explore non-relational data offerings, provisioning and deploying non-relational databases, and non-relational data stores with Microsoft Azure.

This part comprises the following chapters:

- *Chapter 9, Exploring Non-Relational Data Offerings in Azure*
- *Chapter 10, Provisioning and Configuring Non-Relational Data Services in Azure*

9

Exploring Non-Relational Data Offerings in Azure

In the previous chapters, we explored Azure SQL Database, Azure Database for PostgreSQL, Azure Database for MySQL, and Azure Database for MariaDB. Now, let's explore scenarios for using these relational database management systems to store transactional data.

In recent years, NoSQL databases and non-relational repositories have gained great relevance in the market, specializing in the storage of organizations' data in an optimized and appropriate way for each type of data.

In DP-900, we have seen the growth of questions about these non-relational databases so that a professional is prepared to make the right decisions about their Azure projects.

In this chapter, we will learn about Azure Table storage, Azure Blob storage, Azure Files storage, and Azure Cosmos DB, and explore scenarios for using each of them. We will also understand different **application programming interfaces** (**APIs**) such as the Azure Cosmos DB API, the Core (SQL) API, the MongoDB API, the Table API, the Cassandra API, and the Gremlin API.

By the end of this chapter, you will be able to understand the different non-relational data services offered on Azure. We will cover the following technologies:

- Azure Blob storage
- Azure Files storage
- Azure Table storage
- Azure Cosmos DB

So, let's explore these services.

Exploring Azure non-relational data stores

In this chapter, we'll understand the characteristics of Azure *non-relational data stores*, the differences between the services that are offered, and the most commonly used scenarios for each.

Exploring Azure Blob storage

Azure Blob storage is a limitlessly scalable storage service that can store structured, semi-structured, and unstructured data in the form of **binary large objects** (**blobs**). This service can be used to store objects of a variety of types, such as videos, images, JSON files, XLSX files, and CSV files.

Files in Blob storage are stored in a container, in an Azure storage account, and can be accessed through *Azure Storage Explorer*, a free Azure tool, or via an API. To better understand this hierarchy, take a look at *Figure 9.1*.

The permissions settings of Azure Blob storage are granular; you can create read-only, write-only, edit-only, or variations of these permissions, within storage as a whole or by a container.

Azure Blob storage can still be organized into folders, such as Windows folders, which makes it easier to prioritize your objects, as shown in *Figure 9.1*:

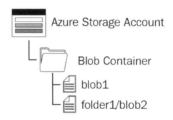

Figure 9.1 – Azure storage account structure

We have three types of blobs in Azure Blob storage:

- **Block blobs**: A block blob is treated as a collection of blocks. Each block can be up to 100 MB in size. A block blob can contain up to 50,000 blocks, with a total size of more than 4.7 TB. The smallest amount of data that can be read or written as a single drive is the block. Block blobs are best for storing large, distinct binary items that don't change much.

- **Page blobs**: A page blob is a 512-byte-sized page group. It is designed to handle random read and write operations; if necessary, you can get and save data to a single page. A page blob can store up to 8 TB of data. Azure deploys virtual disk storage to virtual machines using page blobs.

- **Append blobs**: A block blob optimized to append other blob blocks. Only new blocks can be added to the end of an append blob; existing blocks cannot be updated or deleted. Each block can be up to 4 MB in size. An additional blob can be just over 195 GB in size.

There are three access levels available in *blob storage*, which help balance access latency and storage costs: hot, cool, and archive. The default layer is *hot*. This layer is for blobs that are accessed frequently. Blob data is kept on high-capacity media. You can still configure *cool* and *archive* storage to minimize costs for data that is not accessed frequently. Data in the *cool* layer has only lower performance but can be used immediately, while the *archive* layer moves the data to an external store, and to restore that volume, you must wait for a request made in the Azure portal, which can take hours.

> **Important note**
> You can define file life cycle management policies in Azure Blob storage. This means that you can set a maximum period for a file to remain in storage without being used, and then it can be moved to another layer, such as cool or archive, or be deleted.

Azure Blob storage is the foundation of storage in Azure, but there is a configuration for it to meet data analytics projects. Let's get to know Azure Data Lake Storage Gen2, the Azure Blob storage configuration for data analytics.

Azure Data Lake Storage Gen2

One of the options you have when using Azure Blob storage is to configure in the data lake storage format, which uses an organization pattern within the container that can be used by data analytics tools, such as Azure Synapse Analytics, Azure Databricks, and other vendors.

To configure Azure Blob storage as Azure Data Lake Storage, we need to activate the **Hierarchical Namespace** feature on the Azure Blob storage configuration page, and after that, the Azure Blob storage begins to behave as illustrated in *Figure 9.2*:

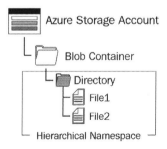

Figure 9.2 – The Azure Data Lake Storage Gen2 structure

Azure Data Lake Storage Gen2 combines Azure Data Lake Storage Gen1 and Azure Blob storage's capabilities. For instance, Data Lake Storage Gen2 offers scale, file-level security, and filesystem semantics. You will also receive low-cost, tiered storage with high-availability/disaster recovery capabilities because these capabilities are built on Blob storage.

Cloud stores can have several usage scenarios, but when the migration of a file server is needed, a common scenario within an organization's data center, the ideal service to receive these files is Azure Files storage. Let's discuss it next.

Exploring Azure Files

It is very common to find a massive volume of files stored on traditional filesystem servers in organizations, which centralize user and department documents for conditional access by other users and applications. To be the target of these servers, Azure has the *Azure Files* service.

Migrating a file server to Azure Files means optimizing and modernizing the traditional hardware-based format itself and managing the documents that are often critical to organizations.

In Azure Files, the file server can be accessed by the industry-standard **Server Message Block** (**SMB**) and **Network File System** (**NFS**) protocols, and the high availability of documents is ensured by the Azure services' **service-level agreement** (**SLA**).

In the following screenshot, we can see the hierarchy of services between **Azure Storage Account**, **Azure Files**, and the user, who is represented by the computer that is accessing the files.

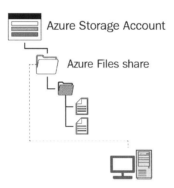

Figure 9.3 – Azure Files structure

Azure Files is also a configuration format of a storage account, and this format has the capacity to store up to *100 TB in only one storage account*, has a per-file size limit of up to 1 TB, and supports up to *2,000 simultaneous connections* from users and applications accessing the service.

One of the most practical ways to copy files to Azure Files is by using the free Azure tool called **AzCopy**, through APIs, or through the Azure portal. You can also use **Azure File Sync**, an application that maintains synchronization between a file server and Azure Files.

Another way to work with Azure Files is to map the repository within operating systems, such as on a traditional file server, which makes it possible for a user to access and save files to Azure Files in a very practical way.

Now that we've covered repositories for documents, let's talk about repositories that are semi-structured for data, starting with Azure Table storage, which complements the options of non-relational databases in Azure.

Exploring Azure Table storage

We can describe Azure Table storage as a *key-value* pair storage system, as explored in *Chapter 4, Working with Non-Relational Data,* where each item is represented by a row with columns, containing data fields that must be stored as shown in *Figure 9.4.*

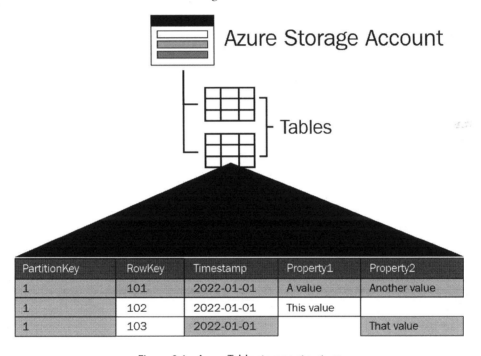

Figure 9.4 – Azure Table storage structure

An important thing to remember if you are new to the concepts of NoSQL is not to confuse this type of table structure with the tables of a SQL relational model. In this case, the tables store semi-structured data and labels about that data.

All records in this database must have a *unique key* (composed of a partition key and a row key) and a `Timestamp` column, informing the date/time when this record was created. When a record is edited in the database, another record is created with a new `Timestamp`, informing the date/time of the change.

> **Important note**
> Unlike SQL databases, Azure Table storage uses the concept of denormalized tables. These are large tables with all their fields related to the registry and that have no relationships with their resources.

Azure Table storage splits a table into *partitions* to help ensure quick access. Partitioning is a method of joining related rows based on a shared property or partition key. Rows with the same partition key will be grouped into a database. Partitioning can help with the organization of data, as well as scalability and performance, in the following ways:

- Partitions are self-contained and can expand or shrink as rows are added or removed from a partition. A store can have as many partitions as it wants.

- You can include the partition key in the search criteria while searching for data. This reduces the number of **input and output** (**I/O**) operations or reads and writes required to identify the data, which helps reduce the amount of data to be analyzed and increases the speed.

The key in an Azure Table storage table comprises two elements:

- **Partition key**, which identifies the partition that contains the line

- **Row key**, for each row on the same partition

Items in the same partition are stored in line key order. If an application adds a new row to a table, Azure ensures that the row is placed in the correct position in the table. This scheme allows an application to quickly run point queries that identify a single row and range queries that fetch a contiguous block of rows in a partition.

Now that you know about the non-relational data repositories in Azure, we'll explore the capabilities of non-relational databases, better known as NoSQL.

Exploring Azure NoSQL databases

In Azure, there are a few options for deploying NoSQL databases, from deploying an open source database such as MongoDB, Cassandra, or Neo4j running in a virtual machine IaaS, through HBase databases in the Azure HDInsight service, to Azure Cosmos DB.

Azure Cosmos DB is the main Azure offering to implement a NoSQL database. It's the NoSQL database most asked about in the questions of the *DP-900* test and is the most used in modern projects, so let's explore it next.

Exploring Azure Cosmos DB

In this section, we will learn about the *concepts* of Azure Cosmos DB, and in *Chapter 10, Provisioning and Configuring Non-Relational Data Services in Azure*, we will explore it further by performing its provisioning and configuration.

Azure Cosmos DB is a *multimodal, globally distributed NoSQL database* system on Azure, which means that depending on its setting, it may have different operating characteristics and infrastructure architecture. It is highly scalable and requires no manual maintenance, which greatly facilitates its use in projects with NoSQL.

The formats that Azure Cosmos DB can configure are as follows:

- **Documents**
- **Graphs**
- **Key-value tables**
- **Column family stores**

This is depicted in the following diagram:

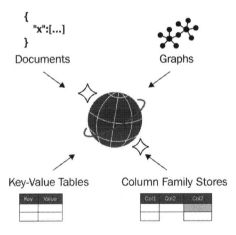

Figure 9.5 – Azure Cosmos DB format types

Azure Cosmos DB APIs

An API is a communication programming interface, used by developers to connect two or more services, and it can be used for applications to connect in databases.

Distinct database management systems have different APIs, and Azure Cosmos DB has its own and supports others, such as MongoDB, Gremlin, Table, PostgreSQL, and Cassandra. These multiple APIs let our apps use Azure Cosmos DB just like any other database.

Cosmos DB works with enormous volumes of data by using *indexes* and *partitioning* to deliver rapid read and write performance. Multi-region writes can be enabled by adding the Azure regions of your choice to your Cosmos DB account, allowing global scalability of the applications.

Since APIs are the primary means of interacting with a Cosmos DB database, let's learn about the different types of APIs that are supported by the database.

Core (SQL) API

The Core (SQL) API is the native Azure Cosmos DB API, which works by managing JSON files in document format and using SQL language for all of its operations. Query results in this API generate new JSON files, as shown in the following example. Here, a SQL query is executed on an Azure Cosmos DB database with the SQL API:

```
SELECT *
From customer
Where email="marcelo@outlook.com"
```

The output of the query will be represented as follows, with the collection of `customer`:

```
## JSON FILE - Resultset##
{
    "_id": 345,
    "first_name": "Marcelo",
    "email": "marcelo@outlook.com"
}
```

Now that we know about the Core (SQL) API, let's learn about the other options available in Azure Cosmos DB.

MongoDB API

This API aims to maintain Cosmos DB database compatibility with the most widely used NoSQL interface worldwide, based on the open source MongoDB database. This API has file management very similar to the Core (SQL) API but based on **Binary JSON** (**BSON**). Data manipulations can be done using MongoDB library features, such as the **Mongo Query Language** (**MQL**). In the following example, we can see the same operation that we analyzed before in SQL, now using the MongoDB interface:

```
db.customers.find({email: "marcelo@outlook.com"})
```

The output of the query will be similar to the return of the SQL API, querying the `customer` collection:

```
## JSON FILE - Resultset##
{
    "_id": 345,
    "first_name": "Marcelo",
    "email": "marcelo@outlook.com"
}
```

You are now familiar with the Core (SQL) API and Mongo DB API, the two options that work well with document format databases. Next, let's learn about other Azure Cosmos DB APIs.

Table API

The Table API is used when you need a *key-value pair-based database*, very similar to Azure Table storage, covered earlier in this chapter.

Data manipulation in this type of Azure Cosmos DB is based on specific **Software Development Kits (SDKs)** that interact with the database endpoint and operate the tables.

> **Important note**
> The Cosmos DB Table API is similar conceptually to Azure Table storage, covered earlier in this chapter, but it has different architecture, limits, and behaviors. To evaluate all the differences, this URL to the Cosmos DB documentation provides a full comparison: `https://docs.microsoft.com/en-us/azure/cosmos-db/table/table-api-faq`.

The following is an example of using the Table API to query customer data, based on record 78 of the table:

```
https://endpoint/Customers(PartitionKey='1',RowKey='78')
```

We still have two more API options in Azure Cosmos DB. Let's now look at the Cassandra API, one of the most widely used open source projects in the world.

Cassandra API

Based on the open source Apache Cassandra project, the Azure Cosmos DB Cassandra API creates an interface for the database and manipulates its data using the SQL language-operated *column store* concept. The following is an example of a Cassandra database structure:

ID	Customer_Name	Account_Executive
1	Jason	
2	Ryan	Will
3	Will	Jason

Figure 9.6 – A sample column store table in a Cassandra database

The query can be performed like this:

```
Select *
From customers
Where Customer_Name="Ryan"
```

This query would return the filtered list only by `Customer_name="Ryan"`.

Now, let's learn about the API that behaves more privately in Azure Cosmos DB because it's a *graph database*, the Gremlin API.

Gremlin API

The Gremlin API is an API that originates from the open source graph computing framework called **TinkerPop**, which focuses on mounting databases that represent corrections between data in a correlational format.

Entities are defined as **vertices**, which are connected with other vertices to form a *graph*, as shown in the following diagram:

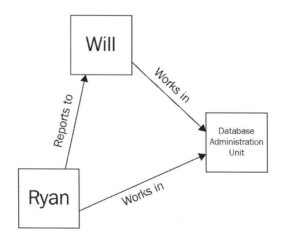

Figure 9.7 – An example of a graph database

The example shows **Ryan**, who reports to **Will** and works with **Database Administration Unit**, just like **Will**. In this example, we have two vertices, employees, that is, Will and Ryan, and another is the unit.

The *Azure Cosmos DB Gremlin API* has its own language to create a web of relationships and manipulate data. The following is an example based on *Figure 9.7*:

```
 g.addV('employee').property('id', '3').property('firstName',
Ryan)
g.V('3').addE('reports to').to(g.V('1'))
```

Now, the following query retrieves all the Employee vertices, ordered by ID:

```
g.V().hasLabel('employee').order().by('id')
```

This script is just a simple example of how to manipulate graph databases using the Gremlin pattern. If you have projects involving this type of database, it is important to know about the data manipulation language in more detail, but for the DP-900 exam, this is the fundamental knowledge required.

This completes our explanation of all the Azure Cosmos DB APIs and the non-relational data offerings in Azure.

So, as we've finished exploring the main storage services and non-relational databases in Azure, shall we summarize?

Summary

Non-relational data is indispensably important to organizations, and knowing where to store this data to meet the needs of a project can contribute greatly to its success. In this chapter, we were able to go through storage offerings for non-relational data, including the *Azure NoSQL* database options.

In this chapter, we explored Azure Table storage, Azure Blob storage, Azure Files storage, and Azure Cosmos DB.

In the next chapter, we will go into more detail about Azure Cosmos DB, provisioning a database in Cosmos DB and evaluating its settings and characteristics.

Sample questions and answers

Let's evaluate a few sample questions in preparation for the exam before starting the next chapter:

1. What constitutes an Azure Table storage key?

    A. Partition key and row key

    B. Table name and column name

    C. Row number

    D. Non-structured data

2.   What should you do with an existing Azure storage account to enable Azure Synapse Analytics to use it as a data lake?

   A.   Add an Azure Files share

   B.   Create Azure Storage tables for the data you want to analyze

   C.   Upgrade the account to enable a hierarchical namespace and create a blob container

   D.   Start data ingestion

3.   Why would you use Azure Files storage?

   A.   To share files that are stored on-premises with users located at other sites

   B.   To enable users at different sites to share files

   C.   To store large binary data files containing images or other unstructured data

   D.   To store video and audio files only

4.   Which Azure Cosmos DB API should you use to store and query JSON documents?

   A.   Core (SQL) API

   B.   Cassandra API

   C.   Table API

   D.   Gremlin API

5.   Which Azure Cosmos DB API should you use to interact with data in which entities and their relationships are represented as vertices and edges in a graph?

   A.   MongoDB API

   B.   Core (SQL) API

   C.   Gremlin API

   D.   Table API

Answer key

1-A 2-C 3-B 4-A 5-C

10

Provisioning and Configuring Non-Relational Data Services in Azure

In this chapter, we will learn how to provision and configure Azure Cosmos DB, a non-relational data service in Azure.

In this chapter, we will look at content that will cover the skills measured in the *Describe how to work with non-relational data on Azure* section of the DP-900 certification study guide, available on the official certification website.

By the end of this chapter, you will be able to understand the following topics:

- Provisioning non-relational data services in Azure
- How to provision and configure Azure Cosmos DB
- Exploring an Azure Cosmos DB database
- How to provision an Azure storage account and Azure Data Lake Storage

Technical requirements

This is a chapter that has hands-on exercises. To follow along in this chapter, you will need the following technical requirements:

- A computer with Windows 10 or above with internet access
- An active Azure account (`http://www.azure.com`)
- Access to the book's code repository on GitHub (`https://github.com/PacktPublishing/Microsoft-Certified-Azure-Data-Fundamentals-Exam-DP-900-Certification-Guide`)

Provisioning non-relational data services

In addition to preparing for the DP-900 exam, this book will give you basic knowledge to start your data projects using Azure. An important part of this training is to carry out the hands-on exercises proposed in the book, as well as in this section.

In this section, we will provision an Azure Cosmos DB database, *a non-relational database*. We will configure the basic settings in this service and explore them, in addition to provisioning an Azure storage account and Azure Data Lake Storage.

So, let's go to the Azure portal and walk through the necessary steps.

Provisioning Azure Cosmos DB

The first step is to find the Azure Cosmos DB session in the Azure portal, as shown in the following screenshot:

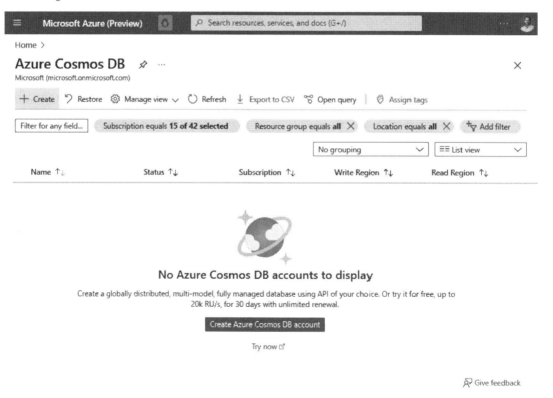

Figure 10.1 – The Azure Cosmos DB page

Let us now provision Cosmos DB by following these steps:

1. First, click the **Create** button in the main menu or the **Create Azure Cosmos DB account** button in the center of the screen.

2. Remember the Cosmos DB APIs? This is the time to select which API you want this new database of yours to use, as shown on the following screen:

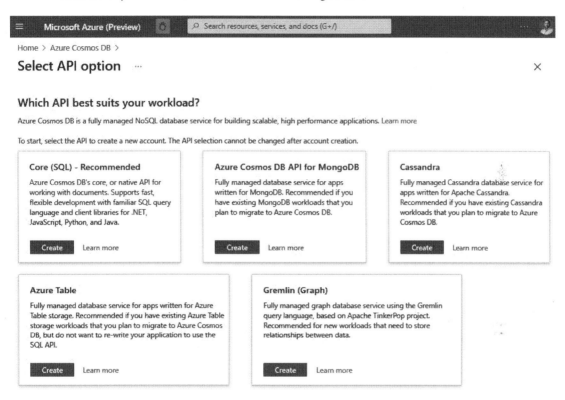

Figure 10.2 – Azure Cosmos DB – API selection page

As you can see, the options are **Core (SQL) - Recommended**, **Azure Cosmos DB API for MongoDB**, **Cassandra**, **Azure Table**, and **Gremlin (Graph)**. To follow this exercise, we will go to the recommended option and click on **Create** below **Core (SQL) - Recommended**.

> **Note**
>
> The preceding selection involves considerably different options in the Cosmos DB architecture, so you cannot change an API from an already created database.

Basics

In the basic settings, you can adjust the following settings:

- **Resource group**: **packt** (created previously)
- **Account Name**: **mycosmosdba**
- **Location**: **(US) East US**
- **Capacity mode**: **Provisioned throughput**
- **Apply Free Tier Discount**: **Apply**
- **Limit total account throughput**: **selected**

With these settings, your Cosmos DB API Core (SQL) will be implemented in the East US region using a dedicated capacity for its throughput. This is important because Cosmos DB's processing capability is not based on colors and RAM but rather on a unit of measure called a **request unit** (**RU**).

An RU is an abstraction of the capacity of CPU, RAM, IOPS, and memory resources required for the operation of the database in question.

Microsoft also provides an *RU calculator* that makes it much easier to define the initial scenario. It can be found at `https://cosmos.azure.com/capacitycalculator/`.

> **Important note**
>
> There is an article in the official Cosmos DB documentation called *Convert the number of vCores or vCPUs in your nonrelational database to Azure Cosmos DB RU/s*, which can be found at `https://docs.microsoft.com/en-us/azure/cosmos-db/convert-vcore-to-request-unit`. It is very useful for anyone who is used to estimating the capacity of databases using the traditional model with cores and RAM.

We then proceed to the next configuration section called **Global Distribution**.

Global Distribution

This setting allows you to configure a geographically redundant cluster, with multiple read replicas and availability zone-based replicas. The distribution options will impact the architecture that the Cosmos DB deployment will have after provisioning. Configure the following settings:

- **Geo-Redundance**: **Disable**
- **Multi-region Writes**: **Disable**
- **Availability Zones**: **Disable**

Networking

In this section, you can define which networks can access your Cosmos DB:

Connectivity method: If you want the private use of applications and users within your virtual network in Azure, you must select **Private endpoint**; otherwise, you can opt for **All networks** or **Public Endpoint** (**selected networks**), where you have the option to list the networks that can perform this connection.

Backup Policy

Now, it's time to ensure a recovery of data from your database. Two alternative backup policies are offered by Azure Cosmos DB:

- **Periodic**: Scheduled by the administrator with intervals in the backup creation and retention policy

- **Continuous**: Automatic backup that copies all data stored into the Cosmos DB database in a backup file for restore

  Once the account has been created, you won't be able to change backup policies.

Select the **Continuous** option and click on the **Encryption** section.

Encryption

Data encryption is essential, especially for databases with public endpoints. Therefore, Cosmos DB always applies at-rest encryption when the data is rested in the database, and automatically decrypts when a query is performed. The encryption key can be configured on this page, and you can use the key managed by Cosmos DB itself or choose a custom key:

- **Data Encryption**: **Service-managed key**

Tags

As with all provisioning in Azure, you can define tags that help you in cloud governance.

We will now proceed to the **Review + create** button. If you've configured the aforementioned settings, your screen should look like the following:

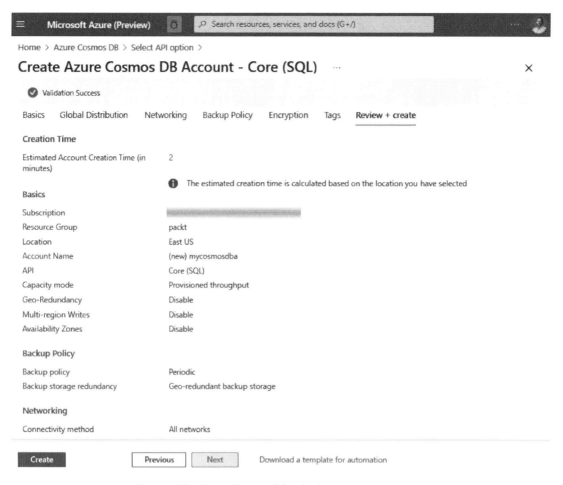

Figure 10.3 – Azure Cosmos DB – the Review + create page

Click **Create**, wait for provisioning to finish, and go to the service to review your settings.

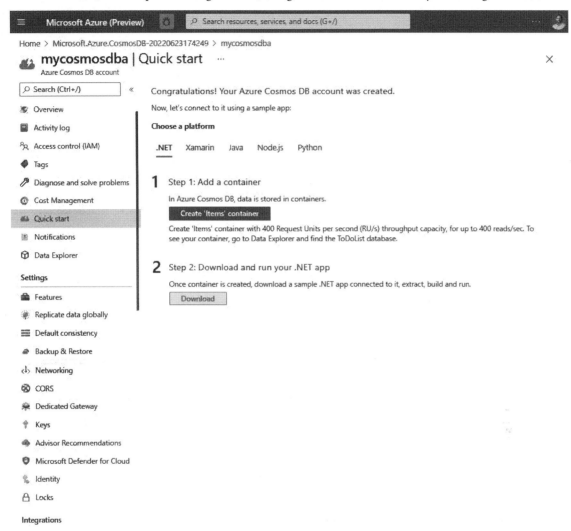

Figure 10.4 – Azure Cosmos DB – the settings page

Because this Cosmos DB intent is new, Azure offers a *wizard* to assist beginners in using Cosmos DB, asking whether you would like to add a container (a concept similar to SQL database tables; it is a logical separation of the server in your document store).

Anyway, it is not necessary to create containers immediately, so click on **Overview** on the left-hand side:

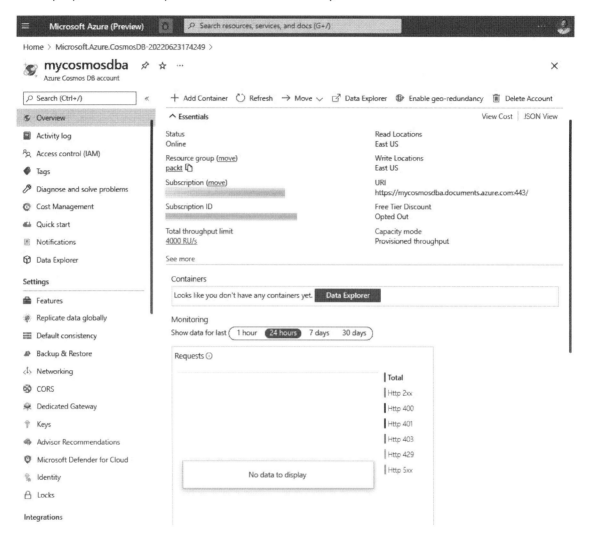

Figure 10.5 – Azure Cosmos DB – Overview

This page will introduce you to the key settings and monitors that demonstrate the behavior of your Cosmos DB database, where you can adjust the settings in Azure Cosmos DB, which we will cover in the next section.

Configuring Azure Cosmos DB

Let's list the top settings in an Azure Cosmos DB database. These settings are important in environments that will be used in projects but are also important for answering questions on the DP-900 test.

To know more, follow along the side menu items on the Cosmos DB page as follows:

- **Access control (IAM)**: This is where you control the user access to your Cosmos DB. On this page, you must configure the different access profiles and the action permissions for each profile, and then add users to those profiles.

- **Diagnose and solve problems**: This is the knowledge base for problems in Cosmos DB. It can be used by the database administrator to see how to perform a certain configuration and obtain reliable references for service documentation.

- **Replicate data globally**: This is a very different feature of Cosmos DB, where you can configure automatic replicas of your database with geographic distribution. This option is interesting for global projects, where the database being distributed globally can help with the latency and availability of your solution:

Figure 10.6 – Azure Cosmos DB – Replicate data globally

- **Default consistency**: This is the consistency level setting of Cosmo DB. As explained in *Chapter 4, Working with Non-Relational Data*, NoSQL databases have the ability to manipulate the level of data consistency between their databases, which creates flexibility for some types of eventual consistency applications.

Other important settings in all databases are **Backup & Restore**, to ensure continuity of your database, and **Networking**, to configure access allowed to a database over the network layer – for example, which IPs can access your database or not.

Now that we know the main configurations of an Azure Cosmos DB database, let's create a sample database and explore the NoSQL database a little more.

Creating a sample Azure Cosmos DB database

To create a Cosmos DB sample database, follow the following steps:

1. On your Cosmos DB instance settings page, click the **Data Explorer** link.
2. On this page, you have access to tutorials and links to the product documentation, as follows:

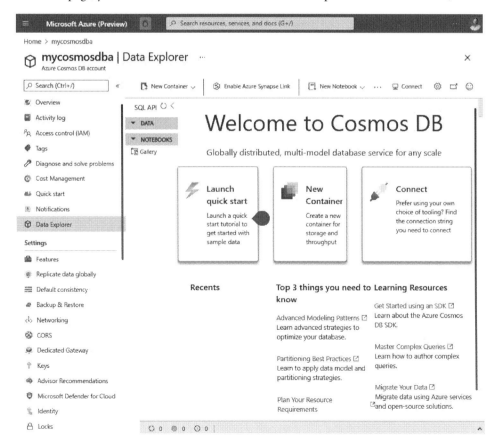

Figure 10.7 – Azure Cosmos DB – Data Explorer

3. Now, let's click **Launch quick start** so that Cosmos DB already recommends you some default settings for a sample database called `SampleDB`. Click **OK** to confirm the creation of this container.

4. The Cosmos DB wizard itself will guide you to open `SampleContainer`.

5. On the **Data Explorer** screen, you can explore creating items using the **New Item** link, and then update and delete items from this container. These are CRUD operations running directly on the database.

6. The wizard directs you to the **Connect** screen, which shows all the settings necessary for your application to connect to the database, as shown in the following screenshot:

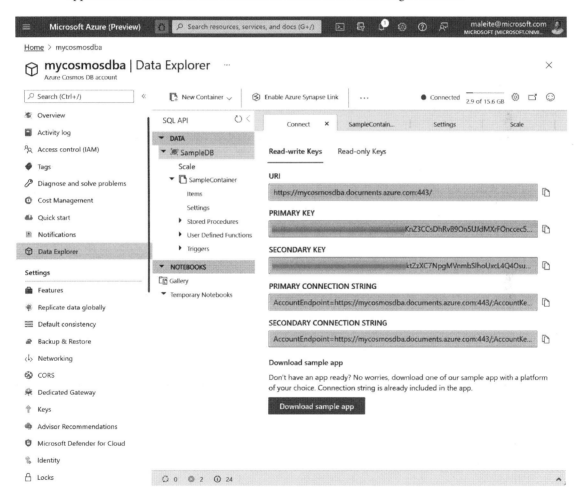

Figure 10.8 – Azure Cosmos DB – Data Explorer – Connect

7. Now, to explore the data by query, hover over the `SampleContainer` container:

    A. You'll see three points; click on them.

    B. In the list of options, click on **New SQL Query**.

    C. Keep the suggested query, `SELECT * FROM c`, and click the **Execute Query** button in the top menu, which returns the following:

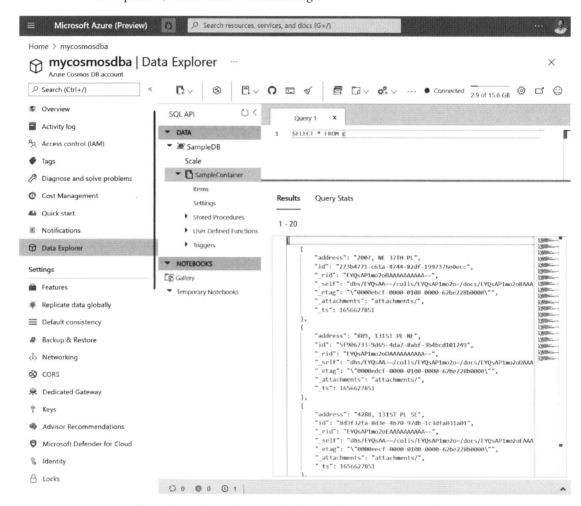

Figure 10.9 – Azure Cosmos DB – Data Explorer – query execution

8. Now, we can further explore this database using the knowledge we already have about the SQL language. Try some variations of the SELECT commands, as follows:

```
SELECT c.id, c.address FROM c WHERE CONTAINS(c.address,
"Any St.")
```

The knowledge required for DP-900 certification is gained by exploring the Azure data services and not experience of a full implementation. Based on this, this exploration of the options and process of creating a Cosmos DB database will help you with any questions related to this content on the test.

Now that we've evaluated the Cosmos DB database, let's evaluate Azure storage accounts and Data Lake Storage.

Provisioning an Azure storage account and Data Lake Storage

A lot of unstructured data, such as videos, images, and audio, are better stored in *object store* repositories than in database systems because of the database systems' limitations and the flexibility of object store repositories.

Therefore, in Azure, we have *Azure storage accounts* that are secure, flexible, and scalable storage for these types of unstructured data files.

In the next walk-through, we will explore provisioning an Azure storage account and its configuration in Azure Data Lake Storage Gen2:

1. Go back to the Azure portal home page and search for Storage Accounts.

2. Click **Create** and fill out the form with the following data:

   - **Subscription**: Select your subscription
   - **Resource Group**: packt
   - **Storage account name**: datalakepackt
   - **Region**: **(US) East US**
   - **Performance**: **Standard**
   - **Redundancy**: **Locally redundant storage (LRS)**

3. Click on **Next : Advanced** > and configure the following settings:

    *   Do not change any configuration of the security section

    *   In **Data Lake Storage Gen 2**, click the **Enable hierarchical namespace** checkbox:

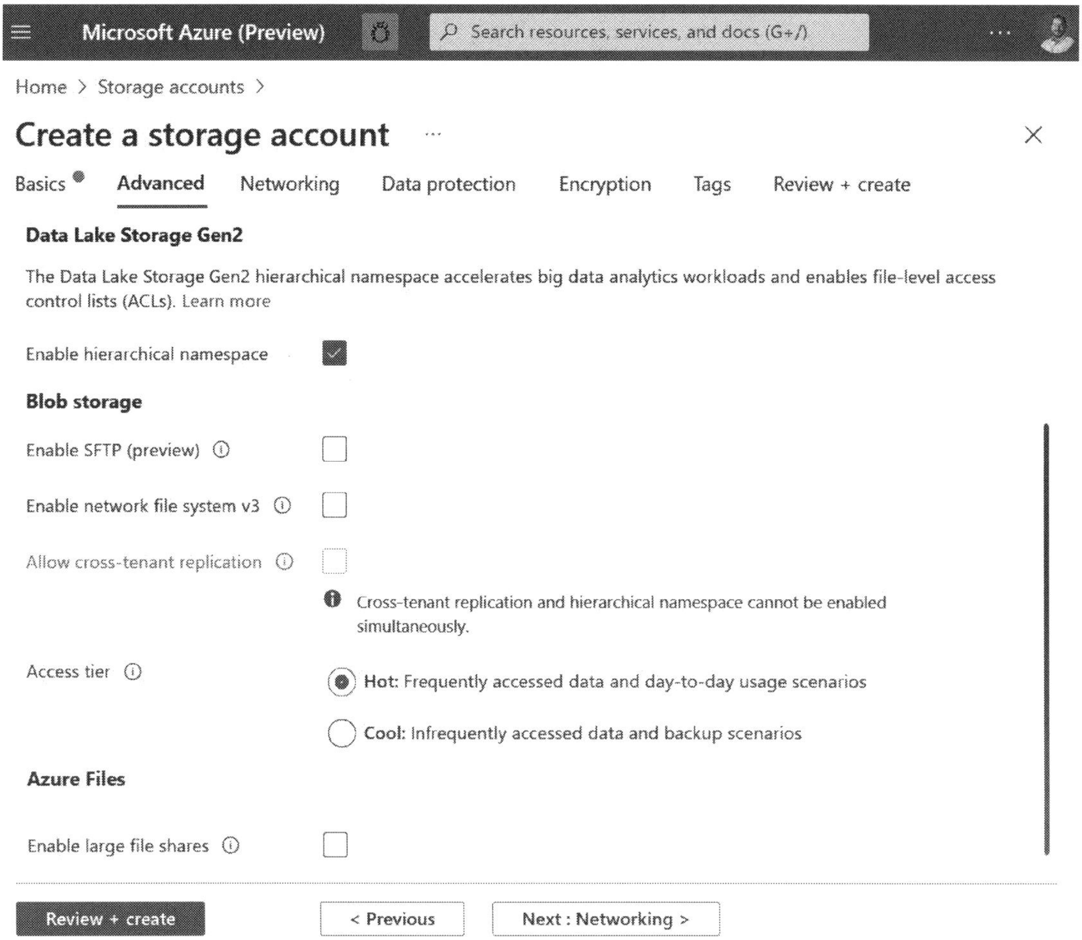

Figure 10.10 – Azure storage account – Data Lake Storage Gen2 configuration

> **Important Note**
>
> With this configuration active, your storage account begins to behave hierarchically, using folders, such as Windows folders, but compatible with data analytics tools that usually connect to **Hadoop Distributed File System** (HDFS) standards. Azure Data Lake Storage provides native support for POSIX-compliant **access control lists** (ACLs)

4.   Click **Review + Create** in the top menu and then the blue **Create** button to provision your storage account – Data Lake Storage Gen2.

5.   After provisioning, go to this storage account. In the settings, you can download the **Azure Storage Explorer** tool. This tool is important to manipulate the files in your new data lake.

In this section, we explored the main repositories for unstructured data in Azure, which were Azure Cosmos DB for the database system and an Azure storage account for unstructured data stored in the object store.

Summary

Non-relational databases are important for the specialization of data storage present in modern software, and knowing how to use the different Azure offerings is essential for the assembly of a *robust* architecture.

In this chapter, we explored provisioning non-relational data services, provisioning and configuring an Azure Cosmos DB database for the first time, how to explore an Azure Cosmos DB database, and how to provision an Azure storage account as data lake storage.

In the next chapter, we will enter the fourth part of our book, *Analytics Workload on Azure*, exploring the key components of data analytics in Azure. But first, let's cover a few more questions related to NoSQL databases that might come up in the DP-900 exam.

Sample questions and answers

Before you move on to the next chapter, try answering the following questions:

1.   The Azure Cosmos DB _____ API enables the use of SELECT statements to retrieve documents from Azure Cosmos DB.

   A.   Core (SQL)

   B.   Gremlin

   C.   MongoDB

   D.   Table

2.   What is a characteristic of non-relational data?

   A.   Forced schema on data structures

   B.   Flexible storage of ingested data

   C.   Entities may have the same fields

   D.   Each row has the exact same columns

3. Complete this sentence: _____ natively support the analysis of relationships between entities.

    A. Document databases

    B. Key-value stores

    C. Graph databases

    D. Column family databases

4. Which Azure storage solution is compatible with HDFS, **Azure Active Directory** (**Azure AD**), and POSIX-based **access control lists** (**ACLs**)

    A. Azure Table storage

    B. Azure Data Lake storage

    C. Azure Queue storage

    D. Azure Files

5. Select the answer that correctly completes the sentence. You have data that consists of video and audio documents. You need to store the data in an Azure environment that ensures availability and security. You should use _____ as the data store.

    A. Azure Cosmos DB

    B. Azure Table storage

    C. Azure Blob Storage

    D. Azure Files storage

Answer key

1-A 2-B 3-C 4-B 5-C

Part 4: Analytics Workload on Azure

This part will provide complete coverage of the knowledge and skills required for the *Skills measured* under the *Describe an analytics workload on Azure* section of the exam syllabus.

You will learn about the fundamentals of database concepts in a cloud environment, get basic skills in cloud data services, and build your foundational knowledge of cloud data services within Microsoft Azure. You will explore the processing options available for building data analytics in Azure. You will explore Azure Synapse Analytics, Power BI, and other analytics services in Azure.

This part comprises the following chapters:

- *Chapter 11, Components of a Modern Data Warehouse*
- *Chapter 12, Provisioning and Configuring Large-Scale Data Analytics in Azure*
- *Chapter 13, Working with Power BI*
- *Chapter 14, DP-900 Mock Exam*

11

Components of a
Modern Data Warehouse

In this chapter, let's explore the components of a modern data warehouse on Azure, understanding the different services such as Azure Databricks, Azure Synapse Analytics, and Azure HDInsight.

This chapter looks at content that will map to the skills measured in *Describe common elements of a modern data warehouse* in the DP-900 certification.

This chapter will be important in your data analytics projects in Azure, as we will explore the different data use cases using Azure tools.

By the end of this chapter, you will be able to understand the following:

- Describing modern data warehousing
- Azure data services for modern data warehousing
- A case study for data analytics on Azure
- Databricks, Azure HDInsight, and Azure Data Factory
- Real-time data analytics – Azure Stream Analytics, Azure Data Explorer, Spark Streaming, and Delta Lake

Describing modern data warehousing

Created in the 80s, the **data warehouse** (**DW**) concept is "*a subject-oriented, integrated, non-volatile, variable data repository over time to support management decisions*" (C. J. Date, Introdução a Sistemas de Bancos de Dados. eighth edition, Rio de Janeiro Campus, 2004).

In other words, a data warehouse is a database that organizes an organization's information, leaving the data more aligned with the nomenclature of company affairs so that it can be consumed by reports and applications.

Some important concepts when dealing with a data warehouse are as follows:

- **Extract, transform, and load** (ETL): This is the technique used to extract the information from the source relational databases, organize this data, and load only the result into the DW.

- **Data mart**: This is a logical subset of the data warehouse, usually divided by department, subject, or views required by users.

- **Business intelligence** (BI): This is a technology-driven process to analyze data and present actionable information to help executives, managers, and other enterprise end users make informed business decisions.

- **Massively parallel processing** (MPP): This is the hardware and software architecture behind traditional data warehouse tools. There are multiple parallel processing units in the database, rather than sequential processing as in a relational database.

In *Chapter 13, Working with Power BI* we will continue learning about data analytics and exploring Microsoft Power BI, which is important for some questions in the DP-900 certification and a great tool to create reports and dashboards from a data warehouse.

Looking at the following diagram, we can evaluate the flow of information in a data warehouse:

Figure 11.1 – Data warehouse data flow

The traditional data warehouse found problems with expanding data usage in organizations, so we will learn about these challenges next.

Challenges of traditional data warehouses

With the exponential growth of data in recent years, traditional DW technologies began to face scalability and cost-benefit challenges.

As the solutions had not been designed for cloud computing, most of them needed manufacturer-specific hardware to work in MPP, which created a lock on scalability and impacted the **total cost of ownership** (TCO).

At this time, new technologies such as big data began to gain notoriety in the market, especially the open source **Hadoop** project.

The birth of big data

Hadoop is an open source project published by Apache, derived from a paper by Google engineers in 2003 that described how the parallel processing of their search engine indexing was done.

In recent years, the project has evolved a lot and has been adopted by large organizations in parallel to the large data warehouse projects already existing.

Hadoop solved a great data warehouse challenge, working with unstructured or semi-structured data, with satisfactory scalability and cost/benefit.

Hadoop's architecture is based on **Hadoop Distributed File System** (**HDFS**) storage, and this hierarchical repository organized by folders can store any type of data, structured or not.

To store and process the data in HDFS, the data engineer can use MapReduce, Pig, Hive, and Storm, among other components of the Hadoop project, which can be seen in the following diagram.

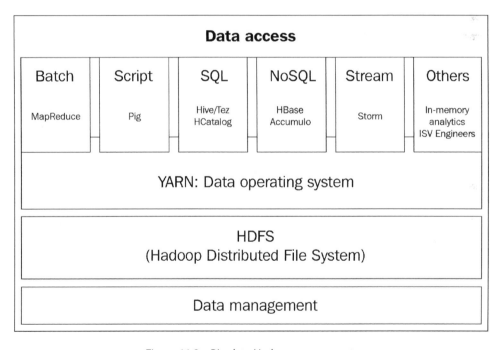

Figure 11.2 – Big data Hadoop components

Each component of Hadoop is responsible for data processing, data access control, governance, and SQL-based data exploration, among others, and each of these components is used by different user roles in a data organization.

Hadoop has undoubtedly contributed greatly to the evolution of data analytics in organizations, and Azure has its distribution, Azure HDInsight.

Azure HDInsight

Azure HDInsight is a **Hadoop PaaS service**, which contains the most used components in big data projects using Hadoop such as Spark, LLAP, Kafka, Storm, and HBase.

If you're planning a project with 100% open source big data standards and want to use components that can be transported to other cloud providers, HDInsight is an interesting option.

Other benefits of this service are as follows:

- **Access control**: With Azure Active Directory integration and Azure RBAC-based controls, Azure HDInsight delivers high levels of security and granularity in access control to your environments.

- **Global scalability**: Azure HDInsight is available in multiple Azure regions around the world, which is a big differentiator compared to other big data solutions.

- **Extensibility**: Azure HDInsight's open source extension pads make us able to use new big data projects in our environments, increasing the possibilities.

- **Cluster types**: HDInsight has a **cluster specialization**, and you can use one or more of these clusters in your project. The types are as follows:

  - **Apache Hadoop**: The foundation of Hadoop with HDFS, MapReduce for processing, and YARN as resource manager

  - **Apache Spark**: A more advanced open source big data processing project

  - **Apache HBase**: A NoSQL database that uses the big data architecture to be highly scalable and performative

  - **Apache Storm**: A streamed data processor for real-time analytics use cases

  - **Apache Interactive Query**: An in-memory cache database

  - **Apache Kafka**: A platform for streaming data ingestion in event format, for real-time analytics use cases

Azure HDInsight use cases can be migrations from legacy Hadoop distribution environments that have complex development in their data modeling, or the use of a particular cluster such as Kafka, widely used in data-streamed projects.

HDInsight is a robust service, but it is big data software. Due to the great simplicity of DWs in modeling data in formats that business areas prefer and delivering high-performance reports, the concept of a modern data warehouse emerged, which we will discuss in the following section.

Modern data warehouse

A modern data warehouse aims to bring the best of big data and data warehouses to a unified, cloud-based architecture capable of serving *all audiences* in a data organization with productive tools.

There are a few factors that have led organizations to pursue a new data analytics model, including the following:

- **Increased data volumes**: The same challenges of DWs were present in big data architectures when we arrived at the data scalability required by today's organizations

- **New types of data**: It is common today for non-structured and semi-structured data to be processed in organizations, but these types of data bring different challenges for governance and organization

- **Data velocity**: Data analytics cases and use in organizations are increasingly requiring speed in the ingestion, processing, and delivery of the result data.

Now that we know the challenges that have generated the need for a new architecture, let's understand how Azure addresses each of these factors.

Azure for the modern data warehouse

Listing the same factors mentioned in the previous section, we will evaluate the ways in which Azure can support organizations:

- **Increased data volumes**: Azure's modern data warehouse architecture is based on and stored using **Azure Data Lake Storage Gen2**, with scalability for petabytes of data and support for unstructured, semi-structured, and structured, organized, and secure data.

- **New types of data**: **Azure Cognitive Services** can help you to structure non-structured data, for use cases such as extracting text-ready solutions from images (Computer Vision), extracting text from audios (speech-to-text) or videos (Video Indexer), and organizing data from a scanned form (Form Recognizer), among others. These services can be added to the modern data warehouse architecture in Azure if there is a related need.

- **Data velocity**: Azure relies on hubs such as **Event Hubs** and **IoT Hubs**, which are event-shaped data capture PaaS services for near real-time scenarios. It also supports near real-time processing in Azure Synapse Analytics, Azure Databricks, and Azure Stream Analytics.

These are just a few examples of services that can be used in your modern data warehouse project. In the next section, we will detail the most used services in this type of architecture.

Exploring Azure data services for modern data warehouses

When we think of modern data warehouse architecture, we think of the process consisting of data analytics, which can be summarized in the following phases:

1. Data ingestion and preparation (ELT)

2. Making data ready for consumption (modeling)

3. Providing access to this data (reporting or API connections)

In this chapter, we will explore the possibilities of services that Azure offers to implement these phases. In *Chapter 12, Provisioning and Configuring Large-Scale Data Analytics in Azure*, there is a hands-on exercise that will help us understand in practice phases 1 and 2, and then in *Chapter 13, Working with Power BI*, we will explore Power BI for reporting.

Let's start with data ingestion and preparation.

Data ingestion and preparation (ELT/ETL)

ELT stands for **extract, load, and transform**, and **ETL** (as mentioned earlier) stands for **extract, transform, and load**. These reflect the process of data being extracted from transactional databases (relational or non-relational, as we saw earlier in this book), loaded into a repository, and transformed for consumption.

We can see a complete Azure-based modern data warehouse architecture in the following figure:

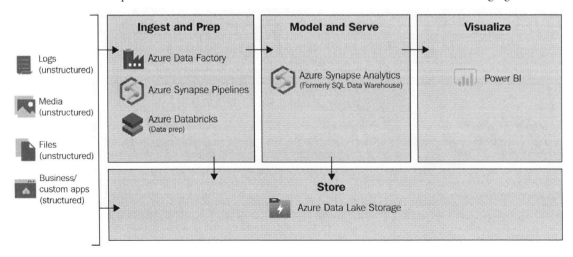

Figure 11.3 – Modern data warehouse architecture reference

Now let's get into the details of these different solutions.

Data storage – Azure Data Lake Storage Gen2

Azure Data Lake Storage Gen 2 is the best storage option for storing data in a modern data warehouse. As we saw in *Chapter 10, Provisioning and Configuring Non-Relational Data Services in Azure*, Azure Data Lake Storage Gen 2 is a type of storage account that relies on compatibility with big data protocols and hierarchical document structuring.

A data lake is a collection of data that is kept in its original form, typically as files or blobs, and then transformed to model consumption needs.

Azure Data Lake Storage is a versatile solution for both staging repositories, which are passages from unfiltered data sources, and data lake layer storage.

It's common to split the data lake in layers, such as *Bronze*, *Silver*, and *Gold*, or *Raw*, *Curated*, and *Trusted*, to organize the data flow from the data source, preparing/modeling the data for the data consumption.

Azure data analytics services such as Synapse Analytics, Azure Databricks, and Azure HDInsight use Azure Data Lake Storage Gen2 as their central data repository.

Now that we know about the default repository for all analytics services in Azure, let's evaluate the services that orchestrate the data in the architecture.

Data ingestion – Azure Data Factory and Azure Synapse Analytics

Systems that are used for process automation often play a crucial role in operations and cannot have interference that compromises their performance and availability. Therefore, a widely used technique for data analytics is **data ingestion**, copying a dump from a source base to an analytical repository, which in the concept of a modern data warehouse is implemented with Azure Data Lake Storage Gen2.

To perform data ingestion, Azure has two tools: **Azure Data Factory** and **Azure Synapse Pipelines**. They are virtually the same, with more than 100 native data connectors that will connect to the most widely used database formats in an organization.

Azure Data Factory has a differential for organizations that use **SQL Server Integration Services** (**SSIS**) and are migrating to Azure because it can run an SSIS integration runtime, which processes SSIS packages in Azure Data Factory without any change.

Both Data Factory and Azure Synapse Pipelines rely on the **mapping dataflows** feature, which is a visual-interfaced data preparation module, making data engineering work much easier.

The two tools also work with linked services to connect the source databases and can run pipelines or simple copies of data using the **Copy data activity** feature.

Another option, for those who want to develop a data preparation routine by programming on notebooks, is to perform the processing of Spark notebooks in Azure Databricks or the processors of Azure Synapse Analytics (Spark, SQL, and Pipelines); we will explore them now.

Data preparation – Azure Databricks

Azure Databricks is a PaaS service on Azure developed by Microsoft in partnership with Databricks, a company founded by the creators of the open source projects Apache Spark, Delta Lake, and MLflow.

Databricks is now a reference in big data solutions with high-speed, notebook-based, and easy cluster administration Spark processing. This causes it to be used in some data preparation scenarios, replacing Data Factory and Synapse Pipelines.

Azure Databricks can be used in data preparation project scenarios, machine learning development, and data exploration and modeling with the data lakehouse concept, which simulates the functions of a DW directly in Azure Data Lake.

In the following diagram, we can learn a little more about Databricks integrations, as well as their features:

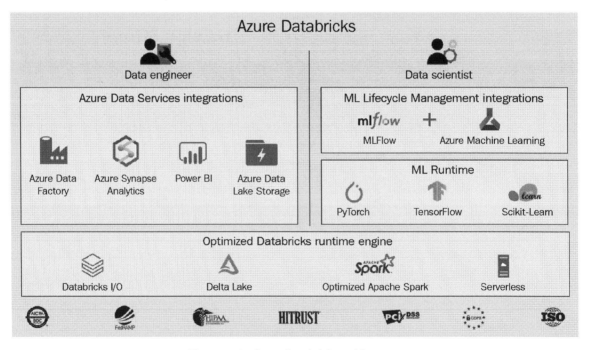

Figure 11.4 – Azure Databricks architecture

Supporting Scala, Python, Java, R, and SQL languages, Databricks notebooks are flexible and quick to operate and support other open source data projects that can further extend Azure Databricks capabilities.

Some important features of Azure Databricks are as follows:

- High-speed connections to Azure storage solutions, such as Azure Blob Storage and Azure Data Lake, as well as Spark clusters that automatically scale and terminate to reduce costs

- The MLflow project to develop machine learning models is one of the most used open source projects

- Indexing, caching, advanced query optimization, and **Databricks Enterprise Security** (**DBES**) support administration, optimization, governance, and environmental security

Now that we've learned about Azure Databricks, let's evaluate the other code-based data preparation option, which is also the primary Azure solution for data warehouses: Azure Synapse Analytics.

Modern data warehouse – Azure Synapse Analytics

Azure Synapse Analytics is a suite that supports services that support the entire data analytics flow, from data ingestion, preparation, modeling, and delivery.

> **Important note**
>
> For DP-900 certification, it is not necessary to implement a modern data warehouse architecture because, in the test, only concepts are required. But to complement the learning, in the next chapter, we will explore Azure Synapse Analytics with a hands-on exercise to provide the foundations for your data analytics projects, and you can explore the Synapse configurations that can be asked about in DP-900.

In the following screenshot, we can look at the Azure Synapse Analytics components available in the side menu:

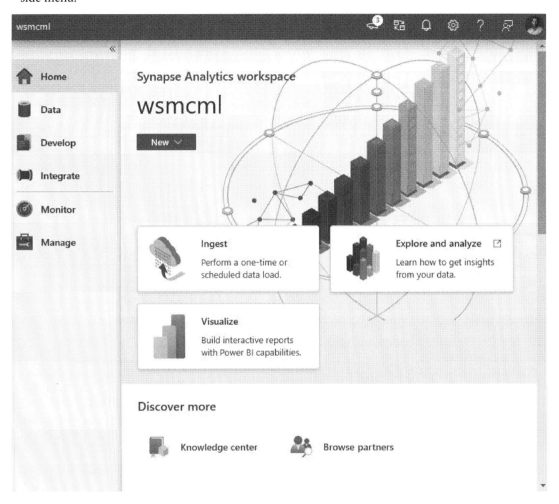

Figure 11.5 – Azure Synapse Analytics workspace

The first item, **Home**, directs you to the **Home** workspace, where you can access tutorials, a knowledge base library, and analyze implementation partners and objects you've recently accessed.

The second item, **Data**, is where you can configure your data repositories, which are Azure Data Lake Storage Gen2, an Azure SQL database, or Azure Cosmos DB, among other options.

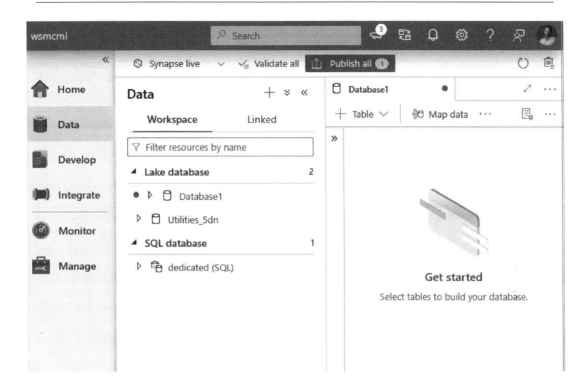

Figure 11.6 – Azure Synapse Analytics – Data

The **Develop** option brings you to an interface for data exploration with the possibility of creating notebooks and SQL scripts to run in Synapse Analytics clusters for data exploration and transformation. The different types of processing that Azure Synapse Analytics has are as follows:

- **Serverless SQL pool**: A pool to run SQL-based scripts using a shared capacity in Azure. A very cost-effective service for some use case implementations. It is built in and always available on Synapse, which means you don't need to provision the cluster, as it's already there waiting to be triggered by a SQL script.

- **Dedicated SQL pool**: This is the evolution of the Azure SQL DW service, another pool to run SQL-based scripts, but in this case, dedicated to your infrastructure. In addition to stable and guaranteed performance, this allows you to materialize your DW database in this pool, which is different from serverless where you can run the scripts but not keep tables and models saved permanently; in the Dedicated SQL pool, this is allowed. The interesting thing is that this database is MPP, a SQL DW inheritance, and that it greatly optimizes queries in large databases.

- **Apache Spark pool**: This is a Spark processing cluster, like Azure Databricks or an Azure HDInsight Spark cluster, but more integrated with other Azure services and with some improvements on the Spark processing created by the Microsoft product team. You can read about these in detail and understand these improvements in the official documentation of Azure Synapse Spark pool here:

  ```
  https://learn.microsoft.com/en-us/azure/synapse-analytics/spark/
  apache-spark-overview
  ```

  Azure Synapse Analytics is a great tool for designing and developing machine learning models using the Azure ML library created by Microsoft.

- **Data Explorer pool**: This is a new processing format, derived from the Azure Data Explorer service. As it is not yet required for the DP-900, we will not delve into it, but it is a specialized pool for processing high volumes of logs, with a highly scalable and cost-effective platform.

In the following figure, we can see this section in Azure Synapse Analytics:

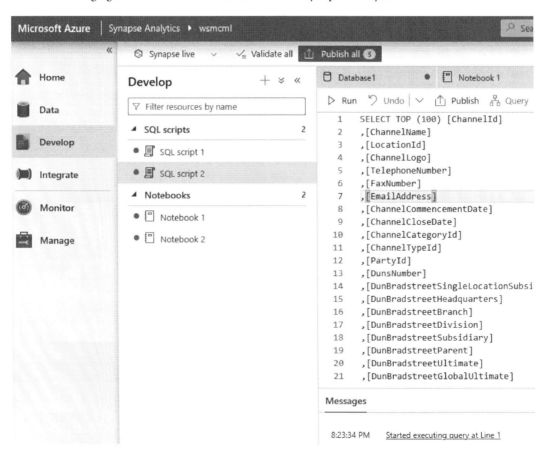

Figure 11.7 – Azure Synapse Analytics – Develop

In this same **Develop** section, as seen in *Figure 11.7*, you can create your mapping data flow for data preparation.

The **Integrate** item brings Azure Data Factory functionality into Azure Synapse Analytics, and this module is called Azure Synapse Pipelines. In the following figure, we can observe that we can assemble a data pipeline, a link connection, a simple copy of data between two structures, access a gallery of examples, and even import from pipeline templates:

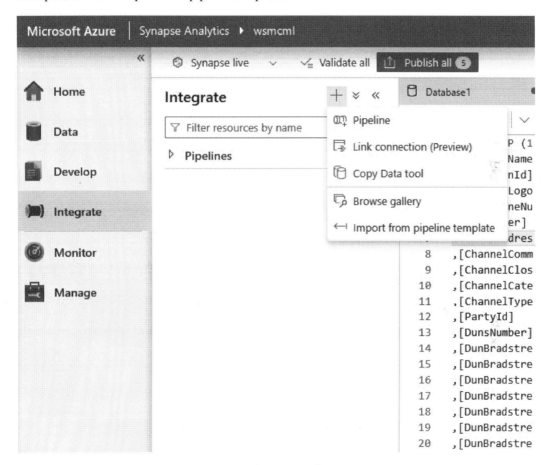

Figure 11.8 – Azure Synapse Analytics – Integrate

The next item is environment management, with **Monitor** being the place to track pipeline executions, connection status, and cluster pools, among other important environment statistics to keep the environment running:

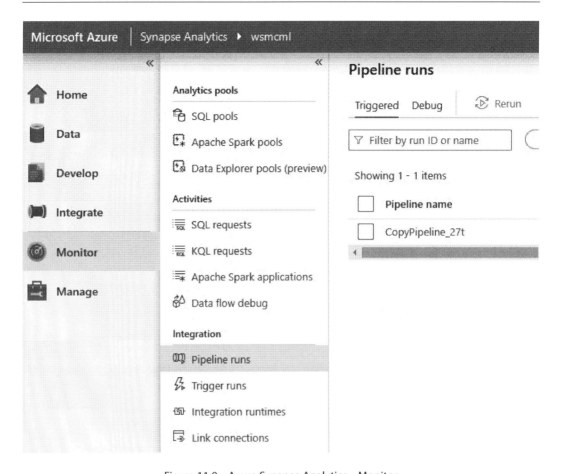

Figure 11.9 – Azure Synapse Analytics – Monitor

The general administration of the tool takes place on the **Manage** page. In this section, we can configure security and access profiles for Azure Synapse objects; the provisioning and sizing of processing pools, our connections, and integrations; GIT versioning control; and our templates in the gallery:

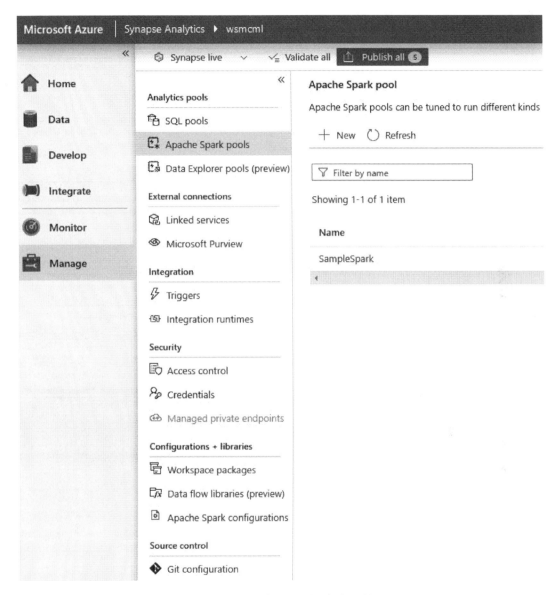

Figure 11.10 – Azure Synapse Analytics – Manage

With this section, we close the overall exploration of the modern data warehouse service Azure Synapse Analytics, but so far, we have talked about data that is loaded into Data Lake through batch loads. Sometimes though, we need to capture the data in streaming, for near real-time solutions. That's what we're going to explore in the next section.

Real-time data analytics – Azure Stream Analytics, Azure Synapse Data Explorer, and Spark streaming

Some analytical use cases aim to monitor near real-time processes to assist in decision-making. For these cases, waiting for a dump from the source database to the target database is not effective; for this reason the concept of a **data stream** emerged.

In Azure, there are some service options for working data streams; let's explore each of them.

Azure Stream Analytics

This is an Azure PaaS service and is very simple and efficient. Usually accompanied by the Azure event queue service, called **Azure Event Hubs**, Azure Stream Analytics consists of running SQL scripts on each of the events that arrive to be processed; that is, it is a data passing service, with some filtering, groupings, transformations, and so on.

The following figure reflects the data flow performed by Azure Stream Analytics:

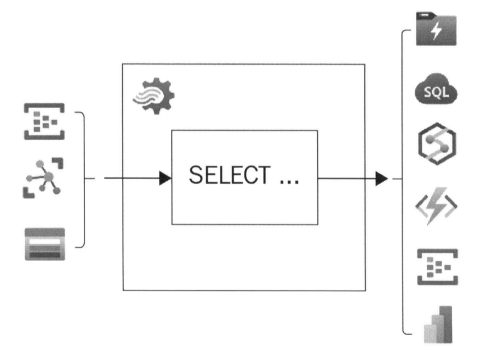

Figure 11.11 – Azure Stream Analytics concept

We have the option to use a Stream Analytics job, which uses shared processing power (serverless), or provision a dedicated cluster.

Another interesting option is the integration of Azure Data Explorer within Azure Synapse, so let's get to know it now.

Azure Data Explorer and Azure Synapse Data Explorer pools

Azure Data Explorer is a standalone analytics service on Azure, developed to process large volumes of data, especially logs, IoT device sensor data, website navigation telemetry, and others, and is very fast and cost-effective.

Azure Data Explorer has its own data exploration language called **Kusto Query Language** (**KQL**) and is optimized for log and time data analysis.

With support for ingesting and outputting results in the event format, Azure Data Explorer can be used as a near real-time processing solution in a data stream or to process large volume of data to store the results in an Azure Data Lake.

KQL queries can be created in the **Develop** section of the Azure Synapse Analytics workspace, and Data Explorer pools can be configured in the **Manage** section.

Azure Synapse Data Explorer pools are derived from **Azure Data Explorer**, but with all native integration with the Azure Synapse Analytics workspace.

There is also a standard open source option, which is based on the Apache Spark Streaming project. Let's discuss that next.

Apache Spark Streaming

Apache Spark can be provisioned on Azure in three different PaaS services: Azure HDInsight, Azure Databricks, and Azure Synapse Analytics Spark pools.

Spark supports running code developed in notebooks based on different languages (Python, Scala, and Java, for example), using parallel processing in multiple clusters to improve performance.

All these options rely on the **Spark Structured Streaming** library, which aims to process data in event format, based on an **application programming interface** (**API**) for data input and output.

When you need to include streaming data in a data lake or Apache Spark-based analytical data store, Spark Structured Streaming is a very interesting option, and I encourage you to go further in your study in the documentation (`https://learn.microsoft.com/en-us/azure/architecture/example-scenario/data/stream-ingestion-synapse`) before implementing this kind of use case, but for the DP-900 certification, this overview will help you to answer the questions.

Delta Lake

Delta Lake is a modern architecture pattern for data lakes, based on delta tables that store metadata from the data stored in a data lake. In other words, Delta Lake records all transactions in a data lake, creating data lineage (that represents rastreability from the data generation to the data consumption, recording all transformations during the process).

This technology supports schema enforcement, transactional consistency, and other data warehouse features, but directly into the data lake, based on Spark routines.

Delta Lake can organize real-time data streams, with batch-loaded data, into containers for data exploration based on SQL queries.

We can work with Delta Lake on Azure Synapse Analytics and Azure Databricks.

With these data stream options, we've finished the concepts and tools for deploying a modern data warehouse to Azure.

Summary

It is common in the modern data warehouse that the largest value of all company data is generated, where reports become insights capable of changing processes and supporting critical decision-making, among other things.

Azure has fantastic services for implementing a modern data warehouse, and its primary service is Azure Synapse Analytics, which seeks to simplify all analytical processes in the same Workspace interface; we will explore this in more detail in the next chapter.

In this chapter, we explored the concepts of a modern data warehouse and Azure data services to implement a modern data warehouse such as Azure Synapse Analytics, Azure Databricks, Azure HDInsight, Azure Data Factory, and Azure Data Lake.

We'll resume our hands-on exploration in the next chapter.

Sample questions and answers

Try to answer the following questions to test your knowledge:

1. Which two Azure data services enable clusters of Apache Spark?

    A. Azure Synapse Analytics

    B. Azure Data Factory

    C. Azure Databricks

    D. Azure Cosmos DB

2. You use the Azure Data Factory service to create a data ingestion and transformation solution. Data from an Azure SQL database is required. Which two sources should you employ?

   A. Linked service

   B. Copy data activity

   C. Azure Databricks notebook

   D. Dataset

3. How should you name the data that you want to consume for processing using an Azure Data Factory component?

   A. Pipelines

   B. Datasets

   C. Linked services

   D. Notebooks

4. For which reason should you use a modern data warehouse?

   A. Perform sales forecast analyses

   B. Explore daily sales transactions

   C. Monitor sales performance KPIs

   D. All of the above

5. Which of the components of Azure Synapse Analytics allows you to train AI models using Azure ML?

   A. Synapse Pipelines

   B. Synapse Spark

   C. Synapse Studio

   D. Synapse SQL Pool

Answer key

1-A C 2-A, B 3-B 4-D 5-B

12
Provisioning and Configuring Large-Scale Data Analytics in Azure

In the previous chapter, we explored the components of a modern data warehouse in Azure. Now, let's see how to use the Azure Synapse Analytics toolset to implement our data analytics projects on Azure.

This chapter will look at content that will map to the *Describe an analytics workload on Azure* section of *Skills measured* in the DP-900 certification. You can take a look at the detailed requirements of DP-900 on the official website: `https://docs.microsoft.com/en-us/certifications/exams/dp-900`.

This hands-on chapter is a complement to our previous chapter to dive deeper into the Azure Data Analytics tools.

By the end of this chapter, we will have covered the following topics:

- Common practices for data loading

- Data storage and processing

- Azure Synapse Analytics:

  - Synapse Studio

  - Synapse Pipelines

  - Synapse SQL pools – serverless and dedicated

  - Synapse Spark pools

  - Synapse Link

  - Synapse Data Explorer

  - Synapse and Azure Machine Learning

Technical requirements

This is a chapter that contains hands-on exercises – to practice together with me, please pay attention to the following technical requirements:

- A computer with Windows 10 or a newer OS and internet access

- An active Azure account (`http://www.azure.com`)

- Access the book code repository on GitHub (`https://github.com/PacktPublishing/Microsoft-Certified-Azure-Data-Fundamentals-Exam-DP-900-Certification-Guide`)

Understanding common practices for data loading

To start an analytics database, we need to load data from transactional databases, where the data that is generated by enterprise systems is stored.

In Azure, we have some options for performing *data ingestion* as we covered in *Chapter 11*, *Components of a Modern Data Warehouse*, using batch loads and data streaming, concepts we also learned about in *Chapter 5*, *Exploring Data Analytics Concepts*.

In this chapter, we'll explore *Azure Synapse Analytics* so that you can materialize that knowledge to help you answer *DP-900* questions and have a foundation for your Data Analytics projects in Azure.

So, let's start step by step.

Provisioning an Azure Synapse workspace

To get started, let's navigate the Azure portal (`http://portal.azure.com`) and search for the **Azure Synapse Analytics** session. When you're in the Azure Synapse Analytics session, click the **+ Create** button to provision a new workspace and fill out the form with the following settings:

- **Subscription**: `coredba`
- **Resource group**: **(US) East US**
- **Managed resource group**: `packetmanaged`
- **Workspace name**: `packt`
- **Use Spark on Cosmos**: Not selected
- **Region**: **East US 2**
- **Select Data Lake Storage Gen2**: **From subscription**
- **Account name**: Click **New** and fill the name in as `packtdatalake` as depicted in the following screenshot:

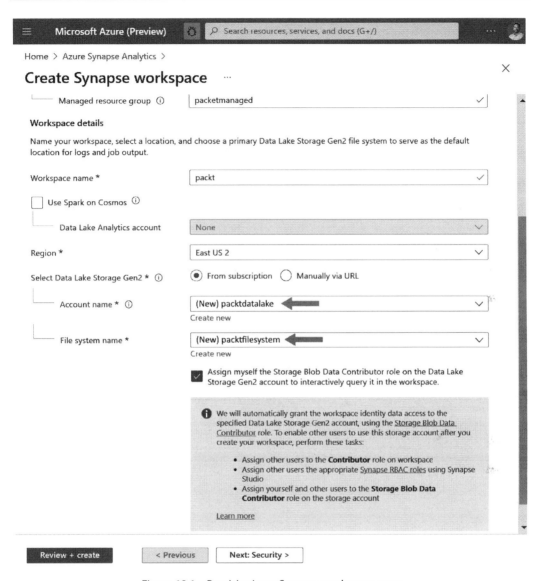

Figure 12.1 – Provisioning a Synapse workspace page

- **File system name**: Following the same process, click **New** and fill the name in as `packtfilesystem`

- **Assign myself the Storage Blob Data Contributor role on the Data Lake Storage Gen2 account to interactively query it in the workspace.**: Yes, check the checkbox to create the proper permission for your user for this storage

Now, click **Next: Security** > to move forward with this Azure Synapse workspace configuration.

Now, we can fill in the admin username and password for the SQL database pool of Synapse Analytics. Fill this form with the following settings:

- **Use both local and Azure Active Directory (Azure AD) authentication**: Yes, check the checkbox
- **SQL Server admin login**: `packtadmin`
- **SQL password**: `Pass@word#123`
- **Confirm password**: `Pass@word#123`
- **Double encryption using a customer-managed key**: Disable

With the basic security settings configured, click **Next: Networking** > to configure the network settings, and fill them in as follows:

- **Managed virtual network**: Disable (this configuration is important for productive projects, to add your Synapse Workspace to an Azure vNet, but for the moment, we don't need this configuration)
- **Allow connections from all IP addresses**: Yes, check the checkbox

> **Important note**
> The **Allow connections from all IP addresses** setting will configure the Azure Synapse workspace firewall to accept access requests from any computer but considering the user authentication as the access control layer. If you want to increase protection by manually setting the IP of the computers that will access the database, you must remove this option and add the IPs.

Go to **Next:** >, then click on the **Review + create** > button, and then click on the blue **Create** button to provision the Azure Synapse workspace.

Wait for it to provision and after the process is complete, click the blue **Go to resource group** button. Then, you can access the **packt** resource group and administer all services provisioned so far in this resource group.

Click on the **packt** Synapse workspace and as soon as you open the Synapse workspace settings page, click **Open** to open Synapse Studio, as shown in the following screenshot:

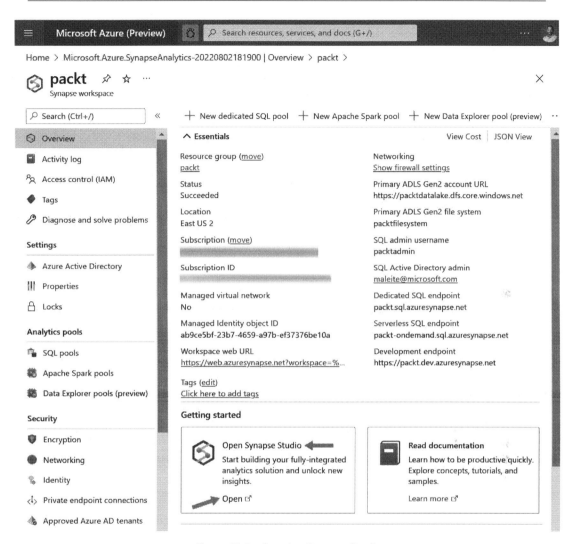

Figure 12.2 – Opening Synapse Studio

You will notice that another window will open in your browser when accessing `azuresynapse.net`. This is the central portal of your Synapse Analytics, Azure Synapse Studio, where you can connect to your data sources, perform complex data preparations, model your data, and even create reports in an integrated Power BI instance.

Now that the environment is set up, let's dive into data ingestion.

Practicing data load

In this exercise, we will explore Azure Synapse Pipelines, which is the module dedicated to performing data ingestion processes, with **Extract, Transform, and Load** (ETL) and **Extract, Load, and Transform** (**ELT**) as we know from *Chapter 5*, Exploring *Data Analytics Concepts*. To access it, click on the **Integrate** item in the panel of icons on the left-hand side of the page, opening the page as follows:

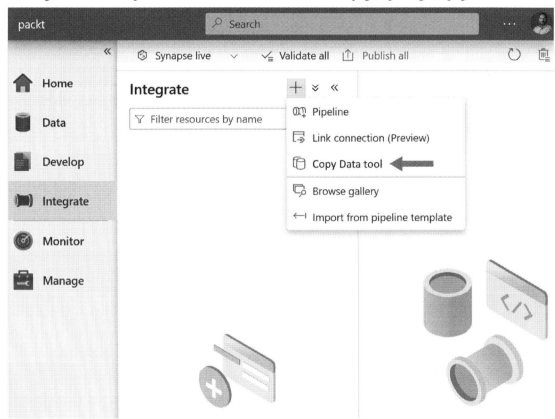

Figure 12.3 – Copy Data tool in Azure Synapse Pipelines

Then, click on the + icon and then **Copy Data tool**.

In Azure Synapse Pipelines, you can create more complex data pipelines in addition to the data copy, so there is also a **Pipeline** section, but for this simple exercise, we will use the **Copy Data tool** feature.

When accessing the **Copy Data tool** feature, a **wizard** (or set of forms) will appear and the first question is whether we want a **Built-in copy task** or a **Metadata-driven copy task** functionality. **Built-in copy task** is simpler, but sometimes we need to analyze the metadata before making our copies and that's where **Metadata-driven copy task** is used.

Let's select **Built-in copy task**.

Next, you will be asked about the running recurrency of this copy. In a real project, it is very important to evaluate the update window of your data from the data source databases and the availability of this data in the analytical database in Azure Synapse Analytics.

For this exercise, we will select **Run once now** and then click the blue **Next** > button.

In the **Source** data store section, you have *more than 90 connectors* for the most diverse types of data sources used on the market, including relational databases, SQL, NoSQL, Azure document stores, and other cloud storages, files, and APIs.

Click + **New connection** to set up a new connection.

Search for Azure SQL Database in the list and click on it.

Let's use Azure Synapse Analytics by connecting to the Azure SQL database that we provisioned in *Chapter 7, Provisioning and Configuring Relational Database Services in Azure*, and then filling out the form with the following access information:

- **Name**: SQLDatabasePackt
- **Description**: Our Study SQL Database
- **Connect via integration runtime**: AutoResolveIntegrationRuntime

> **Important note**
>
> Azure Synapse Pipelines and Azure Data Factory use an agent called the integration runtime as a bridge between the data source and the service in Azure. There are three types of integration runtime available:
>
> **Azure Integration Runtime (Auto-resolve)** – Used to make connections to data sources in Azure. This runtime is native to Azure Synapse Pipelines and Azure Data Factory and is therefore managed by Azure.
>
> **Self-hosted Integration Runtime** – Used to connect to data sources outside of Azure. This integration runtime needs to be installed on a server that will bridge this role between connections, minimizing security risks and network latency on your connections.
>
> **Azure-SSIS Integration Runtime** – Used to run **SQL Server Integration Services** (**SSIS**) packages on Azure Data Factory or Azure Synapse Pipelines. This integration runtime deploys an SSIS server on Azure and it's frequently used for SSIS solutions for migrating from legacy systems.

Select the **Connection string** option and then fill out the following settings:

- **From Azure subscription**: Yes, check the checkbox
- **Azure subscription**: Your Azure subscription used in your exercises
- **Server name**: `coredba`
- **Database name**: `coredb`
- **Authentication type:** `SQL authentication`
- **User name**: `administrador`
- **Password**: `Pass@word#123`
- **Always encrypted**: No

> **Important note**
>
> Azure reserves some words such as administrator, admin, and others, to avoid security issues. That's why I have used **administrador** (which means administrator in Portuguese). In your projects, you can use something such as `admin2022` and variations of this kind for creating this admin login, but to make sure you can follow all the exercise steps mentioned in this book, use **administrador**.

After these settings, click **Test connection** in the lower-right corner of the page.

If an error occurs, you may have to add a white-listing rule on the Azure SQL firewall of your `coredba` SQL server.

To do this, open another tab in your browser (so that you don't lose the configuration you were doing with Azure Synapse Pipelines), go to the Azure portal (`http://portal.azure.com`), and look for the SQL server session.

Select `coredba` and then the **Networking** option. You will see an **Allow Azure services and resources to access this server** option. Click on this option and save the changes depicted as follows:

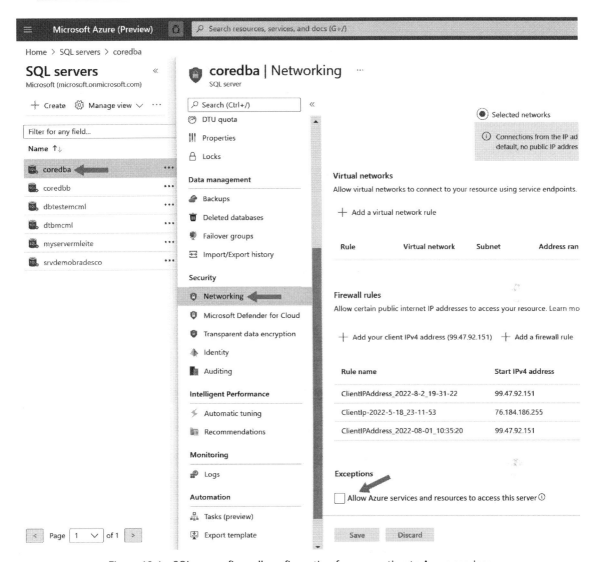

Figure 12.4 – SQL server firewall configuration for connection to Azure services

With these settings configured, return to the tab of your browser that is open on the Azure Synapse Pipelines connection page and click on the **Test connection** button in the lower-right corner of the page.

You should now receive a message saying **Connection successful** as follows and you can click the blue **Create** button:

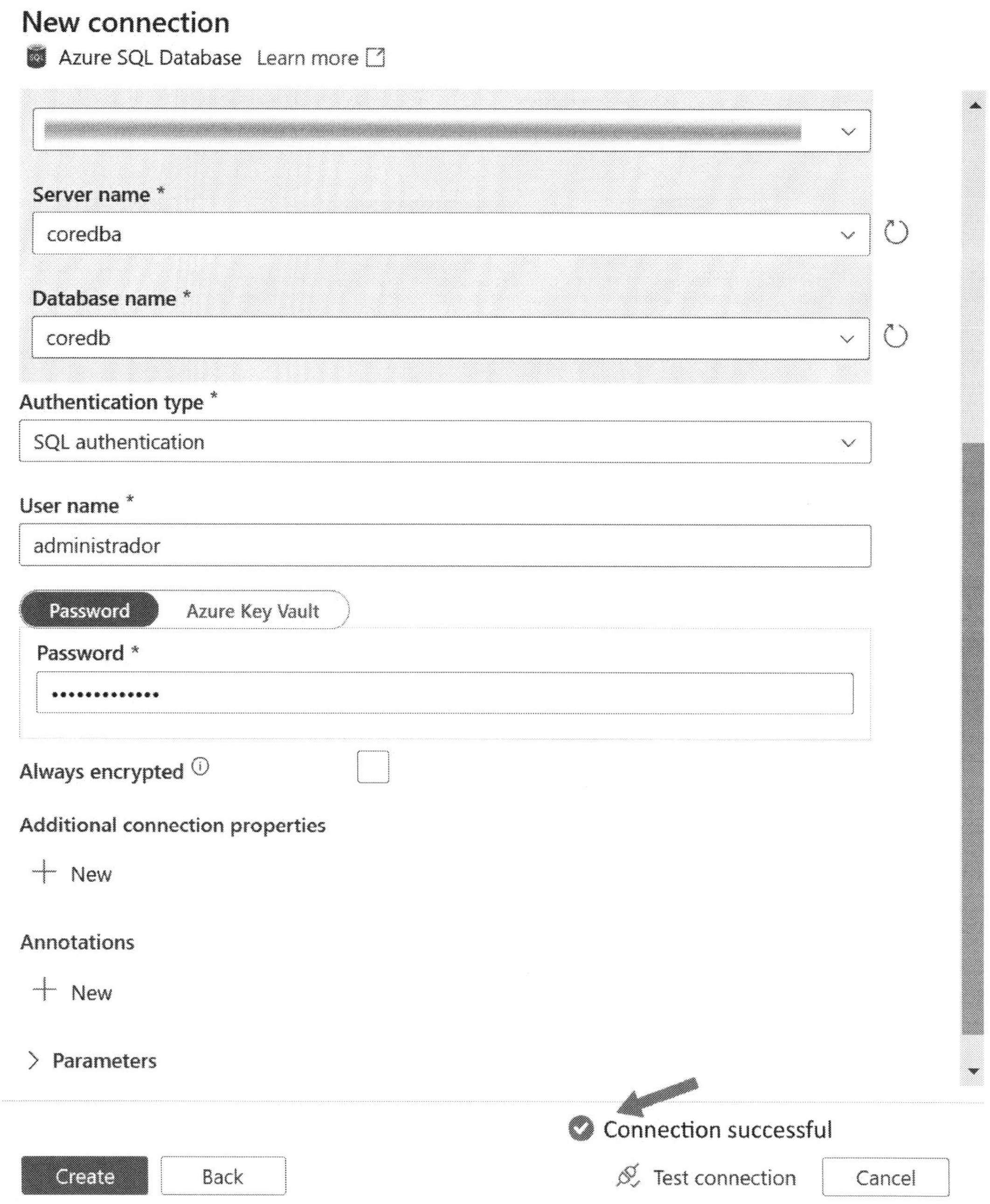

New connection

Azure SQL Database   Learn more ☐

Server name *

coredba

Database name *

coredb

Authentication type *

SQL authentication

User name *

administrador

(**Password**   Azure Key Vault)

Password *

••••••••••••

Always encrypted ⓘ   ☐

Additional connection properties

\+ New

Annotations

\+ New

\> Parameters

✓ Connection successful

Create   Back   🔌 Test connection   Cancel

Figure 12.5 – Azure Synapse Pipelines testing the connection

In the next *wizard* step of Azure Synapse Pipelines, you can select the entities of the connection that you want to copy. Select the `dbo.student_data` table and click the blue **Next** > button.

In the next step, you can add filters to this copy. We will not use these filters in this exercise, so you can click the blue **Next** > button.

Now, it's time to select the destination of this data copy. To do this, we can select `Azure Data Lake Storage Gen2` provisioned when the Azure Synapse workspace was created. Please fill out the form with the following values:

- **Target type**: `Azure Data Lake Storage Gen2`
- **Connection**: `packt-WorkspaceDefaultStorage`
- **Integration runtime**: `AutoResolveIntegrationRuntime`
- **Folder path**: `packtfilesystem`
- **File name**: `studentdata.parquet`

The other fields can remain blank and you can click on the blue **Next** > button.

On the **File format settings** page, we will configure the format of the file that will be created in this data lake, containing the student data we are copying from the Azure SQL database. Select **Parquet**, leave the rest of the settings as their defaults, and click on the blue **Next** > button.

Parquet is a very popular data compression format in data lakes and is interpretable by several different big data and data analytics tools.

In the **Settings** section, we will configure the *task* for this data copy pipeline so that we can put a name to the task and define whether it will have a data consistency check or not, in addition to other settings.

For this exercise, name the task `CopyPipeline_packt` and then click the blue **Next** > button.

Review your settings and then click the blue **Next** > button again.

Azure Synapse Pipelines will run your data copy pipeline, bringing the contents of the `coredba` database tables into your Azure Data Lake instance.

Ideally, all four processes succeed, as shown in the following screenshot, and then you can click the blue **Finish** button:

Figure 12.6 – Azure Synapse Pipelines deployment page

In this way, you complete the process of *data loading*. Now, with the data stored in Azure Data Lake connected to Azure Synapse Analytics, we are going to explore where this data was stored.

Data storage and processing

In the left-hand menu in *Azure Synapse Studio*, click on the **Data** icon. In this section, you will be able to see all the connections made by your Azure Synapse Analytics environment.

Navigate to **Azure Data Lake Storage Gen2** | **packt** | **packfilesystem** to view the `studentdata.parquet` file created by your data-loading pipeline as follows:

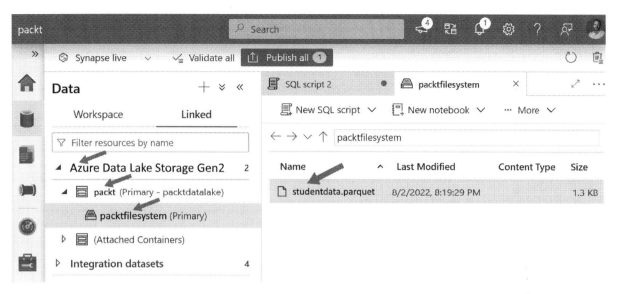

Figure 12.7 – Azure Data Lake exploration on Azure Synapse Studio

Let's query this data. For this, right-click on the filename and the **New SQL script** option > **Select TOP 1000 rows**. This consultation will be carried out by Azure Synapse serverless SQL pool, which is the default option for queries in Azure Synapse.

Azure serverless SQL pool

In this way, the SQL script to query the first 1,000 records of this file will already be created by Azure Synapse Analytics, as will a window to run this script. In this window, you can see **Connect to: Built-in**, the serverless SQL pool endpoint, and then you can click the **Run** button to run the query as follows:

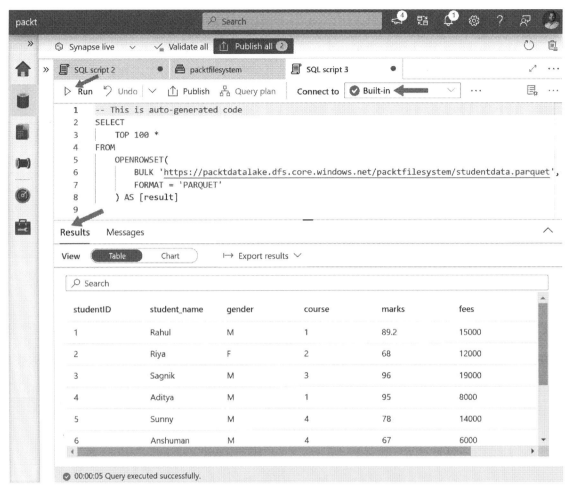

Figure 12.8 – SQL query execution using Azure Synapse serverless SQL
pool consulting Azure Data Lake Storage Gen2 data

This query can be found in the GitHub repository of this book by opening the Chapter12 folder in GitHub and seeing the //Step 1 query in the Chapter12.sql file.

As we can see, from a simple note, we run a query on the data that is stored in the semi-structured `studentdata.parquet` document using SQL. *Serverless SQL pool* is a very interesting processor for performing this type of exploration directly in Azure Data Lake, using the processing power shared with other Azure users, for a very efficient query performance.

However, sometimes, we need to create a (SQL-standard) relational database dedicated to our project so that it is used as a data warehouse, so that's when we use Azure Synapse dedicated SQL pool.

Azure dedicated SQL pool

To explore *Azure dedicated SQL pool*, first, we need to create this dedicated pool. Access the **Manage** item from the left-hand menu in Azure Synapse Studio.

On this page, you can administer not only the dedicated pool but also other processors such as a *serverless SQL pool* or a *Spark pool*.

In the **SQL pools** section, click **New** and fill in the following settings:

- Dedicated SQL pool name: `packtdedicatedsqlpool`
- Performance level: `DW100c`

Click on the blue **Review + create** button and then on the blue **Create** button.

Provisioning should take a few minutes, as it is a slightly more complex operation for Azure, but as soon as you finish, you should notice that it will be flagged as `Online` in your list of SQL pools.

Let's explore this dedicated SQL pool. For this, let's copy a data table from the SQL database to the dedicated SQL pool database.

Return to the **Integrate** item in the left-hand menu of Azure Synapse Studio. Then, click on the + button and the **Copy Data tool** option.

Leave the **Properties** section settings as their defaults and click on the blue **Next** > button.

Under **Source**, select **Azure SQL Database** and the **AzureSqlDatabase1** connection, which is the connection we created in the previous section of this chapter. In this way, you should be able to explore the tables present in this database, select the `dbo.student_data` table for our exercise as follows, and click on the blue **Next** > button:

Copy Data tool

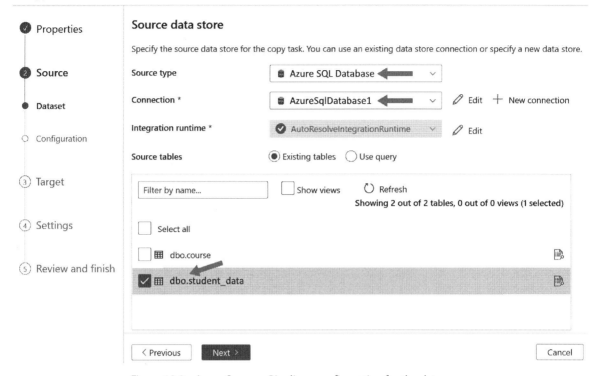

Figure 12.9 – Azure Synapse Pipelines configuration for the data copy

Under **Source | Configuration**, keep the settings as their defaults and click the blue **Next** > button again.

In the next section, we will configure the destination – fill in the following settings according to the following figure:

- **Target type**: Azure Synapse dedicated SQL pool
- **Connection**: packtdedicatedsqlpool
- **Auto-create a destination table with the source schema**: Click on this item as shown in the following screenshot:

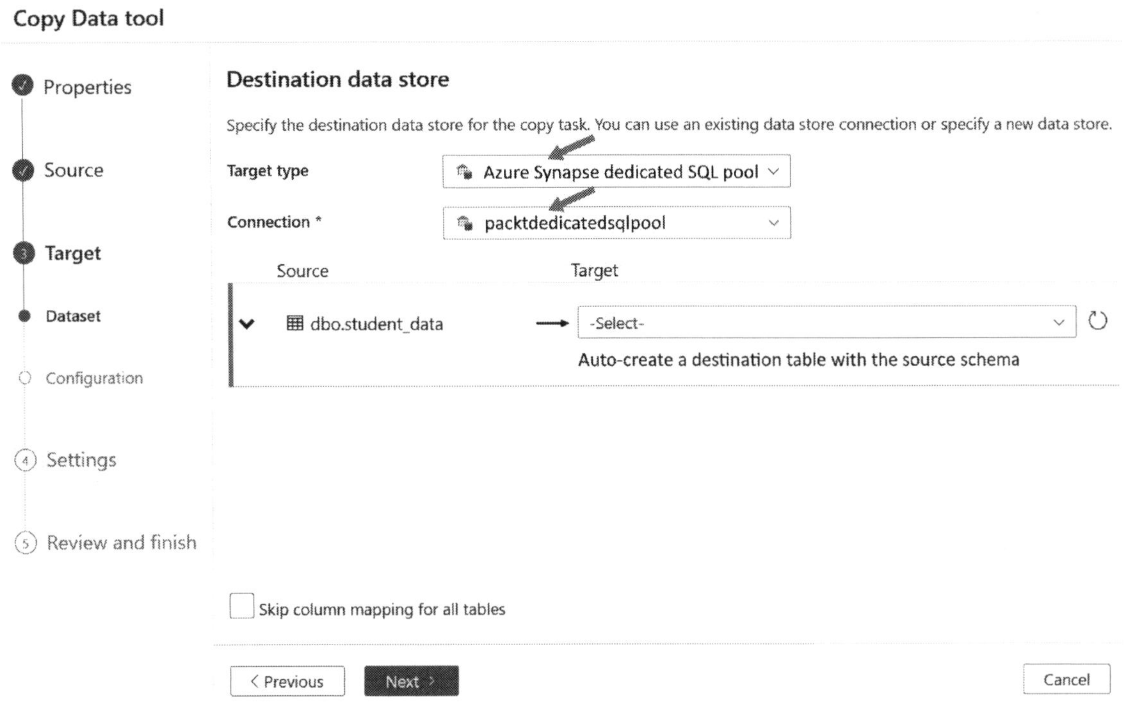

Copy Data tool

- Properties

- Source

- **Target**

- Dataset

- Configuration

- Settings

- Review and finish

Destination data store

Specify the destination data store for the copy task. You can use an existing data store connection or specify a new data store.

Target type   Azure Synapse dedicated SQL pool ∨

Connection *   packtdedicatedsqlpool   ∨

Source   Target

∨ ⊞ dbo.student_data ⟶ -Select-   ∨ ↻

Auto-create a destination table with the source schema

☐ Skip column mapping for all tables

< Previous   **Next >**   Cancel

Figure 12.10 – Azure Synapse Pipelines destination data store configuration

Keep the name of the table to be generated as dbo.student_data and click on the blue **Next >** button.

In the following section, **Column mapping**, Azure Synapse will help you define the columns that will be created in your dedicated SQL pool if you need to change a data type or the name of a column.

> **Important note**
>
> There are different data types between the SQL Server standard (used by Azure SQL Database) and the Azure Synapse SQL dedicated pool pattern, due to the architectural differences between the two software. Data types supported by Azure Synapse dedicated SQL pool can be found in the official Azure documentation here: https://docs.microsoft.com/en-us/azure/synapse-analytics/sql/develop-tables-data-types.

Go to the **Next >** button and fill out the form with the following settings:

- **Task name**: CopyPipeline_packt2
- **Copy method**: Bulk insert

Keep the other settings as recommended and then click on the **Next** > button again twice to start running your Azure Synapse Pipelines package. Your result after execution should be like the following print, validating the execution of the data copy:

Deployment complete

Deployment step	Status
Validating copy runtime environment	✓ Succeeded
❯ Creating datasets	✓ Succeeded
❯ Creating pipelines	✓ Succeeded
❯ Running pipelines	✓ Succeeded

Datasets and pipelines have been created. You can now monitor and edit the copy pipelines or click finish to close Copy Data Tool.

Figure 12.11 – Azure Synapse Pipelines deployment complete

Click on the blue **Finish** button and return to the **Data** item in the left-hand menu of Azure Synapse Studio. Browse the items: **Workspace**, **SQL database**, **packtdedicatedsqlpool (SQL)**, and then **Tables**.

Under **Tables**, you will find the dbo.student_data item. Right-click on this table, click on **New SQL script**, and then click on the **Select TOP 1000 rows** option to get the result as follows:

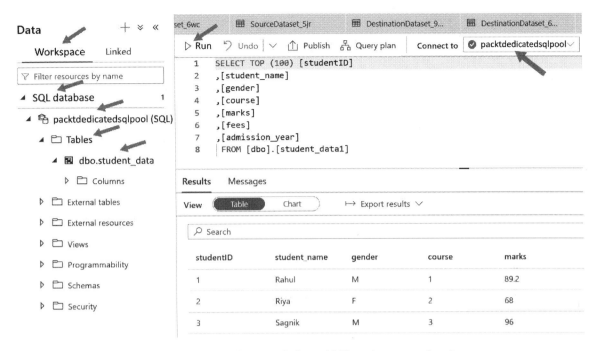

Figure 12.12 – Azure Synapse dedicated SQL pool query exploration

You have this query available in the GitHub repository of this book in the Chapter12 folder as //
Step 2 in the Chapter12.sql file.

Using this logic, you can move semi-structured and structured data to new or existing tables from
the dedicated SQL pool to generate your data model.

You can also use standard SQL Server tools to connect to and administer the dedicated SQL pool,
such as SQL Server Management Studio, Visual Studio Data Tools, and Azure Data Studio.

Now, let's prepare the Synapse dedicated SQL pool, our data warehouse, for the next chapter of this
book, where we will explore a model of facts and dimensions using Power BI. To do this, return to the
GitHub repository, the Chapter12 folder, and copy the //Step 3 query in the chapter12.
sql file.

Paste this query into the dedicated SQL pool query executions window and click the **Run** button. The
script will create the tables and add records to the proposed data model.

Now that we know the data processing options using SQL pools and we explored these possibilities,
let's learn about Azure Synapse's third data processing option, Spark pools.

Azure Spark pools

A major breakthrough with Azure Synapse Analytics is it having a powerful standard open source parallel processor, *Apache Spark*, as a data processing option, using big data techniques within Azure Synapse Studio.

One or more Spark pools can be provisioned in Azure Synapse Studio and each pool is the representation of a parallelized processing Spark cluster. Here are some important settings for each Spark pool:

- **Name**: The name of your Spark pool.

- **Capacity**: The sizing of the servers and the number of servers that will be part of the cluster. You can opt for a GPU server within this configuration and still set whether you will have auto-scaling in this pool or not.

- **Spark Runtime**: This option defines whether your Spark pool will implement some libraries in your installation, such as Python and Java.

> **Important note**
>
> If you are planning to mount a Spark pool, I recommend this official configuration documentation for Azure Synapse Spark pools. In it, you will find all the details relevant to their implementation:
>
> ```
> https://docs.microsoft.com/en-us/azure/synapse-analytics/spark/
> apache-spark-pool-configurations
> ```

To provision your *Spark pool*, access **Manage** on the left-hand menu of Azure Synapse Studio and then click on **Apache Spark pools**.

On this page, you can create your Spark pool by clicking **New Apache Spark pool**. The following settings page should open for you to fill in:

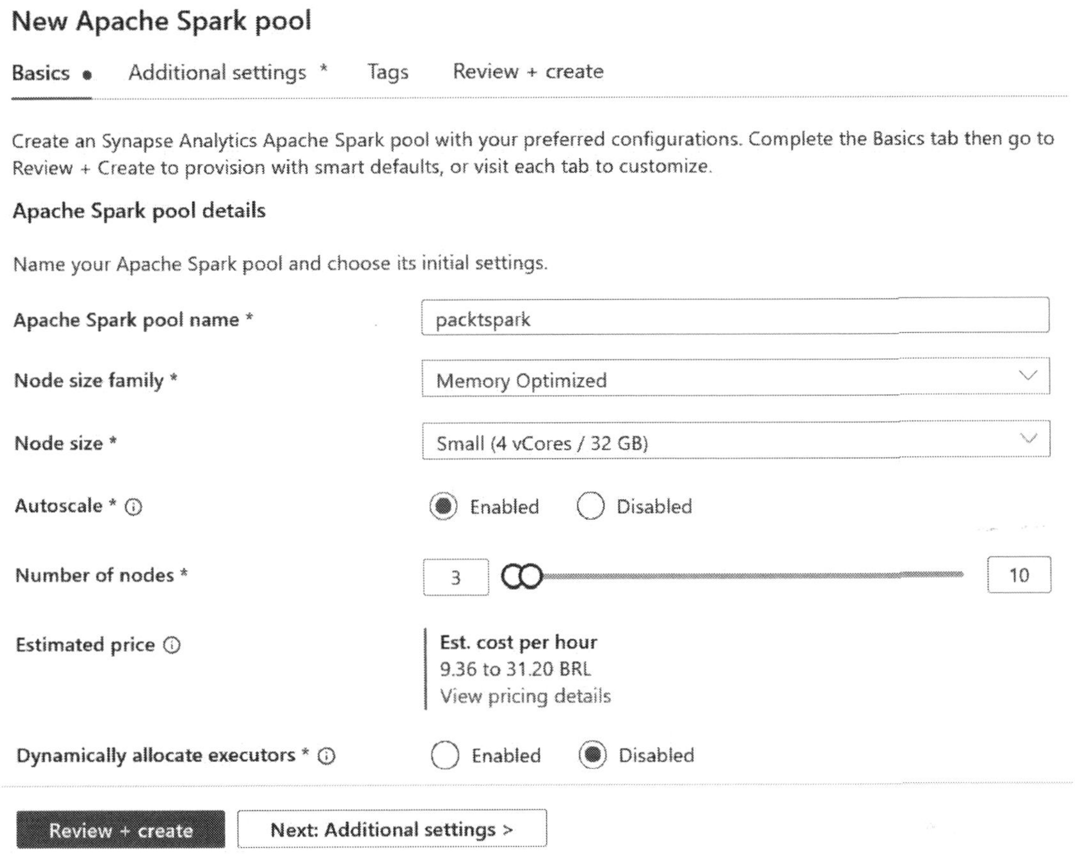

New Apache Spark pool

Basics •   Additional settings *   Tags   Review + create

Create an Synapse Analytics Apache Spark pool with your preferred configurations. Complete the Basics tab then go to Review + Create to provision with smart defaults, or visit each tab to customize.

Apache Spark pool details

Name your Apache Spark pool and choose its initial settings.

Apache Spark pool name *	packtspark
Node size family *	Memory Optimized ⌄
Node size *	Small (4 vCores / 32 GB) ⌄
Autoscale * ⓘ	◉ Enabled ◯ Disabled
Number of nodes *	3 ⚭————————————— 10
Estimated price ⓘ	**Est. cost per hour** 9.36 to 31.20 BRL View pricing details
Dynamically allocate executors * ⓘ	◯ Enabled ◉ Disabled

[Review + create]   [Next: Additional settings >]

Figure 12.13 – Azure Synapse Spark pool provisioning page

Fill the form out with the following information:

- **Apache Spark pool name**: packtspark
- **Node size family**: Memory Optimized
- **Node size**: Small (4 vCores / 32 GB)
- **Autoscale: Enabled**
- **Number of nodes: 3**
- **Estimated price: 9.36 to 31.20 BRL**
- **Dynamically allocate executors: Disabled**

Click on the blue **Review + create** button and then on **Create** to begin pool provisioning.

After confirming that your Spark pool is available for use, Azure Synapse Studio alerts you to navigate to the **Develop** item in the left-hand menu.

Click on the + button and then on **Notebook**, as shown in the following figure:

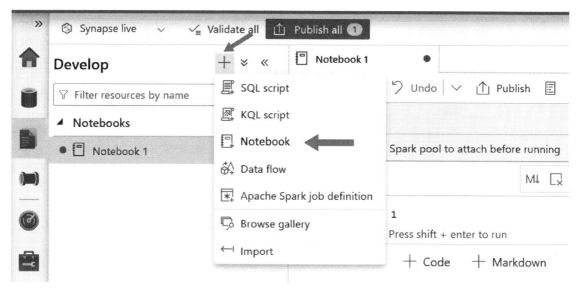

Figure 12.14 – Azure Synapse Studio | Develop – new notebook page

In your new notebook, set the options at the top as shown in the following screenshot. These settings indicate which *Spark pool* your notebook will run in and what notebook interpretation language you want for processing:

Figure 12.15 – Azure Synapse Studio | Develop – Notebook configurations

To test some Spark processing, you can search for sample notebooks on the internet or use the Solutions Gallery in Azure Synapse Studio to search for references from Spark notebook implementation use cases. The gallery can be accessed from the **Develop** menu by clicking on the + button and then on **Browse gallery**:

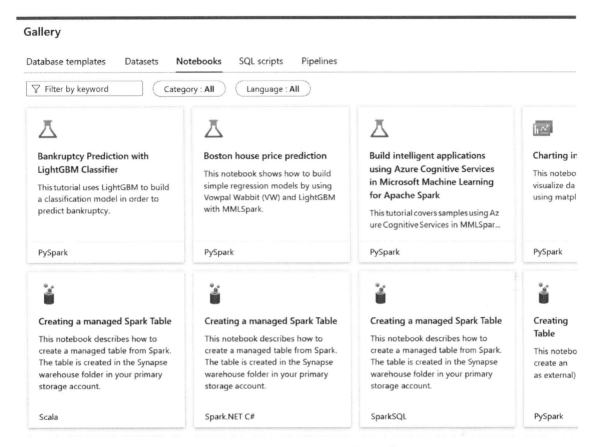

Figure 12.16 – Azure Synapse Studio – gallery

If you want to test notebook execution, I suggest following the tutorial available at this link: `https://docs.microsoft.com/en-us/azure/synapse-analytics/machine-learning/quickstart-gallery-sample-notebook`.

For this notebook, we will give a complete example, both of running Apache Spark in Azure Synapse and building a machine learning model for it.

> **Case**
>
> As our goal in this book is mainly to prepare you for the DP-900 certification, it is not necessary that you practice writing Spark scripts and executing notebooks, as this is not required knowledge. However, if you want to explore Spark pools further, I suggest starting with this Power BI data exploration and report creation tutorial based on Spark processing: `https://docs.microsoft.com/en-us/azure/synapse-analytics/spark/apache-spark-to-power-bi`.

With this, we have completed our exploration of the main data processors in Azure Synapse Analytics. In the next section, we will cover an overview of the other relevant components, depending on the use case.

Azure Synapse Link

One of the most time-consuming activities for a data engineer is the ingestion of data because they must evaluate whether it is necessary, along with the complexity of streaming data in near real time, whether batch loads meet, and with what recurrence in the load.

Azure Synapse Link is a recent Azure project for **hybrid transactional/analytical processing** (**HTAP**), which aims to simplify this process of data ingestion.

Link enables Synapse SQL pools to access data from transactional databases (SQL and NoSQL) directly by synchronizing data for a read replica, which creates a near-real-time interface.

Currently (as of August 2022), the available links are as follows:

- SQL Server
- Azure SQL Database
- Azure Cosmos DB
- Dataverse

Each link has a process for implementation. To deploy Azure Synapse Link to SQL Server, for example, you need to run a series of configurations, which are described at the following link: `https:// microsoftlearning.github.io/mslearn-synapse/Instructions/Labs/09- Synapse-link-sql.html`.

Azure Synapse Link, while very important for increasing your productivity when deploying data projects in Azure, is not necessary for the DP-900 exam. The goal of including these components here is so that you have a knowledge base and can research the situations you will face in real-life projects.

So, let's get to know another Azure Synapse Analytics processor, Azure Synapse Data Explorer.

Azure Synapse Data Explorer

This is a version of Azure Data Explorer within Azure Synapse Studio. Data Explorer is a time data processor, which is very interesting for event log processing use cases.

You can use Azure Synapse Data Explorer in data preparation routines, time series anomaly detection, and near real-time processing cases, among other things.

The difference with this version of Data Explorer is that because you are within Azure Synapse Studio, you can integrate this log processing into other processes using notebooks or SQL scripts in your data project.

To create an Azure Synapse Data Explorer pool to evaluate the service, go to the **Manage** item in the left-hand menu of Azure Synapse Studio and then click **Data Explorer pools (preview)**:

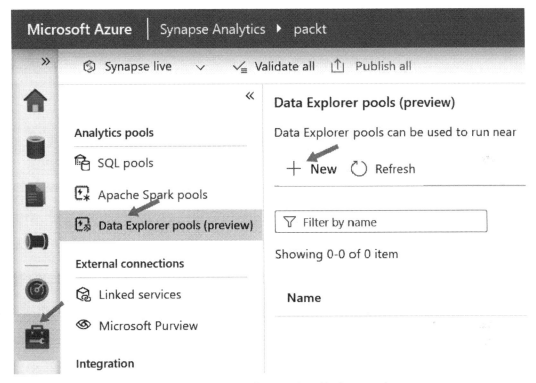

Figure 12.17 – Azure Synapse Data Explorer pools

In addition to processing data, data organizations extract great results through the use of machine learning on the part of data scientists. Therefore, your project may often need Azure Machine Learning, an Azure platform dedicated to working with machine learning models.

Wait, aren't we talking about Azure Synapse? Let's now understand the integration that exists between these two services.

Azure Machine Learning

Machine learning is a subset of artificial intelligence, which uses computers to *learn* based on statistical algorithms. Machine learning models can be developed based on notebooks in *Azure Synapse Spark pools* or in the specialized tool *Azure Machine Learning*, which is a dedicated platform for developing, deploying, and managing machine learning models.

This powerful tool can be implemented based on the concepts of **machine learning operations** (**MLOps**) to automate the life cycle of a machine learning model.

Azure Synapse can integrate with Azure Machine Learning so that the two services work together, providing all the necessary resources for data scientists.

To integrate Azure Machine Learning into Azure Synapse Studio, go to the **Manage** item in the left-hand menu, navigate **Linked Services** | **New**, and then search for `machine learning` in the list of services as follows:

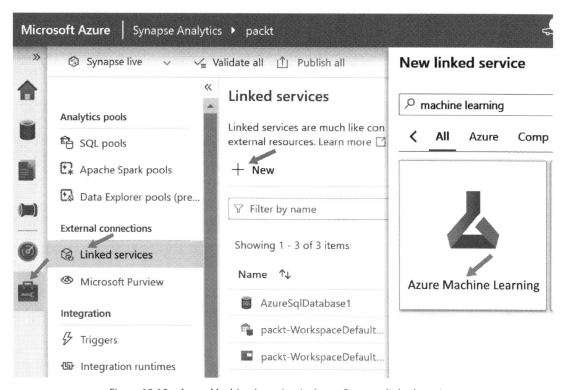

Figure 12.18 – Azure Machine Learning in Azure Synapse linked services

In the form that will open, you will have to provide the configuration parameters for Azure Synapse to connect to an Azure Machine Learning instance.

After successful integration, you will have one more possibility to call on the machine learning models developed in Azure Machine Learning directly in Azure Synapse Analytics, as shown in the following example of running a model on the `student_data1` table from our *dedicated SQL pool*:

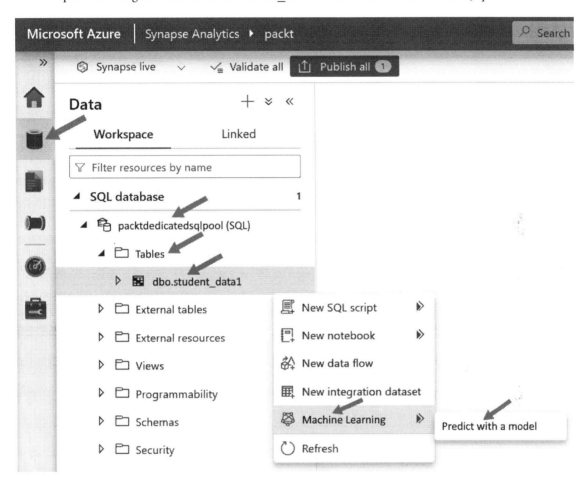

Figure 12.19 – Azure Synapse with Azure Machine Learning integration

With that, we've covered all the most important Azure components for starting out with large-scale data analytics.

Summary

To implement a project with large-scale data analytics, Azure offers a variety of solutions, such as *Azure Synapse Analytics*, *Azure Databricks*, *Azure HDInsights*, *Azure Machine Learning*, and *Azure Data Explorer*, among others.

The DP-900 exam requires the knowledge to explore these options, with a greater focus on the motivations for using each tool, and has some more detailed questions based on *Azure Synapse Analytics*, which is the main Azure platform for these projects. The knowledge gained in this chapter and our exploration of the tool is not only very important for answering these questions but also for directing your path when it comes to a real-life project.

To sum up what we covered in the chapter, we started by exploring the SQL pools further – serverless and dedicated – executing SQL scripts to exercise them. Then, we had an overview of the Spark pools, Data Explorer pools, Azure Synapse Link, and the integration of Azure Synapse with Azure Machine Learning.

In the next chapter, we will turn this data into rich reports, indicators, and presentations of our results through the use of *Power BI*.

Sample questions and answers

Let's go through a few more possible questions about large-scale data analytics from the *DP-900* test:

1. Which of the Azure data services enables clusters of Apache Spark and SQL pools?

    A. Azure Databricks

    B. Azure SQL Database

    C. Azure Synapse Analytics

    D. Azure Spark

2. Select the true statement:

    A. ETL can reduce the transfer of sensitive data to destination systems.

    B. ELT transforms data by using a computer resource independent of the source system and destination system.

    C. ELT can reduce the transfer of sensitive data to destination systems.

    D. ETL transforms data by using a computer resource independent of the source system and destination system.

3. Complete the sentence: _____ presents content defined by a query.

    A. An index

    B. A view

    C. A stored procedure

    D. A notebook

4. Complete the sentence: If you need to process data that is generated continuously and near real-time responses are required, you should use _____.

   A. Scheduled data processing

   B. Buffering and processing

   C. Streaming data processing

   D. Batch data processing

5. Complete the sentence with the best option:

   _____ analytics is a technique that suggests the steps you should take to accomplish a goal or aim.

   A. Descriptive

   B. Prescriptive

   C. Diagnostic

   D. Predictive

Answer key

1-A 2-B 3-B 4-C 5-B

13

Working with
Power BI

The previous chapter showed us, through hands-on examples, how to use the most important Azure Data Analytics services, but how can we present the results after the data analysis? We will cover this topic in this chapter by exploring *Power BI*, which is the frontend platform of Microsoft.

This chapter contributes to the *Skills Measured* part of the *Describe an analytics workload on Azure* part of the DP-900 certification since a few questions about Power BI are included in the exam, but we will explore this a little bit more to give you the foundations to help you get started with your projects.

In this chapter, we'll discuss the concepts and different components of Power BI and explore the tool using a hands-on exercise that will connect Power BI with the Azure Synapse Analytics SQL Pool database we created in *Chapter 12, Provisioning and Configuring Large-Scale Data Analytics in Azure*.

By the end of this chapter, you have an end-to-end view of a modern data warehouse with a business intelligence solution that supports your projects in this area that can help you answer possible DP-900 questions.

In this chapter, we will cover the following topics:

- Using Power BI
- The building blocks of Power BI
- Exploring Power BI Desktop
- Exploring Power BI service
- Other versions of Power BI – Premium, Embedded, and Report Server
- Power BI mobile app

So, let's start by discussing the concepts surrounding Power BI.

Technical requirements

To be able to follow the hands-on sections of this chapter, you will need a Power BI account. If you don't already have one, now is a great time for you to create a free trial account. To register, you can go to `https://go.microsoft.com/fwlink/?LinkId=874445`.

You can find this chapter's example file in this book's GitHub repository at `https://github.com/PacktPublishing/Microsoft-Certified-Azure-Data-Fundamentals-Exam-DP-900-Certification-Guide/tree/main/Chapter13`.

Introducing Power BI

Power BI is a complete **business intelligence** (**BI**) tool that's composed of various apps and services to meet any needs in terms of data consumption and analysis.

With Power BI, it is possible for a *business user*, with no technical skills, to create data source connections between different databases such as SQL Server, Oracle, Excel spreadsheets, and CSV files, among others, and create self-service analyses.

Power BI's simplicity and similarity to the other software in the Office 365 suite make it a *leader* in the self-service BI market, which is a branch of BI that allows the end user to perform their own analysis and not just consume pre-built reports.

Power BI can be used to create reports that visualize data stored in databases or to create near-real-time reports that are used for *immediate decision-making*. In addition to these capabilities, it also has tools for applying AI models to the data, assisting in its exploration and complex *data modeling*.

Now, let's get to know the components of the Power BI tool.

The building blocks of Power BI

Power BI is a multi-component solution that is used in a sequence of activities, often by different user profiles, from creating connections and data work to developing a report, and from publishing this report to consuming the information provided by it.

The following figure represents this Power BI flow, which starts with Power BI Desktop, which involves developer users, through to Power BI Service, where reports are published, and even Power BI App, where reports are consumed by business users:

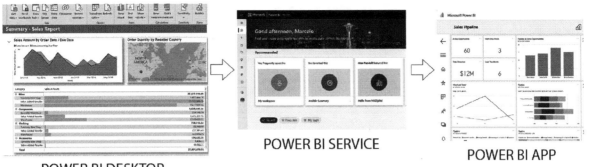

POWER BI DESKTOP   POWER BI SERVICE   POWER BI APP

Figure 13.1 – Power BI's basic suite of tools and services

Let's understand each of these components:

- **Power BI Desktop**: This is a Windows desktop tool for report development and data modeling. It has advanced connection, modeling, and data visualization capabilities.

- **Power BI Service**: This environment is used to share reports and data models so that other members of your organization can consume them. This service focuses on all administration, parameterizations, connections, and access controls to reports.

  Power BI Service is organized by *workspaces*, which are containers that are similar to Windows folders, where each user owns their workspace and can view the other workspaces that have been shared with it.

- **Power BI App**: This tool provides free apps for Windows, Mac, Android, and iOS for reporting, exploring, and connecting to Power BI Service.

In addition to these fundamental components, there are additional versions of Power BI that come in the form of licenses, as follows:

- **Power BI Pro license**: Power BI Pro is a Power BI license that's needed to access Power BI Service, as well as to access Workspaces so that you can share reports with other users. It's unusual to come across license-related questions in the DP-900 exam, but for completeness, the Power BI Pro license can be used in two ways:

  - A license is needed for all users that will share reports in one organization, independent of whether these users will be publishers or viewers on Power BI Service

  - A license is needed just for publisher users, as well as a license for Power BI Premium per capacity, to enable unlimited users to read the reports

- **Power BI Premium license**: This is a special type of *workspace* in Power BI Service that increases the capabilities of the traditional workspace, providing greater service limits and additional features. Power BI Premium licenses can be activated in two modes:

  - **Per Capacity**: The workspace will be a dedicated capacity resource for the organization, with unlimited read-only user access for free. To publish in this environment, you need a Power BI Pro license. Power BI Premium per capacity license gives the organization rights to deploy a Power BI report server, which we will cover in the next topic.

  - **Per User**: The workspace will have the specialized features of the Premium license, but it will just be enabled for the users that have Power BI Premium per user. All features found in Power BI Pro can be found in Power BI Premium per user.

> **Important note**
>
> Paginated reports are reports that have been formatted so that they can be printed or distributed. Typically, they fit on a standard print page, hence the name paginated reports. They are a unique feature of Power BI Premium workspaces. They are not created in Power BI Desktop; instead, they are created in a specialized tool called **Power BI Report Builder**. Go to the following URL to download Power BI Report Builder: `https://www.microsoft.com/en-us/download/details.aspx?id=58158`.

- **Power BI Report Server**: This is a version of Power BI Service that can be deployed manually in any Windows Server in the cloud, in data centers on-premises, and more. It's used to host Power BI reports on-premises or in Azure Virtual Machines. Its features compared to Power BI Service are limited, because the purpose of Power BI Report Server is to host the reports, wherever they are. However, it doesn't have all the Power BI Service features such as management, collaboration, and artificial intelligence to help with report exploration.

- **Power BI Embedded**: This is a Power BI reports host service that *embeds* these reports into development applications. Power BI Embedded can be provisioned in a Power BI Premium per capacity license, reserving part of your dedicated capacity, or on the Azure portal, provisioning a Power BI Embedded instance.

Now that we've had an overview of the components of Power BI, let's look at some of them in more detail.

Exploring Power BI Desktop

Power BI Desktop is a complete tool for BI report development. The purpose of this book is not to cover all the products, but to show you the main features, such as connections, data modeling, and report creation.

To start using Power BI Desktop, you need to download and deploy the application on your system. It can be found on the Microsoft website at https://www.microsoft.com/en-us/download/details.aspx?id=58494 or in the Windows Store, the Windows operating system app store.

After installing Power BI Desktop on your computer, open the application so that we can start exploring. When you open Power BI Desktop, the following window will appear:

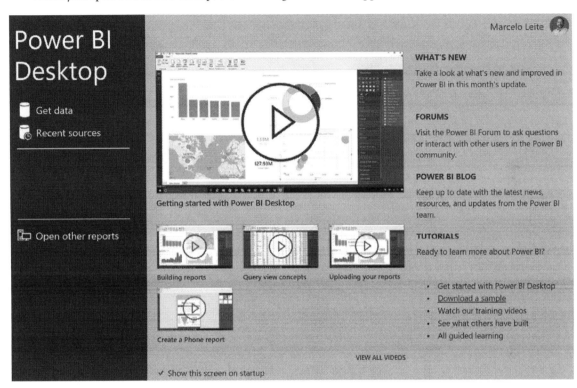

Figure 13.2 – Power BI Desktop home window

In this window, we have access to introductory Power BI videos and their resources, as well as blog access links for updates, discussion forums, tutorials, and samples. This is also where we can start creating our connections in databases.

Creating a Power BI file

Let's start creating our first Power BI file:

1. Click the **Get data** button in the home window.

2. Search for `Azure Synapse Analytics SQL` in the list of connectors and fill in the following information:

   • **Server**: `packt.sql.azuresynapse.net`.

   • **Database**: Keep this field empty; we will not select one specific database. Instead, we will connect to the entire server instance of this Azure Synapse SQL dedicated pool.

   • **Data Connectivity mode**: `Import`.

> **Note**
>
> Power BI allows two types of connection – **Import**, which copies data from the data source for Power BI to run the scripts locally, or **DirectQuery**, which sends the query to the data source, which only returns the result to be displayed in Power BI.

3. If Power BI asks you to authenticate, click **Database** in the left-hand menu and fill in the following data. Then, click the yellow **Connect** button:

   • **User name**: `packtadmin`

   • **Password**: `Pass@word#123`

> **Important note**
>
> If you are unable to establish this connection, return to Azure Synapse Analytics workspaces, go to Synapse Studio, and click **Manage** in the left-hand side menu. Here, check whether **packtsqldedicatedpool** is turned on or not. If it's **paused**, click to turn it on; leave its **Status** set to **Online**.

4. You should be directed to a window that shows all databases, tables, and fields per table that are available in this database. Click to select entities (columns/tables if your data is table-based). Here, we will select `dim_customer`, `dim_product`, and `fact_sales`. Then, click the yellow **Load** button, as shown here:

Navigator   □ ✕

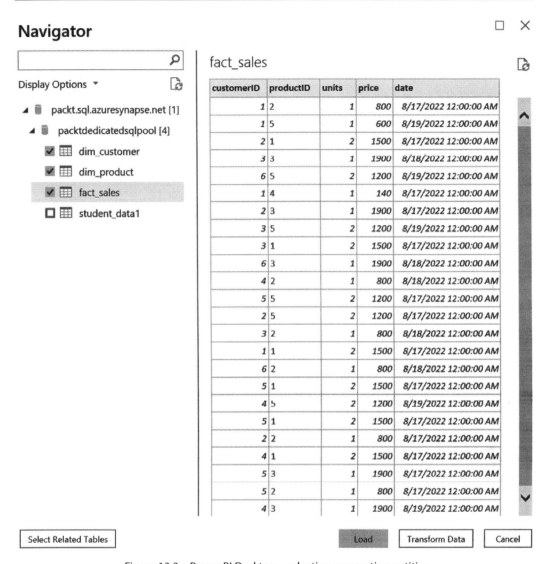

Figure 13.3 – Power BI Desktop – selecting connection entities

As we can see, in addition to selecting only the entities that we want to import into the Power BI model, we also have the **Transform Data** button so that we can prepare the data. **Transform Data** will open Power Query, a Power BI module dedicated to data transformations and preparations.

After clicking the **Load** button, we have to wait a few seconds. Power BI has already understood the schema of this entity (or the multiple entities if you are connected to multiple at the same time) and imported the metadata from this data source into your Power BI file. This metadata is used to create reports, perform data preparations, and more.

Creating a connection

After loading, start exploring the top menu, where you have the option to create a connection, manage existing connections in the file, or open Power Query to perform data preparation, among others.

The left-hand side menu contains three items – one for *reporting* development, one shows the tabular entities of the *data model*, and one where we can visualize the data model and its *relationships*:

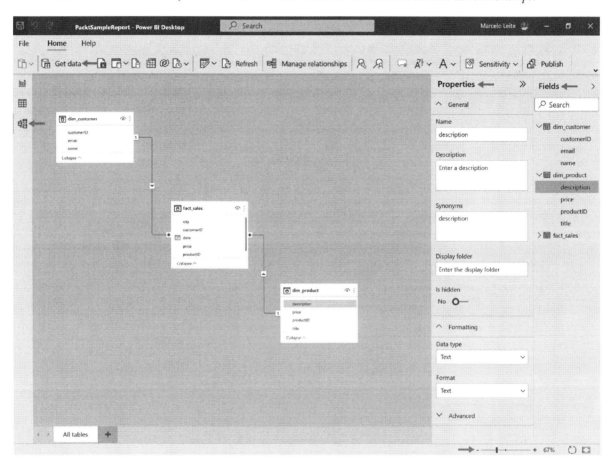

Figure 13.4 – Power BI Desktop – model section

The right-hand side menu consists of different windows. As shown in *Figure 13.4*, we can see **Properties** and **Fields**. These windows are dynamic. With each selection that we make in Power BI Desktop, the settings for the properties of the selected object are changed. The **Fields** window is important as it shows that all the fields can be used to assemble your Power BI reports.

As we can see in the bottom-left corner of Power BI Desktop (*Figure 13.4*), we have the same tab concept as other Microsoft Office 365 Suite tools, where we can have a set of different reports in this same file, plus options to **zoom** in at the bottom right.

In Power BI, we can explore the concepts of *data modeling*, which we covered in *Chapter 5, Exploring Data Analytics Concepts*, because we can create Fact/Dimension tabular models using the Power BI suite or consume them from a data warehouse, as we are doing in this exercise.

Click the **Report** button on the left-hand side menu of the screen. This is the workspace for assembling the reports, So, let's go to the **Fields** window on the right-hand side and select the following fields:

- **Dim_customer**: name

- **Fact_sales**: units

Once you select these two fields, Power BI interprets the relationships between the entities and calculates the number of units that each customer has purchased.

We can explore the chart options to demonstrate these results. For example, you can click on the bars shown in the following screenshot to check the aggregation of the quantities per customer:

Figure 13.5 – Power BI Desktop – the report section

Let's try something. With this chart selected, check the **price** field on the right-hand side. In the **Visualizations** tab, click the **Table** icon to return the chart to tabular format, click the down arrow next to the **price** column, and click **Sum**, as shown in the following screenshot:

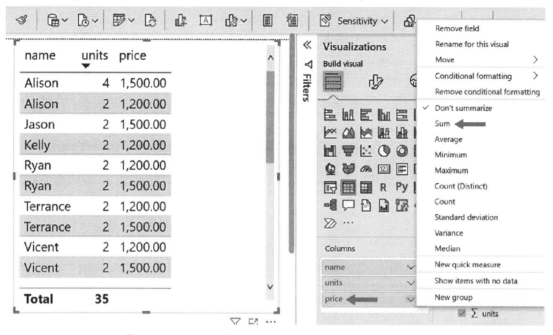

Figure 13.6 – Power BI Desktop – making report adjustments

By doing this, you have adjusted your chart to aggregate total sales per customer, demonstrating the units and total value purchased.

Publishing a report

Following this logic, you can assemble complex reports by using the various graphical and calculation possibilities of Power BI. You can explore other chart types in the **Visualizations** tab, such as line charts, pie charts, and scatter charts.

To facilitate this exploration, we continued to explore Power BI's capabilities; a complete result file of this exploration can be found in this book's GitHub repository. So, go to this book's GitHub repository, go to the `Chapter13` folder, and download and open the `PacktSampleReport.pbix` file in your Power BI desktop application.

> **Note**
> If Power BI returns a message stating that you can't connect to the data source, you must set up a connection to Azure Synapse Analytics, as we explored in the *Creating a connection* section earlier in this chapter, so that you can update the report.

Now, let's click the **Publish** button, which can be found by going to the **Home** tab of Power BI Desktop. Before publishing, Power BI will prompt you to save this PBIX file (Power BI report file), choose a location on your computer, and save it.

After saving this file, Power BI will display a Workspace selection window where you can publish your report to Power BI Service. Select **My Workspace** and click the yellow **Publish** button.

Once the report has been published, you will see the following window in Power BI Desktop, where you have the option to **Open PacktSampleReport.pbix in Power BI**. Click this option, as shown in the following screenshot:

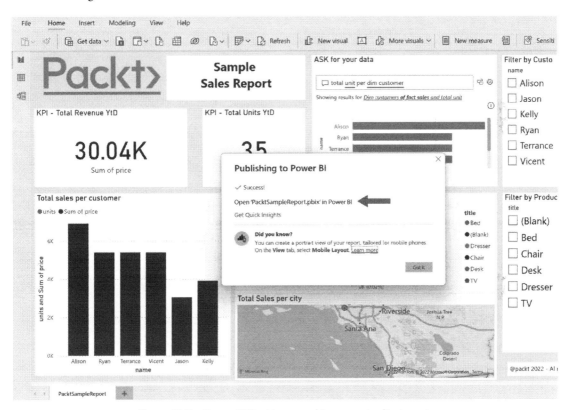

Figure 13.7 – Power BI Desktop – making report adjustments

Your browser will open the respective Power BI page. Now, let's explore Power BI Service.

Exploring Power BI Service

As explained earlier, Power BI Service is where reports are stored and the entire Power BI operation is administered. You can find Power BI Service at `https://app.powerbi.com/`.

In the Power BI Service portal, you can share your reports, define conditional viewing rules with **row-level security** and **column-level security**, package your reports into **apps**, and create interactive dashboards based on one or more reports, among other things:

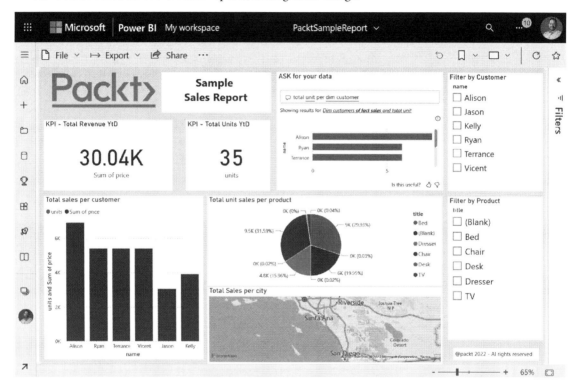

Figure 13.8 – The sample report opened in Power BI Service

From the left menu, you can switch to other sections of Power BI Service. The top menu is where report actions are performed, such as printing, sharing, applying artificial intelligence to the data to get insights (the **Get Insights** button), and subscribing to receive notifications about updates regarding the report data, among others.

Creating a dashboard

To guide this exploration, we will create a dashboard. To do this, look for a **pin** button on the report bar chart, as shown in the following screenshot, and click **Pin visual**:

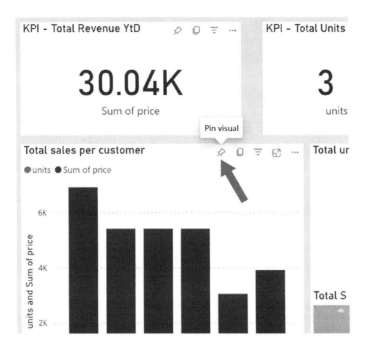

Figure 13.9 – The Pin visual button in Power BI Service

Click the **New Dashboard** option, set **Dashboard name** to PacktDashboard, and confirm this by clicking the yellow **Pin** button:

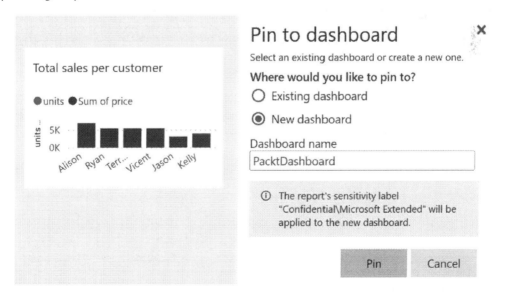

Figure 13.10 – The Pin to dashboard window in Power BI Service

On the dashboard confirmation window, you can access the visuals, and by repeating this pin operation on multiple Power BI report objects, you can create very interesting dashboards that organize various pieces of information.

A Power BI dashboard is a centralized information page that's widely used as a cockpit to monitor indicators of different Power BI reports. A well-designed dashboard only presents the highlights of a story; you can dig into the details in the reports.

Now that we've explored reports and dashboards in Power BI Service, let's get to know the Power BI mobile app.

Power BI mobile app

The Power BI mobile app is used to consume Power BI reports and dashboards, explore data, and interact with platform users.

To get started, download the Power BI mobile app on your Android or iOS phone, or your Windows computer. You can find all these versions at `https://powerbi.microsoft.com/en-us/downloads/`.

Open the app and sign in with your Power BI username and password.

Then, click on **Workspaces** from the left-hand side menu and then on **My Workspace**. On this page, you should find your **PacktSampleReport** report and **PacktDashboard**. Open **PacktDashboard** to begin exploring the dashboard, as follows:

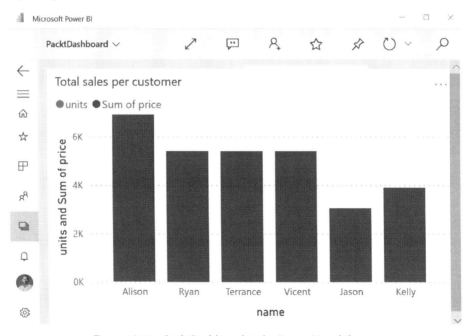

Figure 13.11 – PacktDashboard in the Power BI mobile app

Here, you can explore the top menu options. There are several cool features here, such as the **Comments** button, which allows Power BI users to collaborate and discuss.

This simple dashboard only contains one chart, but you can create dashboards with multiple visuals from different reports, consolidating the most important information on a single page.

To return to our report, click on the bar chart. Here, you can access the chart's details and explore your filter options. You'll also find a button in the top menu called **Open Report**, which will direct you to the **PacktSampleReport** report.

Click on it to access the report through the app:

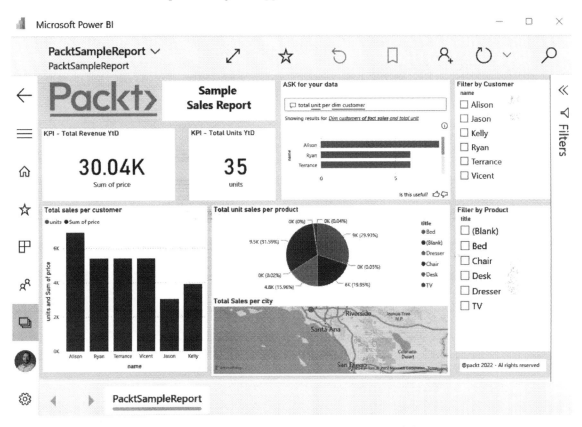

Figure 13.12 – PackSampleReport in the Power BI mobile app

With that, we've explored our Azure Synapse Analytics SQL Pool database using Power BI and consumed it in reports and dashboards using the Power BI mobile app.

Microsoft has specific certifications for Power BI professionals, such as *PL-300 – Microsoft Power BI Data Analytics*, so the questions that are often found in the DP-900 test are simple and related to the topics covered in this chapter.

Now, let's review everything we've learned in this chapter.

Summary

Power BI is a key part of any data analytics project in Azure. For this reason, some basic questions about the service structure have been added to the DP-900 test.

It is important to remember the different modules mentioned in this chapter, namely *Power BI Desktop*, *Power BI Service*, the *Power BI mobile app*, *Power BI Report Server*, *Power BI Premium*, and *Power BI Embedded*.

In the next chapter, we will review all the knowledge you've acquired in this book in terms of commented questions and answers so that you are even more prepared to pass the *DP-900* exam and create data projects in Azure.

But first, let's consider some sample questions and answers related to Power BI.

Sample questions and answers

Try answering the following questions to test your knowledge of this chapter's content:

1. Which of the following advantages doesn't have a direct connection to Power BI's interactive reports?

    A. AI-powered augmented analytics

    B. Easy data preparation and modeling

    C. Advanced analytics with knowledge of MS Office

    D. Ideal for large and medium-sized businesses with the necessary human resources to support data analytics

2. Consider the following statements:

    • S1: Explore and collaborate with the reposts in the Power BI mobile app

    • S2: Connect and ingest data in Power BI Desktop

    • S3: Share dashboards with other users in the organization

    • S4: Create a report and publish it to Power BI Service

Which of the following iterations of the aforementioned sentences best captures the typical flow of events in Power BI?

A. S1-S2-S4-S3

B. S2-S1-S3-S4

C. S2-S4-S3-S1

D. S2-S3-S1-S4

3. Which two scenarios are the best for Power BI paginated reports? Each correct response offers a full resolution:

A. A report that has a table visual with the ability to print all the data in the table

B. A report with a repeatable header and footer

C. A report that has a table visual with the ability to see all the data in the table

D. A report that uses only Power BI visuals

4. Which activity can be performed entirely by using Power BI Service?

A. Data acquisition

B. Report and dashboard creation

C. Data modeling

D. Data preparation

5. For which reason should you use a Power BI dashboard?

A. To develop a new type of report

B. To interact with the data

C. To consolidate information in a single page, with visuals from one or multiple reports

D. To share the report with other data users in the organization

Answer key

1-D 2-C 3-A, B 4-B 5-C

14

DP-900 Mock Exam

Before we start, congratulations on completing all the chapters! Our learning journey started with storage concepts, databases, and data analytics, through key Azure services to implement these concepts, and you're now ready for the *DP-900* certification test.

The *DP-900 – Microsoft Azure Data Fundamentals* exam will provide you with an official Microsoft certification that is intended for professionals who want to certify that they have knowledge of fundamental data concepts and the associated Microsoft Azure data services.

After this fundamental certification, you can specialize in Azure role-based certifications such as *Azure Database Administrator Associate* or *Azure Data Engineer Associate*. To be prepared for these certifications, I suggest you gain experience in implementing projects.

To prepare for any test, we should have a full review of the topics, but it's very important to be prepared to be tested in an exam as well. That's what we're going to do in this chapter: simulate a real exam.

Practice test – questions

This exam simulation is based on *20 questions*, so it'll be fast. First, try to answer the questions without looking at the explanations. When you complete the questionnaire, you can start evaluating the answers and explanations. After evaluating your score, read the explanations carefully, and you can access the reference documentation of issues that you might have missed where you marked incorrect answers.

Core data concepts

1. Select the correct statement:

    A. ( ) **Extract, transform, and load** (ETL) can limit the amount of sensitive data that is transferred to target systems

    B. ( ) **Extract, load, and transform** (ELT) reduces the amount of time needed to copy substantial amounts of data to the target systems

    C. ( ) **Extract, load, and transform** (ELT) transforms data utilizing a computational resource that is not dependent on the source or target systems

    D. ( ) **Extract, transform, and load** (ETL) transforms data utilizing a computational resource that is not dependent on the source or target systems

2. Select an option that best completes the following statement:

    The cloud benefit of increasing or decreasing resources as needed is called _____.

    A. ( ) Scaling

    B. ( ) Networking

    C. ( ) Computing

    D. ( ) Provisioning

3. Structured data is represented in the format of _____.

    A. ( ) Azure Data Explorer

    B. ( ) Document databases

    C. ( ) JSON

    D. ( ) Rows and columns in a table

4. A customer wants to implement a graph database. Select the best use case for this type of database structure:

    A. ( ) Analytical databases

    B. ( ) Reporting

    C. ( ) Exploring complex relationships

    D. ( ) Transactional databases

5. What is the objective of data normalization?

    A. ( ) Compiling complex SQL queries for data exploration

    B. ( ) Ideal for storing documents in tables

    C. ( ) Better performance for transactional databases

    D. ( ) Minimizing the number of tables in a database

Relational data on Azure

Answer the following questions:

1. Select the best option to complete the following sentence:

    _____ physically sorts the data in a table based on the values in a specified column.

    A. ( ) A view

    B. ( ) A clustered index

    C. ( ) A stored procedure

    D. ( ) A non-clustered index

2. When moving an existing SQL Server on-premises solution, which PaaS service offers the best compatibility?

    A. ( ) Azure SQL Database (single database)

    B. ( ) Azure SQL Database (elastic pool)

    C. ( ) Azure SQL Managed Instance

    D. ( ) Azure SQL Virtual Machines

3. Select the true statement about Azure SQL Managed Instance:

    A. ( ) It has a planned maintenance window

    B. ( ) You must purchase a SQL Server license

    C. ( ) It can only support one database

    D. ( ) You can connect to the operating system of the server

4.   Which of the following claims best describes a relational database?

   A.   ( ) A table's columns must all be of the same data type

   B.   ( ) Stores and organizes data points with defined relationships for fast access

   C.   ( ) The same table's rows can have various column combinations

   D.   ( ) A table's rows can store documents

5.   Which SQL statement is used to query rows and return data from tables?

   A.   ( ) QUERY

   B.   ( ) CREATE

   C.   ( ) SELECT

   D.   ( ) INSERT

Non-relational data on Azure

Answer the following questions:

1.   Which of the following options best completes this sentence:

   On Azure Table storage, you need to optimize the data retrieval. You should use _____ as query criteria.

   A.   ( ) Properties

   B.   ( ) Row keys

   C.   ( ) Partition and row keys

   D.   ( ) Partition keys

2.   Which of the following Azure data service options is recommended to implement a new graph database?

   A.   ( ) Azure Data Lake

   B.   ( ) Azure Blob Storage

   C.   ( ) Azure Table

   D.   ( ) Azure Cosmos DB

3. Complete the sentence. Using _____, I can provision Azure storage using a JSON file:

    A. ( ) **Azure Resource Manager (ARM)**

    B. ( ) The Azure portal

    C. ( ) The Azure **command-line interface (CLI)**

    D. ( ) Azure PowerShell

4. You are developing a solution with Azure Cosmos DB, and after your development, you want to delete all resources. What's the sequence of steps to perform this deletion?

    · 1—Access the resource group where Azure Cosmos DB was implemented

    · 2—Using the Azure portal, search for resource groups

    · 3—Type the resource group name and click on **Delete**

    · 4—Click on **Delete Resource Group**

    A. ( ) S1 – S2 – S3 – S4

    B. ( ) S2 – S1 – S3 – S4

    C. ( ) S1 – S3 – S4 – S2

    D. ( ) S2 – S1 – S4 – S3

5. You want to implement an Apache Spark cluster for data science. Which Azure services can be used for this scenario?

    A. ( ) Azure Synapse Analytics

    B. ( ) Azure Databricks

    C. ( ) Azure HDInsight

    D. ( ) Azure SQL Database

Modern data warehouse analytics on Azure

Answer the following questions:

1. What's the language used in Azure Synapse Data Explorer to explore data?

    A. ( ) SQL

    B. ( ) Java

    C. ( ) KQL

    D. ( ) T-SQL

2. Select the use case for implementing a data warehouse:

    A. ( ) Printing a receipt of a sales order

    B. ( ) Searching for the sales order status

    C. ( ) Recording sales transactions

    D. ( ) Exploring sales from last year

3. Select an answer that correctly completes the following sentence:

    The library that provides data stream processing for Apache Spark processes in Azure Databricks and Azure Synapse Analytics is called _____.

    A. ( ) Spark Structured Streaming library

    B. ( ) Spark Unstructured Streaming library

    C. ( ) Spark Streaming library

    D. ( ) Apache Spark does not support data stream processing

4. You are using Azure Data Factory, implementing data ingestion from Azure SQL Database. Which resources should you use for this connection? You can choose more than one answer for a complete solution.

    A. ( ) Dataset

    B. ( ) Copy data activity

    C. ( ) Linked service

    D. ( ) Azure Databricks notebook

5. You are using Power BI paginated reports. Which of these use cases can be implemented using Power BI paginated reports?

    A. ( ) Reports with a repeatable header and footer

    B. ( ) Reports formatted for printing

    C. ( ) Reports with custom dashboard visuals

    D. ( ) Reports with the ability to print the entire data in a table

Practice test – answers and explanations

Now that you have marked up your answers to the questions, in the following sections, we'll discuss how we can eliminate incorrect choices and mark the correct answer for these questions.

Core data concepts

1. Select the correct statement:

    A. ( ) **Extract, transform, and load** (**ETL**) can limit the amount of sensitive data that is transferred to target system.

    B. ( ) **Extract, load, and transform** (**ELT**) reduces the amount of time needed to copy substantial amounts of data to the target system.

    C. *(X) Extract, load, and transform (ELT) transforms data utilizing a computational resource that is not dependent on the source or target system.*

    D. ( ) **Extract, transform, and load** (**ETL**) transforms data utilizing a computational resource that is not dependent on the source or target systems

Explanation

- Option A is *incorrect* because, in ETL processes, it is often not evaluated whether the data is sensitive or not. For this analysis, it is interesting to add other tools—such as Microsoft Purview, for example.

- Option B is *incorrect* because ELT does not reduce the time to copy data between systems. Copy time varies with the total size and complexity of the data type being processed in ELT.

- Option C is **correct** because the main feature of the ELT process is that the data is first extracted from the data source, then uploaded to a data lake, and then transformed using modern data warehousing and big data techniques.

- Option D is *incorrect* because, in ETL processes, the transformation of the data occurs at the runtime of the data ingestion process—that is, the data is already copied under transformation to the analytical environment.

Here is a link to the reference documentation:

https://docs.microsoft.com/en-us/azure/architecture/data-guide/relational-data/etl

2. Select an option that best completes the following statement:

    The cloud benefit of increasing or decreasing resources as needed is called _____.

    A. *(X) Scaling*

    B. ( ) Networking

    C. ( ) Computing

    D. ( ) Provisioning

Explanation

- Option A is **correct** as it is the scalability of the cloud that allows us to increase or decrease our resources as needed

- Option B is *incorrect* because networking is the connectivity capability of the cloud

- Option C is *incorrect* because computing is what is provided by the cloud for the execution of processes

- Option D is *incorrect* because provisioning is the process we do to instantiate a new cloud service

Here is a link to the reference documentation:

```
https://docs.microsoft.com/learn/modules/explore-provision-deploy-
relational-database-offerings-azure/2-describe-provision-relational-
data-services
```

3. Structured data is represented in the format of _____.

   A. ( ) Azure Data Explorer

   B. ( ) Document databases

   C. ( ) JSON

   D. *(X) Rows and columns in a table*

Explanation

- Option A is *incorrect* because Azure Data Explorer is a semi-structured Azure data processing tool

- Option B is *incorrect* because document databases generally store semi-structured data

- Option C is *incorrect* because it is a document type widely used for semi-structured data storage

- Option D is **correct** because structured data is typically based on tables consisting of rows and columns

Here is a link to the reference documentation:

```
https://learn.microsoft.com/en-us/training/modules/explore-relational-
data-offerings/2-understand-relational-data
```

4. A customer wants to implement a graph database. Select the best use case for this type of database structure:

   A. ( ) Analytical databases

   B. ( ) Reporting

   C. *(X) Exploring complex relationships*

   D. ( ) Transactional databases

Explanation

- Option A is *incorrect* because analytical databases have a different structure than graph databases, such as data lakes and parallelized data processing tools

- Option B is *incorrect* because reporting is the practice of creating reports connected to the database, and not necessarily related to a graph database

- Option C is **correct** because graph databases are designed to define complex relationships and explore those relationships both by queries and in a visual way

- Option D is *incorrect* because transactional databases are databases designed to support business application operations, not necessarily with complex relationships

Here is a link to the reference documentation:

```
https://learn.microsoft.com/en-us/azure/cosmos-db/graph/graph-
introduction
```

5. What is the objective of data normalization?

   A. ( ) Compiling complex SQL queries for data exploration

   B. ( ) Ideal for storing documents in tables

   C. *(X) Better performance for transactional databases*

   D. ( ) Minimizing the number of tables in a database

Explanation

- Option A is *incorrect* because the queries must instead connect the tables that are normalized, but in general, this implementation brings greater organization to the database

- Option B is *incorrect* because normalization is not related to the data types of the tables

- Option C is **correct** because normalization processes can optimize database performance for transactional workloads

- Option D is *incorrect* because normalization in most cases increases the number of tables in the database

Here is a link to the reference documentation:

```
https://learn.microsoft.com/en-us/training/modules/explore-relational-
data-offerings/3-normalization
```

Relational data on Azure

1. Select the best option to complete the following sentence:

   _____ physically sorts the data in a table based on the values in a specified column

   A. ( ) A view

   B. *(X) A clustered index*

   C. ( ) A stored procedure

   D. ( ) A non-clustered index

Explanation

- Option A is *incorrect* because a view is the materialization of the result of a query and the way it is returned, without optimization in the queries of the original table

- Option B is **correct** because, as we explored in *Chapter 3, Working with Relational Data*, the clustered index in a relational database creates a data access control table from a key column, causing access to that data to be optimized

- Option C is *incorrect* because a stored procedure is the storage of a SQL instruction block that can be triggered by other objects in the database and by the application connected to this database, but does not physically materialize a table

- Option D is *incorrect* because a non-clustered index has a separate structure from the data rows that contains a pointer to the data row as a key value

Here is a link to the reference documentation:

```
https://docs.microsoft.com/en-us/sql/relational-databases/indexes/
clustered-and-nonclustered-indexes-described?view=sql-server-ver12
```

2. When moving an existing SQL Server on-premises solution, which PaaS service offers the best compatibility?

   A. ( ) Azure SQL Database (single database)

   B. ( ) Azure SQL Database (elastic pool)

   C. *(X) Azure SQL Managed Instance*

   D. ( ) Azure SQL Virtual Machines

Explanation

- Options A and B are *incorrect* because Azure SQL Database is intended for the development of new cloud-native applications or applications that have already been developed in Azure

- Option C is **correct** because Azure SQL Managed Instance was designed exactly for the purpose of migrating existing databases in SQL Server (versions above SQL Server 2005), maintaining all compatibility to migrate those databases to a PaaS service

- Option D is *incorrect* because despite being an option, Azure SQL Virtual Machines has fewer benefits than Azure SQL Managed Instance because it is an IaaS migration option

Here is a link to the reference documentation:

```
https://learn.microsoft.com/en-us/azure/azure-sql/managed-instance/
sql-managed-instance-paas-overview?view=azuresq3
```

3. Select the true statement about Azure SQL Managed Instance:

   A. *(X) It has a planned maintenance window*

   B. ( ) You must purchase a SQL Server license

   C. ( ) It can only support one database

   D. ( ) You can connect to the operating system of the server

Explanation

- Option A is **correct** because Azure SQL Managed Instance has a planned maintenance window page that can be accessed by the Azure portal and configured to have less of an impact on services

- Option B is *incorrect* because to use Azure SQL Database, we have the option of taking an existing SQL Server license in an enterprise agreement (a Hub benefit), but this action is not mandatory, and we can activate the service and use it as needed by Azure

- Option C is *incorrect* because Azure SQL Managed Instance supports multiple databases

- Option D is *incorrect* because it is not possible to connect to the operating system of the server

Here is a link to the reference documentation:

```
https://learn.microsoft.com/en-us/azure/azure-sql/database/maintenance-
window?view=azuresq4
```

4. Which of the following claims best describes a relational database?

   A. ( ) A table's columns must all be of the same data type

   B. *(X) Stores and organizes data points with defined relationships for fast access*

   C. ( ) The same table's rows can have various column combinations

   D. ( ) A table's rows can store documents

Explanation

- Option A is *incorrect* because columns from a relational database table do not have to have the same data type.

- Option B is **correct** because a relational database stores and organizes its data considering the relationships between the predefined tables. This behavior causes queries to be optimized.

- Option C is *incorrect* because you do not have to have equal rows between tables for the database to be relational.

- Option D is *incorrect* because in some relational databases it is possible to store documents as binaries, but this is not a characteristic that best describes a relational database.

Here is a link to the reference documentation:

```
https://azure.microsoft.com/en-us/resources/cloud-computing-dictionary/
what-is-a-relational-databas5
```

5. Which SQL statement is used to query rows and return data from tables?

   A. ( ) QUERY

   B. ( ) CREATE

   C. *(X) SELECT*

   D. ( ) INSERT

Explanation

- Option A is *incorrect* because there is no SQL statement called QUERY

- Option B is *incorrect* because CREATE is used to create objects in the database and not perform queries

- Option C is **correct** because SELECT is used to create queries that return rows from database tables

- Option D is *incorrect* because INSERT is used to insert new rows into tables in the database and not perform queries

Here is a link to the reference documentation:

```
https://learn.microsoft.com/en-us/sql/t-sql/queries/select-transact-
sql?view=sql-server-ver16
```

Non-relational data on Azure

1. Which of the following options best completes this sentence:

    On Azure Table storage, you need to optimize the data retrieval. You should use _____ as query criteria.

    A. ( ) Properties

    B. ( ) Row keys

    C. *(X) Partition and row keys*

    D. ( ) Partition keys

Explanation

- Option A is *incorrect* because while working on Azure Table storage, properties may not optimize data retrieval

- Option B is *incorrect* because, in addition to row keys, we also have partition keys in Azure Table storage to optimize queries

- Option C is **correct** because it is complete with the top two features for query optimization to Azure Table storage: partition keys and row keys

- Option D is *incorrect* because, in addition to partition keys, we also have row keys

Here is a link to the reference documentation:

```
https://learn.microsoft.com/en-us/training/modules/explore-provision-
deploy-non-relational-data-services-azure/5-azure-tables
```

2. Which of the following Azure data service options is recommended to implement a new graph database?

    A. ( ) Azure Data Lake

    B. ( ) Azure Blob Storage

    C. ( ) Azure Table

    D. *(X) Azure Cosmos DB*

Explanation

- Options A, B, and C are *incorrect* because these services do not support graph databases

- Option D is **correct** because Azure Cosmos DB has the Gremlin API, which supports the assembly of graph databases, and even though it is not the only graph database option in Azure, it is recommended for new projects

Here is a link to the reference documentation:

```
https://learn.microsoft.com/en-us/azure/cosmos-db/graph/graph-
introduction
```

3. Complete the sentence. Using _____, I can provision Azure storage using a JSON file:

    A. *(X) Azure Resource Manager (ARM)*

    B. ( ) The Azure portal

    C. ( ) The Azure **command-line interface (CLI)**

    D. ( ) Azure PowerShell

Explanation

- Option A is **correct** because ARM templates, based on JSON files, are designed for automation in the service provisioning process in Azure

- Options B, C, and D are *incorrect* because the Azure portal, the Azure CLI, and Azure PowerShell can provision Azure storage but do not use a JSON file as a reference for this creation.

Here is a link to the reference documentation:

```
https://docs.microsoft.com/training/modules/explore-provision-
deploy-non-relational-data-services-azure/2-describe-provision-non-
relational-data-services
```

4. You are developing a solution with Azure Cosmos DB, and after your development, you want to delete all resources. What's the sequence of steps to perform this deletion?

    - S1—Access the resource group where Azure Cosmos DB was implemented

    - S2—Using the Azure portal, search for resource groups

    - S3—Type the resource group name and click on **Delete**

    - S4—Click on **Delete Resource Group**

    A. ( ) S1 – S2 – S3 – S4

    B. ( ) S2 – S1 – S3 – S4

    C. ( ) S1 – S3 – S4 – S2

    D. *(X) S2 – S1 – S4 – S3*

Explanation

Option D is **correct** because the correct sequence starts, and in the Azure portal, we search for the **Resource Group Services** category so that we can have a full list of resource groups. After that, it is necessary to access the resource group in question and then click **Delete Resource Group**. To follow, we must enter the name of the resource group and confirm.

Here is a link to the reference documentation:

```
https://learn.microsoft.com/en-us/azure/azure-resource-manager/
management/delete-resource-group?tabs=azure-powershell
```

5. You want to implement an Apache Spark cluster for data science. Which Azure services can be used for this scenario?

   A. *(X) Azure Synapse Analytics*

   B. *(X) Azure Databricks*

   C. *(X) Azure HDInsight*

   D. ( ) Azure SQL Database

Explanation

- Among these options, we found three **correct** ones for implementing an Apache Spark cluster. *Azure Synapse Analytics* has a Synapse Spark pool, *Azure Databricks* is Spark-based, and *Azure HDInsight* has cluster options with Spark.

- Option D is *incorrect* because Azure SQL Database does not support Spark clusters.

Here are a few links to the reference documentation:

- ```
  https://learn.microsoft.com/en-us/azure/synapse-analytics/spark/
  apache-spark-overview
  ```

- ```
  https://learn.microsoft.com/en-us/azure/databricks/getting-
  started/spark/
  ```

- ```
  https://learn.microsoft.com/en-us/azure/hdinsight/spark/apache-
  spark-overview
  ```
  ```

Modern data warehouse analytics on Azure

1. What's the language used in Azure Synapse Data Explorer to explore data?

    A. ( ) SQL

    B. ( ) Java

    C. *(X) KQL*

    D. ( ) T-SQL

Explanation

-   Option A is *incorrect*. SQL is a standard language for databases, but some use cases have specialized technologies. That's why Data Explorer has its own type of language.

-   Option B is *incorrect*. Java is not supported in Azure Synapse Data Explorer.

-   Option C is **correct**. The full name of the Data Explorer-owned language is **Kusto Query Language** (**KQL**), and it's optimized for fast exploration of telemetry- and timestamp-related data.

-   Option D is *incorrect*. T-SQL is not supported in Azure Synapse Data Explorer.

Here is a link to the reference documentation:

```
https://learn.microsoft.com/en-us/training/modules/explore-
fundamentals-stream-processing/8-data-explorer
```

2. Select the use case for implementing a data warehouse:

    A. ( ) Printing a receipt of a sales order

    B. ( ) Searching for the sales order status

    C. ( ) Recording sales transactions

    D. *(X) Exploring sales from last year*

Explanation

-   Option A is *incorrect* because a transactional database is ideal for storing sales order data for printing receipts

-   Option B is *incorrect* because a data warehouse, despite being a data query engine, has as its main objective aggregating information from a period and providing explorations about that data

-   Option C is *incorrect* because a transactional database is ideal for storing record sales transactions

-   Option D is **correct** because to perform last year's sales exploration, you will need to aggregate a large volume of transactions, which makes this workload ideal for a data warehouse

Here is a link to the reference documentation:

```
https://docs.microsoft.com/learn/modules/examine-components-of-
modern-data-warehouse/2-describe-warehousing
```

3. Select an answer that correctly completes the following sentence:

    The library that provides data stream processing for Apache Spark processes in Azure Databricks and Azure Synapse Analytics is called _____.

    A. *(X) Spark Structured Streaming library*

    B. ( ) Spark Unstructured Streaming library

    C. ( ) Spark Streaming library

    D. ( ) Apache Spark does not support data stream processing

Explanation

- Option A is the **correct** name of the data stream library found in the Apache Spark open source project.

- Options B, C, and D are *incorrect* names.

Here is a link to the reference documentation:

```
https://learn.microsoft.com/en-us/training/modules/explore-
fundamentals-stream-processing/6-spark-streaming
```

4. You are using Azure Data Factory, implementing data ingestion from Azure SQL Database. Which resources should you use for this connection? You can choose more than one answer for a complete solution.

    A. ( ) Dataset

    B. *(X) Copy data activity*

    C. *(X) Linked service*

    D. ( ) Azure Databricks notebook

Explanation

- Option A is *incorrect* because a dataset is the result of some data query, not necessarily an Azure Data Factory resource.

- Options B and C are **correct** answers because to implement a copy of data in Azure Data Factory, it is necessary to create a **Copy data** activity, and when making the source connection it is necessary to create a linked service, as we explored in the hands-on exercise in *Chapter 12, Provisioning and Configuring Large-Scale Data Analytics in Azure.*

- Option D is *not the best option*. Azure Databricks can copy data but does not use the capabilities of Azure Data Factory, instead creating a connection customized "as code" in a notebook in Azure Databricks.

Here is a link to the reference documentation:

```
https://learn.microsoft.com/en-us/azure/data-factory/author-
visually?tabs=data-factory
```

5. You are using Power BI paginated reports. Which of these use cases can be implemented using Power BI paginated reports?

   A. *(X) Reports with a repeatable header and footer*

   B. *(X) Reports formatted for printing*

   C. ( ) Reports with custom dashboard visuals

   D. *(X) Reports with the ability to print the entire data in a visual table*

Explanation

- Options A, B, and D are **correct**. Power BI paginated reports are designed for print-ready reports, with the possibility of a repeatable header and footer, and including the entire data from a visual table in the print operation.

- Option C is *incorrect* because Power BI paginated reports are not designed for dashboard visuals.

Here is a link to the reference documentation:

```
https://learn.microsoft.com/en-us/power-bi/paginated-reports/paginated-
reports-report-builder-power-bi
```

Summary

As you can see, the *DP-900* exam questions require an overview of data concepts and Azure data services exploration. Now that you've gone through the concepts, performed the exploration exercises in the Azure portal, and attempted a simulation test, you're ready to take the exam and ace it!

The data market is growing in a very accelerated way, with high demand for skilled professionals in all countries. This is the time to improve your knowledge, get good certifications, and build a *successful career*.

This book was conceived and built with great affection and dedication, and I'm sure you're prepared to start your data projects with Azure.

You can count on me on this journey. You can connect with me on my LinkedIn profile (`https://www.linkedin.com/in/marcelocml/`) and follow my videos on my YouTube channel (`https://www.youtube.com/c/DicasDeDados`).

I would like to see you certified in Azure Data Services soon. All the best!

Index

Symbols

360-degree customer view case study 65, 66
  consolidated view, of customer data 66

A

access control lists (ACLs) 172
ACID properties
  atomicity 15
  consistency 15
  durability 16
  isolation 15
**American National Standards
    Institute (ANSI) 40**
analytical database 9, 71-73
  data ingestion 10
  data processing 10
  data query 10
  example 10, 11
analytical data model 73, 77
  dimensions 78, 79
  exploring 77, 78
  facts 78

analytical data store 73
  data lake 76
  data warehouse 76
  exploring 76
  hybrid approaches 77
analytical workload 17, 18
Apache Hadoop 180
Apache HBase 180
Apache Interactive Query 180
Apache Kafka 180
Apache Spark 180
Apache Spark Pool 188
Apache Spark Stream 193
Apache Storm 180
append blob 148
**application programming
    interface (API) 193**
AzCopy 150
Azure
  SQL Server databases 88
Azure Blob storage 57, 149
  access levels 149
  append blob 148
  block blob 148
  page blob 148

Azure Cognitive Services 181
  Azure Computer Vision 57
  Azure Speech service 57
Azure Command-Line Interface (CLI) 30
Azure Cosmos DB 124, 152, 153
  formats 153
Azure Cosmos DB, provisioning 160, 161
  backup policy 163
  basic settings 162
  encryption 163
  Global Distribution 162
  networking 163
  tags 163-166
Azure Database, for MariaDB 97
  features 97
Azure Database, for MySQL 93
  Backups feature 119
  features 94
  Flexible Server 94
  MySQL Community Edition 93
  Single Server 94
Azure Database for PostgreSQL 95, 124
  connecting to 138-140
  deployment options 96
  Flexible Server 96
  Hyperscale (Citus) 96
  querying 140
  relational data, querying in 137
  Single Server 96
Azure databases
  connection issues, causes 129
Azure Databricks 184
  architecture 185
  features 185
Azure Data Explorer 193
Azure Data Factory 74, 183
Azure Data Lake
  exploring 208, 209

Azure Data Lake Storage Gen2 183
Azure Data Lake Store Gen2 181
Azure data services, for modern
    data warehouse 182
  Azure Databricks 184, 185
  Azure Data Factory 183
  Azure Data Lake Storage Gen2 183
  Azure Synapse Analytics 183-186
  data ingestion 182, 183
  data preparation 182-184
  data storage 183
Azure Data Studio 28, 29, 90, 91
Azure dedicated SQL pool 211-215
Azure Event Hubs 74, 192
Azure File Sync 150
Azure HDInsight 180
  benefits 180
Azure Integration Runtime
    (Auto-resolve) 203
Azure IoT Hub 74
Azure Logic Apps 74
Azure Machine Learning 222, 223
Azure non-relational data stores
  Azure Blob storage, exploring 148, 149
  Azure Data Lake Storage Gen2,
    configuring 149, 150
  Azure Files, exploring 150
  Azure Table storage, exploring 151, 152
  exploring 148
Azure NoSQL databases
  Azure Cosmos DB APIs 153, 154
  Azure Cosmos DB, exploring 153
  Cassandra API 155, 156
  Core (SQL) API 154
  Cosmos DB Table API 155
  exploring 152
  Gremlin API 156, 157
  MongoDB API 154, 155

Azure portal 30

Azure relational database services

Azure Database for PostgreSQL and
MySQL, configuring 119, 120

Azure Database for PostgreSQL and
MySQL, provisioning 110-114

Azure SQL Database, configuring 115-118

Azure SQL Database, provisioning 102-109

configuring 114

provisioning 102

Azure serverless SQL pool 209, 210

Azure Spark pools 216-220

Azure SQL Database 89, 124

advanced threat prevention 90

advantages 90, 98, 99

anomaly detection 90

database auditing logs 90

data, inserting into 133

data, selecting from 134-136

data types 132

disadvantages 99

elastic pool 89, 90

high availability 90

point-in-time restore 90

relational data, querying in 124-128

scalability 90

single database 89

table schemas, altering 133

table schemas, deleting 133

tables, creating 130-132

use cases 98

Azure SQL Database firewall 129

Azure SQL Edge 93

Azure SQL Managed Instance 91

advantages 92

capability mode 91

SQL Server version 92

Azure-SSIS Integration Runtime 203

Azure storage account

provisioning 171-173

Azure Stream Analytics 74, 192

data flow 192

Azure Synapse Analytics 185

components 186

data 187

develop section 189

integrate section 189

manage section 191

monitor section 190

workspace 186

Azure Synapse Analytics Studio

data exploration example 31, 32

Azure Synapse Data Explorer 220, 221

Azure Synapse Data Explorer pools 193

Azure Synapse Link 220

Azure Synapse Pipelines 74, 183

exploring 202-208

Azure Synapse workspace

provisioning 198-201

Azure Table storage 152

partition key 152

row key 152

B

batch load 19

advantages 19

constraints 19

big data 76

evolution 179

Binary JSON (BSON) 154

binary large object (blob) 148

block blob 148

business intelligence (BI) 79, 178

C

Cassandra 59, 62
Cassandra API 155, 156
cluster specialization 180
column family database 60, 61
   elements 61
   example 62
commit process 15
Copy data activity feature 183
core data
   terminologies 3
Core (SQL) API 154
Cosmos DB Table API 155
CRUD operations 15, 56
cube 77
customer relationship management
   (CRM) database 4

D

data 4
   inserting, into Azure SQL Database 133
   selecting, from Azure SQL
      Database 134-136
   semi-structured data 4-6
   storing, in cloud environment 7
   structured data 4
   unstructured data 6
data analyst 26
   tasks 33
   tools 33, 34
data analytics
   case study 81
   exploring 76
database administrator (DBA) 25
   tasks 27
   tools 28

database components 48
   index 50
   stored procedure 49
   trigger 49
   view 48
database management systems (DBMSs) 16
database schema 40
database solutions 8
   analytical databases 9-11
   transactional databases 8
Databricks Enterprise Security (DBES) 185
Data Control Language (DCL) 44
data cubes 73
Data Definition Language (DDL) 44, 45
   instructions 45
data domain
   case study 34, 35
   data flow 27
   workforces 25
data-driven culture case study 81, 82
data duplication challenge 13
data engineer 26
   tasks 31
   tools 31
Data Explorer Pool 188
data files
   semi-structured 56
   structured 56
   unstructured 56
data ingestion 18, 71
   batch load 19
   batch processing 74
   data streaming 20
   processing 73
   stream or real-time processing 74
data lake 71, 76
data lakehouse 76

Data Lake Store
  provisioning 171-173
data loading, practices 198
  Azure Data Lake, exploring 208, 209
  Azure dedicated SQL pool 211-215
  Azure Machine Learning 222, 223
  Azure serverless SQL pool 209, 210
  Azure Spark pool 216-220
  Azure Synapse Data Explorer 220, 221
  Azure Synapse Link 220
  Azure Synapse Pipelines, exploring 202-208
  Azure Synapse workspace,
    provisioning 198-201
Data Manipulation Language (DML) 44-46
  instructions 46, 47
data mart 178
data modeling 79
  example 80
data normalization 40
  example 41, 42
data pipeline 71, 72
  example 72
Data Query Language (DQL) 44-46
  instructions 46, 47
data silos 65
data source connectors 74, 75
data storage
  defining 11
data stream 192
data streaming 20
  advantages 20
  disadvantages 21
  stock market example 20
Data Transaction Language (DTL) 44
data type
  defining 11

data types, Azure SQL Database 132
  reference link 132
data visualization 73
  exploring 79, 80
data warehouse (DW) 76, 177
DBA's tools 28
  Azure Data Studio 28, 29
  Azure portal 30
  SQL Server Management Studio 29, 30
Delta Lake 77, 194
denormalized analytics databases 76
dimensions 73, 77, 78
dimension tables 78
distributed databases 16
document database 59, 60
  benefits 59

E

elastic pool 89, 90
Enterprise Resource Planning (ERP) 4, 82
enterprise-scale business analytics 79
entity 40
Event Hubs 181
eventual consistency 16
  illustration 17
extract, load, and transform
  (ELT) 18, 72, 182, 202
extract, transform, and load
  (ETL) 18, 72, 182, 202

F

fact 73
foreign key 42

G

graph database 62
  edges 62
  nodes 62
  use cases 63
Graph format 56
Gremlin API 156, 157

H

Hadoop 76, 179
  components 179
**Hadoop Distributed File System
(HDFS)** 172, 179
Hadoop PaaS service 180
HBase 62
**hybrid transactional/analytical
processing (HTAP)** 220

I

index 50
  creating 50
Infrastructure as a Service (IaaS) 7
input and output (I/O) operations 152
**International Organization for
Standardization (ISO)** 42
Internet of Things (IoT) 59
IoT Hubs 181

J

JavaScript Object Notation (JSON) 4

K

key performance indicators (KPIs) 73
keyspace 60
  column families 61
key value 78
key-value database, NoSQL databases 58
  example 59
Kusto Query Language (KQL) 193

L

lake database 76

M

machine learning operations (MLOps) 222
mapping dataflows feature 183
massively parallel processing (MPP) 178
measures 77
modern data warehouse 181
  Azure data services 182
  Azure support 181
  data types 181
  data velocity 181
  increased data volumes 181
MongoDB API 154, 155
Mongo Query Language (MQL) 154
multidimensional structure 77

N

network file system (NFS) 150
NewSQL 73
non-relational data
  basic storage 57
  characteristics 13-15, 55, 56, 64

non-structured data 56

semi-structured data 57

types 56

use cases, identifying 64

non-relational data services

Azure Cosmos DB, configuring 167, 168

Azure Cosmos DB, provisioning 160, 161

provisioning 160

non-structured data 56

Optical Character Recognition (OCR) 56

Speech-to-Text (STT) 56

normalization 8, 40

NoSQL database case study

360-degree customer view 64-66

financial institution fraud detection 67

NoSQL databases

column family database 60-62

document database 59, 60

exploring 58

graph database 62, 63

key-value store 58, 59

O

object store 73

online analytical processing (OLAP) 9

online transaction processing (OLTP) 8

P

page blob 148

Platform as a Service (PaaS) 7, 87

Power BI 33, 228

building blocks 228

components 229

dashboard sample 34

Premium license 230

Pro license 229

Power BI App 229

Power BI Desktop 229, 230

connection, creating 234-236

exploring 231

Power BI file, creating 232, 233

report, publishing 236, 237

Power BI Embedded 230

Power BI mobile app 240, 241

download link 240

Power BI Premium licenses

per capacity 230

per user 230

Power BI Report Builder

reference link 230

Power BI Report Server 230

Power BI Service 229

dashboard, creating 238-240

exploring 238

URL 238

predefined schema 76

primary keys 42

profiles

owner 7

read-only 7

read/write 7

Q

queryable formatting 56

R

raw data 71, 77

real-time data analytics 192

relational Azure data services
exploring 87
relational data 39
case study 50-52
characteristics 12, 39
entity 40
querying, in Azure Database
for PostgreSQL 137
querying, in Azure SQL Database 124-128
relationships 40
structures, exploring 40
table 40
**Relational Database Management
Systems (RDBMS) 42**
relationships 40
result set 76
rollback process 15

S

sample Azure Cosmos DB database
creating 168-171
SELECT statement 51
results 51
results, after UPDATE 52
Self-hosted Integration Runtime 203
semi-structured data 4, 57
graph database example 6
key-value database example 6
server message block (SMB) 150
Service-Level Agreement (SLA) 88
snowflake schema 76
Software Development Kits (SDKs) 155
Spark 76
Spark Structured Streaming library 193

SQL command categories 45
Data Control Language (DCL) 44
Data Definition Language (DDL) 44
Data Manipulation Language (DML) 44
Data Query Language (DQL) 44
Data Transaction Language (DTL) 44
SQL database configuration page
access control 116
backups 118
security 119
SQL Dedicated Pool 187
SQL Server IaaS Agent extension
reference link 30
SQL Server IaaS Agent Registration 93
**SQL Server Integration Services
(SSIS) 183, 203**
SQL Serverless Pool 187
SQL Server Management Studio 29, 30
SQL Server, on virtual machines 92
advantages 92, 93
customizations 93
SQL Server Reporting Services 33
star schema 76
stored procedure 49
example 49
stream data ingestion 74
structured data 4
**Structured Query Language
(SQL) 42, 123, 124 30**
advantages 43
command categories 44
disadvantages 43
multiple data views 43
portability 43
scalability 43
standardization 43
Synapse Analytics 31, 32, 124

T

table 40

tables

creating, in Azure SQL Database 130-132

table schemas

altering, in Azure SQL Database 133

deleting, in Azure SQL Database 133

tabular schemas 76

TinkerPop 156

total cost of ownership (TCO) 178

traditional data warehouses

challenges 178

transactional database 8

e-commerce database 8

example 8

relational transactional database 9

transactional workload 15

database management systems (DBMSs) 16

eventual consistency 16, 17

trigger 49

U

unstructured data 6, 56

V

vertices 156

view 48

example 48

Virtual Network (VNet) 92

W

Webshoes case study 21, 22

Workbench

reference link 137

workforces, data domain 25

data analyst 26

Database Administrator (DBA) 25, 26

data engineer 26

Packt.com

Subscribe to our online digital library for full access to over 7,000 books and videos, as well as industry leading tools to help you plan your personal development and advance your career. For more information, please visit our website.

Why subscribe?

- Spend less time learning and more time coding with practical eBooks and Videos from over 4,000 industry professionals

- Improve your learning with Skill Plans built especially for you

- Get a free eBook or video every month

- Fully searchable for easy access to vital information

- Copy and paste, print, and bookmark content

Did you know that Packt offers eBook versions of every book published, with PDF and ePub files available? You can upgrade to the eBook version at packt.com and as a print book customer, you are entitled to a discount on the eBook copy. Get in touch with us at customercare@packtpub.com for more details.

At www.packt.com, you can also read a collection of free technical articles, sign up for a range of free newsletters, and receive exclusive discounts and offers on Packt books and eBooks.

Other Books You May Enjoy

If you enjoyed this book, you may be interested in these other books by Packt:

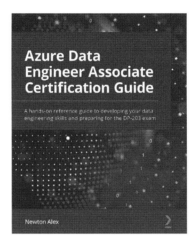

Azure Data Engineer Associate Certification Guide

Newton Alex

ISBN: 9781801816069

- Gain intermediate-level knowledge of Azure the data infrastructure
- Design and implement data lake solutions with batch and stream pipelines
- Identify the partition strategies available in Azure storage technologies
- Implement different table geometries in Azure Synapse Analytics
- Use the transformations available in T-SQL, Spark, and Azure Data Factory
- Use Azure Databricks or Synapse Spark to process data using Notebooks
- Design security using RBAC, ACL, encryption, data masking, and more
- Monitor and optimize data pipelines with debugging tips

Azure Data Engineering Cookbook - Second Edition

Nagaraj Venkatesan, Ahmad Osama

ISBN: 9781803246789

- Process data using Azure Databricks and Azure Synapse Analytics
- Perform data transformation using Azure Synapse data flows
- Perform common administrative tasks in Azure SQL Database
- Build effective Synapse SQL pools which can be consumed by Power BI
- Monitor Synapse SQL and Spark pools using Log Analytics
- Track data lineage using Microsoft Purview integration with pipelines

Packt is searching for authors like you

If you're interested in becoming an author for Packt, please visit `authors.packtpub.com` and apply today. We have worked with thousands of developers and tech professionals, just like you, to help them share their insight with the global tech community. You can make a general application, apply for a specific hot topic that we are recruiting an author for, or submit your own idea.

Share your thoughts

Now you've finished *Microsoft Certified Azure Data Fundamentals (Exam DP-900) Certification Guide*, we'd love to hear your thoughts! Scan the QR code below to go straight to the Amazon review page for this book and share your feedback or leave a review on the site that you purchased it from.

`https://packt.link/r/1-803-24063-6`

Your review is important to us and the tech community and will help us make sure we're delivering excellent quality content.

Download a free PDF copy of this book

Thanks for purchasing this book!

Do you like to read on the go but are unable to carry your print books everywhere?

Is your eBook purchase not compatible with the device of your choice?

Don't worry, now with every Packt book you get a DRM-free PDF version of that book at no cost.

Read anywhere, any place, on any device. Search, copy, and paste code from your favorite technical books directly into your application.

The perks don't stop there, you can get exclusive access to discounts, newsletters, and great free content in your inbox daily!

Follow these simple steps to get the benefits:

1. Scan the QR code or visit the link below:

https://packt.link/free-ebook/9781803240633

2. Submit your proof of purchase

3. That's it! We'll send your free PDF and other benefits to your email directly

Made in the USA
Monee, IL
16 May 2023

33772707R00166